By proving contraries, truth is made manifest.

Joseph Smith, 1844

PERSONAL ESSAYS ON MORMON EXPERIENCE

EUGENE · ENGLAND

· DIALOGUES ·
WITH · MYSELF

ISBN 0-941214-21-4
Printed in the United States of America

Distributed by Signature Books, Midvale, Utah

*This book is for Charlotte,
who brings joy and pain and endures*

CONTENTS

AUTHOR'S FOREWORD

On June 5, 1844, just two days before the publication of the libelous *Nauvoo Expositor,* which provoked a reaction in him that led directly to his murder by a mob, Joseph Smith wrote a generous, expansive letter to a Mr. Daniel Rupp, who had sent him his book on various U.S. religions. Joseph offered to provide information on Mormonism for a subsequent edition and praised the author for letting each church "tell its own story" and then putting those presentations together for comparison, because

By proving contraries, truth is made manifest.

For me this is a climax of tragic awareness in the man I believe has done more for the salvation of humankind than anyone except Jesus Christ. Part of the Prophet Joseph's moral and spiritual heroism is focused for me in his growing insight (and willingness to risk all, including his life, on that insight) that tragic paradox lies at the heart of things and that life and salvation, truth and progress, come only through anxiously, bravely grappling with those paradoxes, both in action and in thought. In the next few days, after facing in writing the "contrary" nature of existence, he grappled in violent action with perhaps the central human paradox, public responsibility versus private integrity—community versus individual values, and he paid with his life for his courageous blend of loyalty to his covenant people, his covenanted Savior, and himself. I have been as true to his example as I know how as I have chosen what experiences to grapple with and have confronted my central inner conflicts as I have written these dialogues with myself.

Ten years ago I became interested in the personal essay as a separate art form. I had already been writing personal essays for ten years and had published others' essays in *Dialogue* without thinking much about the particular literary and religious strengths of the form. But in studying Mormon literature of the nineteenth century and then analyzing what many Mormon writers of my generation were doing that might be part of a recognizable literary tradition, I became convinced, as I wrote in a review of the first anthology of Mormon literature, that the Mormon heritage "shows to best advantage in various forms of personal witness to faith and experience, genres in which the truth of actual living, of quite direct confession, is at least as important as aesthetic or metaphorical truth, [such as] diaries, letters, sermons, lyric poetry, . . . autobiography, . . . and increasingly, the personal essay" (*BYU Studies,* Spring 1975). Since that time the Mormon personal essay has indeed increased in availability and conscious quality.

This collection is an attempt to show by example what the resources of the personal essay can be in a Mormon's search for self and community. I have selected from my work with a variety of purposes: to show something of the range of subject matter and approach possible in the personal essay; to give a personal version of the intellectual and cultural history of Mormonism over the past twenty years; and, of course, to bear witness to the conditions of my own growth of mind and spirit during that period.

I begin with two essays that set forth the theological and historical basis for the unusual potential of the Mormon personal essay. Joseph Smith revealed and lived a restored Christianity that profoundly highlights our tragic predicament: We are eternal, indestructible beings who have unlimited potential for progression, with the example and aid of God, whose work and glory is to bring us the joy of that progression. But we live in a universe of matter/energy, other beings, and natural laws that were not created by God and cannot be destroyed or forced by God, a universe that is, in its fundamental nature, full of opposites, paradoxes, incompletions—all of which cause pain and loss as well as make possible struggle and growth and joy. The fundamental opposition, the most fruitful paradox, is that our lonely eternal selves can only flower into full selfhood in relationship with other eternal selves, particularly

God the Father and Mother, the community of Saints which God establishes on the earth to teach, nurture, and test us, and our own eternal married companion. Those relationships require that we curb our radical egotism in obedience and self-sacrifice, even at the cost of what seems our precious integrity. They require that we enter into genuine dialogue with other selves, appreciate their sometimes contradictory integrity, learn to speak the truth, but in love. As I explain and try to demonstrate in the next four essays we must learn to appreciate, even enjoy, that process of give and take, especially in the Church, which is truly, I believe, "the school of love"–and is that in good part because of the very challenges and struggles that it confronts us with.

Next I define what I believe a Mormon scholar in our time can be–critical and innovative as his gifts from God require but conscious of and loyal to his own unique heritage and nurturing community and thus able to exercise those gifts without harm to others or himself; then I try to demonstrate that role by taking on some of the thorniest theological and ethical issues confronting modern Mormons. First I develop my understanding of the unusual Mormon view of the most important and perplexing theological idea in Christianity–that we can be changed, saved from our universal human sinfulness, by the suffering and death of a being who lived 2000 years ago. I explore the uniquely Mormon idea that our eternal, individual agency is what must be surmounted by Christ–who cannot do it by force but only by using our innate sense of justice to bring us guilt and remorse for our mistakes and then by lifting us out of that immobilizing remorse through his unconditional love that gives us the power, in our personal response, to change, to have "faith unto repentance." Then I explore the unique Mormon response to the perennial problem of explaining evil in a universe created by a supposedly all-powerful God–as well as God's seemingly selective interference in that universe. I do this first through reviewing a popular book on these questions and then through reporting my own experiences in healing family and friends and even my Chevrolet.

After a respite from this heavy going–provided by accounts of my experience with two unique Mormon traditions, traveling to general conference in Salt Lake City and participating in the "Hosanna Shout" at temple dedications, I return to the most pressing ethical dilemmas of the past twenty years: withholding the priesthood from blacks, participation of Mormons in war, and our view of the roles of men and women. I find in all three cases that central Mormon doctrines are the most challenging and exemplary, even exciting, that are available to help with these troubling matters–but that the practices and popular theologies of many Mormons, including myself, come up short. In the same manner, I address the current flurry of anti-Mormonism, sparked by "Ex-Mormons for Jesus" in cooperation with various Evangelical Protestant churches; I defend the solid scriptural basis for our Christian theology and high ethical ideals but recognize our failure to live up to either fully, our need to learn from other Christians who emphasize certain things, such as grace, in ways that may be helpful to us and them, and our responsibility to endure these growing persecutions without overreacting or turning in suspicion on each other.

My final essay is about such enduring–in the face of the unanswerable paradoxes I have explored throughout and the continuing injustice, suffering, and suspicion, as well as wonder and joy and service that our lives as Mormon humans are made up of. It expresses part of what it has been like for me, over the past few years, as I have, in constant dialogue with myself and others–particularly Charlotte, struggled to be faithful in the tragic quest that my testimony of Joseph Smith and his Church have called me to.

Eugene England
Provo, Utah
January 1984

I am grateful to the Association for Mormon Letters, *BYU Studies, BYU Today, Dialogue: A Journal of Mormon Thought, Ensign, Exponent II,* and *Sunstone* for permission to publish certain of the following essays, as indicated in the headnotes. I also gratefully acknowledge the following people: Richard Cracroft and Gene Dalton, for counsel and encouragement; Karen Howard, Melvin Smith, Pamela Lindsay, and Twila Van Leer for typesetting and proofreading; Michael Graves for design and Brian Bates for photography; and Mary Bradford, Clifton Jolley, and Hugh Nibley for reading the manuscript and writing responses for the back cover.

Given at the Rocky Mountain Modern Language Association convention, October 1980; published in *Proceedings, 1979-82* of the Association for Mormon Letters.

CHAPTER 1

JOSEPH SMITH AND THE TRAGIC QUEST

The persistence, indeed supremacy, in our literature of the tragic modes and the persistence and intensity of our interest in tragic experience are somewhat mysterious but undeniable. We are fascinated by extreme suffering and loss–even claim to be exceptionally ennobled through the arts based on them. The great variety of the tragic literary modes, from prose narrative to poetic drama to lyric elegy, from Classical to Shakespearean tragedy–and the variety of intensely argued interpretations of their meaning and value, all attest to a persistently *diverse* understanding of that richly central human experience we call tragic. But on the evidence of the enduring monuments in our literature, it would seem that the *central* issue in tragedy is justice, specifically ultimate justice; the extreme anguish which tragedy confronts and forces us to confront derives, not from mere pain and loss, but pain and loss that touches our deepest concerns, those about the nature of the universe itself. And those concerns are by definition religious. As Paul Tillich has said: "Since religion expresses our ultimate concern, it is greater and more tragic than anything else."[1]

P. A. Christensen, in his essay, "Tragedy as Religious Paradox," convincingly demonstrates that the emerging and unifying element in the richly diverse tragic tradition is the focus on that ultimate desolation, available to us all, when by accident or our own questing we come to feel "the universe has lost its meaning, its moral bearings, its spiritual security."[2] Tragic man, the subject of our greatest literature, unwilling to rest with simplistic and thus secure conceptions of the universe, pushes at the paradoxes his mind and experience uncover, "lives precariously on the growing margin of knowledge," and challenges—or obeys—the Gods of his conceptions in ways that bring, in either case, suffering and loss out of all proportion to his actions. Yet tragic man persists in testing the paradoxes and enduring the suffering. Perhaps he does so because that is the process of all significant learning, of breaking out of confining concepts, out of old seed husks into new life, the process of dying in the old man so a new one can be born; perhaps he does so because it is the ultimate way of courageously confronting the real universe. And we persist in watching and talking about that experience enacted in our literature and in certain heroic lives; perhaps we do so to bear witness to each other of the ultimate value of such ultimately mysterious suffering, to attest to the dignity and authority of such courage and endurance, perhaps because thus we prepare somewhat to face the terror in our own small but equally human lives.

It has been argued by many that Christian tragedy is impossible, because in Christian belief *ultimate* justice is guaranteed by a benevolent God; and some have argued further that *Mormon* tragedy is unthinkable, because justice is not only ultimately guaranteed but already made available, at least after sufficient rationalization, by a just and providential God. It should be clear by now that nothing could be more mistaken. For one thing, ample tragedy already exists, in both the literature and the experience of Christians—including Mormons. And if indeed the central issue—the heart of tragic experience—is ultimate paradox, religious paradox, we might expect to find more of it in profound religious thought and living than elsewhere. Tragedy does not have to do with presence or lack of ultimate guarantees but with present suffering in the face of the paradoxes reality progressively unfolds to the tragic quester. Tragedy is intensified by those discrepancies between our experience and our conceptions of ultimate things that viable religious thinking and living brings when it encourages tragic questing, as I believe Mormonism especially does.

Joseph Smith, the founder of the Mormon faith, is, to us who are his followers, the greatest Christian prophet, in fact second only to Christ in his contribution to mankind; yet he is, I believe, a quintessentially tragic figure—and is best understood as such. Clifton Jolley has shown how Joseph Smith's life took on, perhaps partly by intuitive design but certainly in the mythmaking sensibilities of his devoted followers, the powerful archetypal pattern of the martyred hero.[3] With remarkable fidelity, Joseph, especially in his martyrdom, follows the specific elements of a universal pattern, a shape of sacred meaning, that is, a myth, that forms a mirror by which Mormons focus feeling and understanding about themselves. Jolley quotes Robert Scholes' affirmation that "A myth . . . is the answer to an unspoken question about a matter of great import. . . . Mythic consciousness is related to oracular or prophetic consciousness . . . myths deal only with the eternal." Myth, the prophetic role, and tragedy are strongly linked. The true prophet, the one who takes on archetypal power in a people's consciousness, is, I believe, the ultimate tragic quester; prophetic consciousness is tragic consciousness because by definition it asks the ultimate questions and is led to confront in thought and experience the ultimate paradoxes.

Joseph Smith's life is *mythic* in that it imitates unconscious but universal images and satisfies eternal questions for Mormons; his life is *tragic* because it *raises* ultimate questions for all who are willing to know it and be impelled by it in their own tragic questing. I will describe three major areas where Joseph Smith makes that contribution: 1) in his unique ontology, which poses the most tragically paradoxical universe I know about; 2) in the tragic consciousness and perspective that informs his personality; and 3) in the dramatically tragic events of his life. My intention is simply to open up some areas of investigation and some ways of thinking about them that may help us better understand tragic experience in general and Joseph Smith in particular. I also hope to provide encouragement and perspective for Mormon writers and critics who are contributing to a growing heritage of tragic literature informed by Joseph Smith's life and thought.

As early as 1830, in what became basic scriptures of the Restored Church, Joseph Smith had articulated a foundation for Mormon thought that is inexorably tragic. In the Book of Mormon the prophet Lehi teaches that there is and must be an opposition in all things, paradox at the heart of existence as well as in all moral action. Otherwise, according to Lehi, not only would God's intentions be destroyed but God himself would not exist—nor anything else. Lehi goes on to suggest that for this opposition to operate in bringing about God's purpose—the exaltation, the "joy" that is also the purpose of *man's* existence—it was necessary for Adam (that is, all mortals) to fall (II Nephi 2:11-26). The Book of Moses makes explicit this idea of a "*fortunate* Fall"—that it was a heroic decision by Adam and Eve, in accordance with rather than in opposition to God's plan, a means to enter into a moral universe of choice, where both mistakes and learning, both sin and redemption, are made possible, where, as Adam says, "because of my transgression my eyes are opened, and in this life I shall have joy, and again in the flesh I shall see God" (Moses 5:10-11). But still the Fall is real, tragic, bringing in its train evil, pain, appalling wickedness and sorrow and unanswered questions.

By the time of his death in 1844 Joseph Smith had developed a complete, though not systematic, ontology consistent with these two basic ideas, a compelling foundation for Momon thought and experience that is essentially tragic. The central concept, which has been called "eternalism," is that not only God is eternal, uncreated, indestructible, but so is man at his essential core, his "intelligence," and so are the elements of the universe and the laws that govern the elements and the development of intelligences. "The mind of man–the intelligent part–is as immortal as, and is co-equal with, God himself,"[4] he taught. God has in fact gone through a process such as man is now experiencing and is engaged, as guide and model for man, in an eternal development under the direction of Gods above him–a process and hierarchy that extend to infinity in all directions, backward and forward in time, out into space, and into multiple dimensions of existence.

This expansive vision is certainly adventuresome, exciting in its guarantee of a continuing and challenging existence, one with the potential of joy-bringing progress in a friendly and potent universe and under the guidance of heavenly parents genuinely related to us and perfectly capable of saving us if we so choose. But there are genuinely tragic implications. Eternally *guaranteed* and individually *conscious* existence means there is no escape–from ourselves or from the God who loves us or the universal laws which hold us responsible to ourselves and him. Joseph Smith's cosmos is like modern science's in its ultimate naturalism and rationality. But it is also like Kafka's in that it is a universe filled with a hierarchy of moral intelligences who pursue the individual inexorably, sometimes, as in the Abraham-Isaac myth, forcing us, apparently irrationally, to confront both our sense of self and our real potential for trusting relationship to God. Like Joseph K., or Raskolnikov, or Abraham, we *cannot* escape certain things. A modern Mormon thinker, B. F. Cummings, has put the case this way: "The self is insubordinate, wandering, imperially aloof, solitary, lonely, withdrawn, unvisited, impenetrable"; it "cannot escape from existence nor can it escape from the awareness of its existence" nor from the "inevitable sense of solitude" that is "born of the very fact of individuality,' of "being an eternally identical one." "Individuality has thus its price [that is, cosmic loneliness] as well as its advantages. This aloneness is a fact for men and Gods to live with, for it is inherent in existence." There is a means of escape through conformity to the processes of learning, doing, becoming by which progress comes but a heavy penalty for those who will not conform. "In other words, we are inescapably free to make choices . . . existence itself compels us to make choices of one kind or the other."[5]

As the existentialists have described a similar notion, we are in life "condemned to be free," but in Mormon thought there is no escape even in suicide or death. Nor is there an omnipotent God who will make all things right despite our choices, nor is there the hope of merging our identity into some undifferentiated world soul. We cannot escape the effects, the consequences of the laws—or natural processes—of the universe, some of which are quite specific and bring specific tragic complications. To quote Cummings again:

One of the conditions of [the individual's] progress is his affiliation with others whose goal is the same as his own. Nothing that he can do is of avail to him without these affiliations. Through all eternity he remains an individual but through eternity he will remain a social individual. . . . These very affiliations augment the individual's stature as an individual. The whole concept of progess becomes one of associative progress, but this doctrine of affiliation opens up the way for each individual to develop to the fullest his individual powers.[6]

Of course, the problem is that that doctrine, that condition of the universe, not only allows the individual to develop his fullest powers but in the process confronts him eternally with what seems a central tragic paradox in mortal experience: group values versus individual values, as we see it confronted for instance in *Antigone* and *Billy Budd*. Put another way, it is obedience versus integrity, as we see it confronted in *King Lear* and *The Brothers Karamasov*—and Job and Abraham—and, I believe, in Joseph Smith's life and thought and in much of our best Mormon literature. But in Joseph Smith's cosmology there is not even the ultimate relief claimed by Sophocles in his refrain, "Count no man happy until he is dead." Since in the Mormon view there is no radical difference in the quality of life and the processes of growth for the soul after death, the tragic struggle continues; the facing of these fundamental paradoxes goes on in an eternal quest, whose painful, joyful progress is its own reward. Joseph Smith put the case this way:

How many Gods there are, I do not know. But there never was a time when there were not Gods and worlds, and when men were not passing through the same ordeals that we are now passing through.... You cannot comprehend this but when you can, it will be to you a matter of great consolation.[7]

Part of the tragedy of course is that we do not yet have that consolation of full comprehension but live by faith in our ability to endure with dignity and hope the pain and suffering the tragic paradoxes bring and faith in the reality of the joy and growth the process brings. It is not easy, and the constant temptation is to revert to what P.A. Christensen calls "representative man,"[8] whose imperative is to escape pain, to seek quiet harbors, to find secure absolutes, even at the cost of worshipping idols, those unchanging creations of his own mind that meet his complacent needs, grant special privileges, and maintain untroubled relationships. Mormons themselves, inheritors of the theology of a tragic quester, are tempted to revert to a more primitive and secure, absolutistic theology. As Sterling McMurrin has pointed out, commenting on those among Mormons who have this very understandable tendency to turn away from a difficult, tragic theology, "They are not willing to take their problems to a God who may have problems of his own."[9]

But still the heritage is real. I will merely sketch a few dimensions of the character of Joseph Smith the tragic quester, whose biograpy has yet to be written, but who can be discovered in his letters and diaries and the reports of his speeches. This is from a letter to his wife, Emma, in 1832, during a long mission journey away:

I have visited a grove which is just back of the town almost every day where I can be secluded from the eyes of any mortal and there give vent to all the feelings of my heart in meditation and prayer. I have called to mind all the past moments of my life and am left to mourn and shed tears of sorrow for my folly in suffering the adversary of my soul to have so much power over me as he has had in times past but God is merciful and has forgiven my sins.... I have given my life into [God's] hands. I am prepared to go at his call. I desire to be with Christ. I count not my life dear to me only to do his will.[10]

Those seem to me the energizing poles of Joseph Smith's successful tragic quest; on the one hand a deep sense of sinfulness and failure and on the other absolute yielding to what he was completely confident was a divine purpose and mission. These polarities form the defining outline of the immensely powerful mind and character that fascinated–sometimes horrified–his contemporaries and that we can know through his writings, and those poles determined the persistent tragic action of his life.

The diaries, which we have in Joseph's own hand for 1832-33 and 1835-36, are full of direct petitions to God for himself and others; they reveal intense consciousness of his own failings (December 4, 1832: "Oh Lord deliver thy servant out of temptations and fill his heart with wisdom and understanding"[11]) juxtaposed directly with ingenuous assurance of his own powers (Nov. 28, 1832: "This day I have spent in reading and writing. This evening my mind is calm and serene, for which I thank the Lord; Dec. 1 wrote and corrected revelations"[12]). He records side by side and with exactly the same ingenuous rhetorical directness his miraculous blessing of his brother Samuel's wife in childbirth and a tempestuous bout with his brother William that brought the whole Quorum of Twelve Apostles into disarray and threatened to overthrow the young Church. His sense of integrity impels him to remarkable openness about his uncertainties and mistakes. His early accounts of what might have seemed an amazingly presumptuous claim–a vision of God and Christ–all focus on the forgiveness Christ there offered him for his sins.[13] He confesses to the council of Church authorities, "I am determined to do all that I can to uphold you, although I may do many things inadvertently that are not right in the sight of God."[14] He seems to consciously and constantly act out the implications of the fortunate fall, knowing that adventuresome action in the world will bring him to make mistakes, but these can bring not only pain and conflict but new perspectives, learning, redemption, and growth.

Wilford Woodruff reports Joseph preaching in 1841,

If we did not accuse one another God would not accuse us and if we had no accuser we should enter heaven. . . . If we would not accuse [our accuser] *he would not accuse us, and if we would throw a cloak of charity over his sins he would over ours, for Charity covered a multitude of sins and what many people called sin was not sin and Christ did many things to break down superstition.*[15]

Later Joseph said,

. . . I love that man better who swears a stream as long as my arm, and administering to the poor and dividing his substance, than the long smooth faced hypocrites. I don't want you to think I am very righteous, for I am not very righteous. God judgeth men according to the light he gives them.[16]

He sometimes leavened this theme with humor:

Brethren I am not a very Pious man, I do not wish to be a great deal better than anybody else. If a Prophet were so much better than anybody else was he would inherit a glory far beyond what any one else would inherit and behold he would be alone, for who would be his company in heaven. If I should condescend to be so righteous as the brethren would wish me to be, I should be taken from your midst and be translated as was Elijah.[17]

Yet he knew fully the pain of his tragic quest, both the pain of insight that his visions of the future and of ultimate reality brought him–and the pain of others' incomprehension, even rejection by those closest to him, as the demands increased that were placed on them by his unfolding sense of responsibility to the Kingdom.

During a six-months stay in a primitive Missouri jail, Joseph wrote this, from experience and in awful anticipation:

The things of God are of deep import; and time and experience and careful and ponderous and solemn thoughts can only find them out. Thy mind, O man, if thou wilt lead a soul unto salvation, must stretch as high as the utmost heavens and search into and contemplate the darkest abyss and the broad expanse of eternity–thou must commune with God. . . . None but fools will trifle with the souls of men.[18]

Four years later, on 16 April 1843, he wrote:

O how I would delight to bring before you things which you never thought of, but poverty and the cares of the world prevent. . . . I cannot find words to express myself. I am not learned. But I have as good feelings as any man. Oh that I had the language of the archangel to express my feelings once to my friends, but I never expect to.[19]

Joseph Smith stated with remarkable certainty and openness, beginning in 1842, two years before the event, that he would be killed. And he acted, with a remarkable combination of wistful sorrow and determined assurance, to prepare for that day by completing the temple, giving the endowments and special teachings to about thirty-five of the leaders and their wives, especially teaching and preparing Brigham Young, and very consciously capping his theological legacy with the carefully prepared and revolutionary "King Follett Discourse" just two months before his death. During this time he was constantly clear about his purposes and expected fate:

I know what I say, I understand my mission and business. God almighty is my shield and what can man do if God is my friend. I shall not be sacrificed until my time comes; then I shall be offered freely.[20]

Here we see Joseph's determination that inexorably impelled him onward, like a Lear or an Oedipus, toward a tragic end, but we are also moved by the magisterial courage of his integrity in pursuit of truth and of prophetic responsibility and its legacy of specific insight and achievement. Though the cost may be out of all proportion for Joseph, it is not for us. The conflict of high communal emotion and tragic sense of mission is focused powerfully for us in the following; it is from the report by Wilford Woodruff of a speech in Nauvoo just after Joseph had narrowly escaped from enemies trying to take him back to what he was certain would be his assassination in Missouri. These enemies had in turn been captured by Joseph's friends in a rather comic episode and were now held by the Mormons–in fact, had been treated to a fine meal at Joseph's home and were standing with him:

Before I will bear this unhallowed persecution any longer I will spill my Blood. There is a time when bearing it longer is a sin. I will not bear it longer. I will spill the last drop of Blood I have and all that will not bear it longer say AH. [*Woodruff reports "the Cry of AH rung throughout the Congregation"*] *. . . However you may feel about the high hand of oppression, I wish you to restrain your hand from violence against these men who are around me. My word is at stake a hair of their heads shall not be harmed. My life is pledged to carry out this great work.*[21]

From this point to Joseph's death just one year later, there is a crescendo of events and feelings, of choices and expressions by the protagonist himself, that follow exactly not only the martyred-hero myth Jolley has traced but also the classic shape of tragic drama; and we read through the diaries and speeches with the same awareness of tragic irony, feeling pity and fear and eventual catharsis of a special kind.

But I wish to focus first on Joseph's own tragic consciousness:

August 27, 1843: I prophecy that all the powers of Earth and Hell shall never be able to overthrow [*me*] *for I have obtained it by promise. Melchizedek* [*was given*] *power of an endless life . . . which also Abraham obtained by the offering of his son Isaac. . . . Men will set up stakes and say thus far will we go and no further. Did Abraham when called upon to offer his son, did the Savior, No.*[22]

Joseph, who identified strongly with Abraham, was clearly not about to set limits on his own commitments and go "no further":

29 November 1843: If I do not stand with those who will stand by me in the hour of trouble and danger, without faltering, I give you leave to shoot me.[23]

24 March 1844: Why do not my enemies strike a blow at the doctrine; they cannot do it, it is truth. And I am as the voice of one Crying in the wilderness, repent of your sins and prepare the way for the coming of the Son of Man.[24]

And, on April 7, 1844, he delivered the "King Follett Discourse." It is now clear he knew full well that was his most important speech, the capstone of his life, and the one that would lead most directly to his death because his enemies could not abide the revolutionary but essential doctrine there—the doctrine I have outlined as the foundation of Joseph's tragic ontology. At the end of that speech he said:

I love you all. I am your best friend, and if persons miss their mark, it is their own fault. You don't know me—you never will. You never knew my heart. No man knows my history. . . .If I had not experienced what I have, I could not have believed it myself. I never did harm any man since I have been born in the world. My voice is always for peace. I cannot lie down until my work is finished. I never think evil nor think anything to the harm of my fellowmen. When I am called at the trump and weighed in the balance, you will know me then.[25]

In the tragic drama of Joseph Smith, this was perhaps the *anagnorisis*, the hour of awful realization. Or perhaps that came at the more famous moment on June 23, when, in the midst of an escape from the arrest that he knew would lead to death, he was asked by his wife and friends to return and help protect them and said, "If my life is of no value to my friends it is of none to myself."[26] But for me the *anagnorisis* is focused on June 5, when he wrote, "By proving contraries, truth is made manifest."[27] Just a few days later he was to take an action as Mayor, ordering the destruction of an inflammatory newspaper and its press as a public nuisance, that would lead directly to his martyrdom. In that action he would confront the central tragic paradox of his prophetic calling and make his choice. As other leaders argued for merely fining the libellers and destroying only the printed papers, he was to say, "I would rather die tomorrow and have the thing smashed, than live and have it go on, for it [is] exciting the spirit of mobocracy and bringing death and destruction upon [this people]."[28] So only a few days before that tragic proof of the paradox, the "contrary," of public versus personal responsibility, he wrote, "By proving contraries, truth is made manifest."

And there we have, clearly stated, I believe, the heart of the tragic quest. We do indeed live in a universe where it is only by proving, or testing, contraries or paradoxes, that truth is made manifest. Fifty years earlier, William Blake, certainly another prophetic tragic quester, had said, "Without contraries is no progression," and warned, "Whoever tries to reconcile [the contraries] seeks to destroy existence."[29]

The suffering and loss—and ultimate gain—that are made possible by testing fundamental paradoxes certainly defines the tragic *events* of

Joseph's life. A horribly painful operation on his leg as a boy left him a partial cripple, at least with a limp and a sense of weakness which all his life he compensated for by building enormous strength in his upper body, wrestling and engaging in athletic tests with a zest that became part of his prophetic and legendary charisma. His increasing involvement in building the temporal kingdom in Kirtland, in response to revelation of the full dimensions of his prophetic responsibility to the community of Saints, led to a financial disaster that nearly destroyed the community, threatened his life, and split the Church leadership into factions. These factions quarreled and fought openly in the very temple where a year before Joseph had presided over one of the most spectacular spiritual outpourings in human history–including visitations from Moses, Elijah, and Christ. In Missouri he gave himself as a ransom for his people, was nearly executed, and suffered in a foul prison for six months, brooding helplessly over what his prophetic actions had brought his people to: the Haun's Mill massacre, where men and children were murdered and women raped, and Governor Boggs' extermination order that expelled 15,000 Mormons into the Great Plains winter, attended by the pillage and rapine of the militia-turned-mob. In a letter to the Saints he wrote of being

. . .in this hell, surrounded with demons (if not those who are damned, they are those who shall be damned) and where we are compelled to hear nothing but blasphemous oaths and witness a scene of . . . drunkenness and hypocrisy and debaucheries of every description.

. . . it cannot be found among the wild and ferocious beasts of the forest that a man should be mangled for sport! women be robbed of all that they have–their last morsel for subsistence, and then be violated to gratify the hellish desires of the mob, and finally left to perish with their helpless offspring around their necks. . . .

Oh God where art thou. And where is the pavilion that covereth Thy hiding place.[30]

But the great drama, which is still more directly available to us in our history rather than our literature, is the classic crescendo of triumph and tragedy that occurred in what came to be called the City of Joseph. Like a member of an Ancient Greek audience (who knew in detail the end from the beginning), I watch in fascinated horror as on April 6, 1841, Joseph, who had an almost boyish love of ceremony and celebration, conducts a day of exuberant spectacle in his young city, drilling and parading fourteen companies of the Nauvoo Legion in his splendid Lieutenant-General's uniform, laying the cornerstone of the ambitious temple, followed by a magnificent turkey dinner. And there, prominently in the audience, is John C. Bennett, Joseph's newly appointed counselor, who after a meteoric rise to power will turn against the Prophet and do perhaps most to bring him down. And also there, standing by Joseph at the cornerstone laying, is Thomas C. Sharp, young editor of the *Warsaw Signal*, who is already beginning to find something ominous in this display and who will immediately open a determined campaign against the Mormons that will be climaxed by his acknowledged part in inciting the assassination of Joseph by members of the Warsaw militia and end with his central role in getting the Mormons driven from the state.

The tragic irony is almost unbearable as we hear Joseph, in July 1840, with his city only one year old, prophecying, "These who are now my friends shall become my enemies and shall seek to take my life. I know these things by the visions of the almighty," and then going on in the same speech to proclaim, in the full flush of classic hubris, a prophecy that would, within four years be ironically and tragically fulfilled:

The city of Nauvoo shall become the greatest city in the whole world. . . . We will build upon the top of this Temple a great observatory, a great and high watchtower, and in the top thereof we will Suspend a tremendous bell that when it is rung shall . . . wake up the people of Warsaw, and shall sound in the ears of men [in] Carthage.[31]

He continues, in this account by Howard and Martha Coray:

And if it should be (stretching his hand toward the place and in a melancholy tone that made all hearts tremble) [the] will of God that I might live to behold that temple completed and finished . . . I will say, Oh Lord, it is enough, Lord let thy servant depart in peace.[32]

But he did not live until the temple was finished—nor did he depart in peace, and that was partly because he identified not only with the humble servant, Simeon, but also with the prophet of the covenant, Abraham, who forms for us, in the encounter with God over the sacrifice of Isaac, the fundamental scriptural images of the tragic quest. This is how Stanley Kimball, in his biograpy of Heber C. Kimball, tells the story of Joseph's proving of *that* contrary:

During the summer of 1841, shortly after Heber's return from England, he was introduced to the doctrine of plural marriage directly through a startling test–a sacrifice which shook his very being and challenged his faith to the ultimate. He had already sacrificed homes, possessions, friends, relatives, all worldly rewards, peace, and tranquility for the Restoration. Nothing was left to place on the altar save his life, his children, and his wife. Then came the Abrahamic test. Joseph demanded for himself what to Heber was unthinkable, his Vilate. Totally crushed spiritually and emotionally, Heber touched neither food nor water for three days and three nights and continually sought confirmation and comfort from God. On the evening of the third day, some kind of assurance came, and Heber took Vilate to the upper room of Joseph's store on Water Street. The Prophet wept at this act of faith, devotion, and obedience. Joseph had never intended to take Vilate. It was all a test. Heber had passed the ordeal, as had Vilate. . . . Then and there Joseph sealed their marriage for time and eternity, perhaps the first sealing of this kind among the Mormons.[33]

This was indeed an "Abrahamic" test, and just as that biblical story offends me–that story of the prophet, who also after three days struggle, agreed to obey God's command that he sacrifice his only son as a burnt offering–so the story of Joseph's testing of Heber and Vilate offends me. I can find no way to be at peace with either story, yet I believe that both are true and sacred stories and terribly important. These particular trials are radically different from the daily ones that require that we give up, for the Kingdom, our sins, our weaknesses, our pleasures, the *things* most dear to us, or our mere preferences. Abraham and Heber were asked in the name of God to turn against, in some sense to deny, the very ideas that had brought them to God in the first place and to the higher ethical and spiritual vision to which God had called them–asked to prove loyalty to God (or his servant) by obeying the direction of God or his servant to transgress the very things God had taught them. It is a supreme trial, a paradox, a cross, a mystery. But it will not do merely to say that Joseph or the author of Genesis–or God–made mistakes or that such tests are *unfair*. Unfair or not, the universe, I believe, reveals something crucial about itself in these stories. And it is a failure of the test, and a form of idolatry, simply and easily to choose one of the poles of the paradox of obedience versus integrity, redemptive covenant versus individual freedom, that these tragic myths pose. Thus I do not agree with those who think that the test of Heber was simply a revealing lapse on Joseph's part, and if it reveals a flaw, it is a tragic one in every sense–including its being that which impelled Joseph constantly to that proving of paradoxes by which truth is made manifest. But it is true that this test, also administered to others, who did not pass the test and turned on Joseph, led directly toward his martyrdom.

Joseph's conscious control of that process—his fidelity to it—is seen more clearly in the other major factor in it besides polygamy, that is, his insistence, against all common sense, on explicitly revealing, first gradually, then explosively in the "King Follett Discourse," his radical doctrines concerning the nature of man and God and their relationship. These doctrines were at one and the same time the most important ones for the long-range quality and success of his work as a prophet and the ones most certain to cause his death. As he put it, some would "fly to pieces like glass" because they could not abide the tragic paradoxes and tragic quest such doctrines called them as well as Joseph to embark upon. He was perfectly conscious of what he was doing, and the dramatic tension builds during the last months as he increasingly predicts his own doom while he consciously acts in the quest that will assure it. The tension is increased by a crescendoing litany of requests by Joseph for the prayers of the Saints. He asked that they pray for his failing health, for the aid of the Holy *Spirit* and the help of God to calm the wind because his lungs are becoming progressively weaker; he is losing his breath, his *spiritus*, and his speeches exhaust him. Even the "King Follett Discourse" was cut short by exhaustion and then completed in May—and then reviewed in what is called his "last discourse" on June 16, one week before his arrest:

I never told you I was perfect, but there is no error in the revelations which I have taught—must I then be thrown away as a thing of naught.[35]

[*The Apostle Paul teaches it, but*] *if Joseph Smith says there are Gods many and Lords many they cry away with him, crucify him. . . .*

If Jesus had a father can we not believe that [*that father*] *had a father also. I despise the idea of being scared to death. . . . I have reason to think that the Church is being purged. . . . When things that are great are passed over without even a thought I want to see all in all its bearings and hug it to my bosom—I believe all that God ever revealed and I never heard of a man being damned for believing too much but they are damned for unbelief. When* [*God*] *visited Moses in the Bush, Moses was a stuttering sort of a boy like me—God said thou shalt be a god unto the children of Israel. . . . Did I build on another man's foundation but my own? I have got all the truth and an independent revelation in the bargain—& God will bear me off triumphant.*[36]

As Clifton Jolley has reminded us, Joseph's followers were mostly willing to rest in the satisfying archetypal pattern, the mythic proportions their martyred hero attained in the shape of his life and his death at Carthage–and in the expected revenge by God upon the persecutors of the Prophet that their folk traditions immediately began to compile. But although most Mormons were remarkably content with "Vengeance is mine, saith the Lord," in 1857 a group of them took revenge into their own hands at Mountain Meadows in Southern Utah, massacring an essentially innocent group of emigrants, whose main mistake may have been that they explicitly aroused tragic memories and emotions in their taunts about Joseph Smith. This massacre, where Mormons and Indians killed about 100 men and women and older children, is only now being faced and understood as a Mormon tragedy, one that must be connected in our moral imaginations to the Haun's Mill Massacre, where Mormon men and children were killed and women were raped. And we have yet to confront the extended tragedy in the life and execution of the main scapegoat–John D. Lee–who powerfully raises for us that central tragic paradox of obedience versus personal integrity. Levi Peterson has written a fine essay on the role of Juanita Brooks as a classical tragedian as well as historian in bringing us to face the tragedy, its unbearable pain and loss of innocence–and to achieve some benefit like that of tragic catharsis. He identifies especially Brooks' help in providing a recovered and realistic sense of the heroism and endurance of the people, our spiritual ancestors, who experienced this *agon*, and he shows that, with the knowledge that comes from a testing of the paradoxes vicariously with them, we are able to forgive them and ourselves. We can recover, despite our grief, some measure of innocence, enough at least to endure in a tragic universe.[37]

In my view of tragedy as religious paradox, paradox that is inescapably rooted in the nature of things, catharsis is made available in tragic literature and history and personal experience by its power to help us accept, intelligently, courageously, such a universe and also to accept both our eternal individuality and our need to rely on our common humanity over against such tragic realities. There is available, not the reconciling that Blake warned against, but an ultimate healing of the tension between individual integrity and community obligations in an acceptance of both, especially in the form of covenants, where we freely, based on real experience, make binding promises to divine beings or each other that commit us absolutely to loyalty and ethical action.

Comedy celebrates the human community, especially in the reality and symbol of that ultimate covenant, that ultimate testing of contraries, marriage–as we see in Shakespeare and in Blake, for instance. But so does tragedy, which deals most often with the binding, searing, freeing confrontations of the family–so does tragedy make that celebration of community, despite our having lost some direct sense of that with the loss of the explicitly religious roots of Greek tragedy and our dispensing with the chorus. Besides the values Levi Peterson outlines, those of recovered solidarity with our spiritual ancestors and with moral authority, it is possible, through tragic catharsis, to reach an acceptance of a universe of ultimate paradox and a celebration of the courage of individuals not only to endure but to test the paradoxes of such a universe–and an acceptance of such tragic questers within the human community that is implied by the presence of an audience. The pain of tragic suffering and loss, made necessary in tragic questing, is best coped with through recognition and expression in those forms of art which can effect what Peterson calls that "paradoxical alchemy whereby affirmation and relief arise from pain and despair."[38]

Yes, Christian tragedy is possible; Mormon tragedy is possible–and exists, in fact with some uniquely powerful, though still largely potential, dimensions.[39] Mormon theology, revealed through Joseph Smith, claims that the universe is essentially, as well as existentially, paradoxical–and therefore is irreducibly tragic. Thus Mormon tragedy will not be tragic, as P.A. Christensen claims traditional tragedy is, because of the *failure* of religion, but rather because of the success of religion. Mormon tragedy will reveal not only that false concepts of God and the universe fail man in his confrontation with reality and leave him desolate until he constructs new and better concepts, but it will also reveal the tragedy that comes for a human being–as it did for Joseph–because he has *found* the true God, become his prophet, and fulfilled his mission with fidelity. As St. Paul knew, "It is fearful thing to fall into the hands of the living God" (Hebews 10:31). And in a universe which requires the unimaginable suffering and death of that God himself in order to effect human reconciliation and atonement, perhaps the ultimate call to engage fully in the tragic quest–to be reconciled to its ultimate necessity–comes *from* that God, Jesus Christ, as he expressed it to Joseph Smith: "All these things shall give thee experience, and be for thy good. The Son of Man hath descended below them all. Art thou greater than he?"[40]

NOTES

1. Quoted in Parley A. Christensen, "Tragedy as Religious Paradox," *Western Humanities Review* 12 (Winter 1958): 46.
2. Christensen, p. 40.
3. Clifton H. Jolley, "The Martyrdom of Joseph Smith: An Archetypal Study," *Utah Historical Quarterly* 44 (Autumn 1976): 329-350.
4. Joseph Smith, "The King Follett Discourse: A New Amalgamated Text," edited by Stan Larson, *Brigham Young University Studies* 18 (Winter 1978): 203
5. B. F. Cummings, *The Eternal Individual Self* (Salt Lake City: Utah Printing Co., 1968), pp. 7, 69, 70.
6. Cummings, p. 121.
7. "The King Follett Discourse," p. 205.
8. Christensen, p. 47.
9. Sterling McMurrin, *The Theological Foundations of the Mormon Religion* (Salt Lake City, University of Utah Press, 1965), p. 35.
10. Joseph Smith to Emma Hale Smith, 6 June 1832, published in *BYU Studies* 11 (Summer 1971): 517-23, and in *A Believing People: The Literature of the Latter-day Saints,* Richard H. Cracroft and Neal R. Lambert, eds. (Salt Lake City: Bookcraft, 1974), p. 107.
11. Joseph Smith Diary, 4 December 1832, Joseph Smith Collection, Historical Department of The Church of Jesus Christ of Latter-day Saints, Salt Lake City, Utah.
12. Joseph Smith Diary, 28 November and 1 December 1832.
13. James B. Allen, "Joseph Smith's First Vision," *Dialogue: A Journal of Mormon Thought* 1 (Autumn 1966): 39-41.
14. Joseph Smith Diary, November 12, 1835.
15. *The Words of Joseph*, compiled and edited by Andrew P. Ehat and Lyndon W. Cook (Salt Lake City: Bookcraft, 1980), p. 80; hereafter cited *Words of Joseph.*
16. *Words of Joseph,* p. 204 (14 May 1843).
17. *Words of Joseph,* p. 206.
18. Joseph Smith, Jr., *History of the Church of Jesus Christ of Latter-day Saints*, B. H. Roberts, ed., 7 vols., 2nd ed. rev. (Salt Lake City: Deseret Book Co., 1951), 3:295.
19. *Words of Joseph*, p. 196.
20. *Words of Joseph,* p. 158 (22 Jan. 1843).
21. *Words of Joseph*, pp. 217-218 (30 June 1843).
22. *Words of Joseph,* pp. 245-46.
23. *Words of Joseph*, p. 258.
24. *Words of Joseph,* p. 337.
25. "The King Follett Discourse," p. 208.
26. *History of the Church*, 6:549.
27. *History of the Church,* 6:428.
28. *History of the Church,* 6:442.
29. Quoted in *The Norton Anthology of English Literature: Major Authors Edition*, Abrams, et al., eds. (New York: W. W. Norton, 1975), p. 1323.
30. *History of the Church*, 3:290-91.
31. *Words of Joseph*, p. 417.
32. *Words of Joseph,* p. 418.
33. Stanley B. Kimball, *Heber C. Kimball: Mormon Patriarch and Pioneer* (Urbana: University of Illinois Press, 1981), p. 93.
34. Wilford Woodruff Diary, 21 January 1844, Wilford Woodruff Papers, LDS Church Archives.
35. *Words of Joseph*, p. 369.
36. *Words of Joseph,* pp. 378-82.
37. Levi Peterson, "Juanita Brooks: The Mormon Historian as Tragedian," *Journal of Mormon History* 3 (1976): 47-54.
38. Peterson, p. 54.

39. In literary forms we have drama of high tragic quality in Thomas Rogers' collection, *God's Fools* (Salt Lake City: Signature Books, 1983), see especially *Huebener*, and Robert Elliott, "Fires of the Mind," *Sunstone* 1 (Winter 1975):23-93; flawed but impressive tragic novels in Maurine Whipple, *The Giant Joshua* (Boston: Houghton Mifflin Co., 1941; rpt. Salt Lake City: Western Epics; 1976) and Virginia Sorensen, *The Evening and the Morning* (New York: Harcourt, Brace, and Co., 1949); skillful tragic short fiction in Douglas Thayer, *Under the Cottonwoods* (Provo: Frankson Books, 1977: rpt. Salt Lake City, Signature Books, 1983) and Levi Peterson, *The Canyons of Grace* (Chicago: University of Illinois Press, 1982); and tragic lyrical poems in Clinton Larson, *The Lord of Experience* (Provo, Utah: Brigham Young University Press, 1967) and *The Western World* (Provo: Brigham Young University Press, 1978), see especially "Homestead in Idaho," "To a Dying Girl," and "Jesse."

40 *History of the Church*, 3:301; this passage, in a letter by Joseph Smith from Liberty Jail, appears also in the LDS (Utah) Doctrine and Covenants 122:7-8.

Presidential Address for the Association for Mormon Letters, October 1980; published in the Association's *Proceedings, 1979-1982* and a shorter version in *Sunstone*, May-June 1983.

C H A P T E R 2

OBEDIENCE, INTEGRITY AND THE PARADOX OF SELFHOOD

In his Presidential Address for the Association for Mormon Letters, in 1979, Richard Cummings spoke of "a creeping identity crisis which is gnawing at the very heart of Mormondon."[1] Using the example of his uncle B. F. Cummings' failure to get Church help in publishing, or even selling, his fine book, *The Eternal Individual Self*, and the more well known story of the removal and long exclusion of Joseph Smith's "King Follett Discourse" from B. H. Roberts' *History of the Church*, Cummings discussed what he called "the clash between institutional authority and individual integrity and between the imperative of blind obedience and the claims of reasoned belief." With considerable forthrightness, Cummings spoke of a problem which is for many the most anguishing problem in Mormon experience—the struggle to maintain individual integrity, to be true to ourselves in the face of pressures to obey, to conform, to overlook what seem to Cummings and others to be "clear fallacies or even tyrannies in the strictly authoritarian pattern," especially to keep faith with ourselves in the face of misunderstanding, hostility, even ostracism from our brothers and sisters and disapproval, even disciplinary action, from those in authority over us in the Church.

I believe that issue is indeed central to Mormon experience and literature but in ways that are, in my view, less troubling and at the same time more challenging than Cummings suggested. He saw the problem, at least in terms of our own *decisions*, as essentially a simple one, though the consequences might be difficult and complex: Clearly we are to choose individually reasoned belief over blind obedience, the honor of self over the demands of the group, or what Cummings at one point, referring to the examples of B. F. Cummings and B. H. Roberts, called "individual initiative on behalf of personal integrity in the face of hierarchical hostility or indifference."[2] I sometimes wish the problem were that simple, with the enemies clearly identified and all lined up together and the main challenge being to attack or at least survive them. At other times I am grateful that, in fact, the issue is a genuine paradox, a tragic but fruitful condition of existence, a source of the struggle but also of the supreme joy of growth in this universe in which "there must needs be opposition in all things." In other words the tension between the conflicting values of individual integrity on the one hand and on the other obedience to a God we believe is acting through his servants, a tension which exists at all levels of the Church and from earliest times, is a tension that should *not* be resolved in favor of one or the other of those conflicting values. Rather, the Mormon identity crisis will, I hope, continue, successfully transcended, of course, by each of us in our own way but in ways which maintain both of those values of obedience and integrity as we work out our salvation in fear and trembling–and also as we try to write and appreciate Mormon literature.

Following are examples of some who have confronted this paradox and struggled to remain true to both of the conflicting values, with more or less heroic, sometimes tragic, results. The examples provide enduring images in the Mormon imagination, metaphors if you will, which may help us preserve the paradox as redemptive, rather than merely polarizing it in favor of one value or the other.

Cummings reminded us of the courageous integrity of B. H. Roberts in privately publishing and distributing the "King Follett Discourse" after it had been, without apology or even discussion, excluded by Church authority from his *History*; I will begin with a similarly courageous decision by Elder Roberts that may seem to have come down on the other side of the paradox but which actually, I believe, transcended it. In the early 1890s Elder Roberts, a member of the First Council of Seventy, and Apostle Moses Thatcher engaged in various political activities, even though they were counseled by the First Presidency not to. They were so counseled apparently because of concern about possible neglect of their Church duties. As Truman Madsen tells us in his biography of B. H. Roberts, at one time the conflict was reported in the press, and as a result the two outspoken political activists and the

First Presidency asked forgiveness of each other and were reconciled.[3] But when Elder Roberts was given Church encouragement in 1895 to serve as a delegate from Davis County to the Democratic state convention, he assumed he thus had permission to run for political office and accepted nomination as the Democrats' candidate for Congress; he then was surprised and offended when, at the October General Conference, Elder Joseph F. Smith, a senior apostle and member of the First Presidency–and a Republican–publicly censured both him and Elder Thatcher, who was running for the U.S. Senate. The two Democrats saw the censure as politically motivated and stumped the state, openly decrying such "ecclesiastical interference."[4] Much partisan feeling developed, and when Roberts lost the election by 900 votes he was convinced (for the rest of his life) that the defeat was due solely to the criticism of himself and Elder Thatcher.

After the election members of the Twelve began to discuss whether Elder Roberts should be disciplined because of some of his public statements, but action was postponed until after statehood was conferred in January and then until Roberts finally agreed to meet with the First Presidency and the Twelve in February. Heber J. Grant reports that that meeting was the most painful of his life, as Elder Roberts was immovable in his position, feeling he had acted honestly and fairly and willing to be removed rather than take anything back. A meeting in early March produced the same result, and Roberts was suspended from his office and from acting in the priesthood. At this meeting, Elder Grant records with great admiration, Roberts "held all the brethren at bay"[5]–responding to each of the Apostles in turn, speaking without notes but with perfect memory and composure, thinking brilliantly on his feet; but despite his admiration Elder Grant was appalled at Elder Roberts' adamant position. He and Francis Lyman were appointed to call on Roberts, and after they had talked briefly with him at his home and were about to leave, Elder Grant noticed tears in Elder Roberts' eyes and asked him to be seated again. Now there finally poured forth specific hurts, and the visitors were able to respond effectively.[6] Apparently the key was that Roberts had previously refused to bring up, in his meetings with the Apostles, three separate situations where he had thought he had been intentionally maligned or slighted; as he now brought these forward, in each case Elder Grant had relevant personal knowledge that showed Roberts, to his satisfaction, that he had jumped to false conclusions. Elder Roberts, knowing Elder Grant's perfect honesty, was "non-plussed. . . . This changes things," he said.[7] He promised to think the matter over again and write the two apostles in the morning, which he did, submitting to "the authority of God in the brethren" and confessing that, though he had acted all along in good conscience, after this struggle he felt much better and thanking them for their goodness. Not only Elder Roberts was changed by this experience. Elder Grant records in his journal of that day his great joy at receiving Elder Roberts' letter and that he had learned much, especially about the importance of a private talk such as they had just had, as opposed to the earlier public arraignment before a council of the priesthood.

The story does not end there, however. Elder Roberts' integrity still caused him to resist the so-called "political manifesto," a prohibition against general authorities engaging in non-Church-related work, including political activity, without First Presidency approval. He and Elder Thatcher had previously refused to sign the document because they saw the danger that it could be used to discriminate against one party. Under a deadline at which Elder Roberts' suspension was to become permanent, the First Presidency met with Elder Roberts late into the evening of March 25, after which he walked the streets all night, thinking and praying. He returned in the morning ready to sign, finding the First Presidency had also stayed all night, in tears and prayer. In Conference the next week he confessed publicly that he had been wrong in his opposition. This action then estranged him permanently from political friends and backers, who subsequently avoided him. Elder Thatcher never signed the political manifesto, despite Elder Roberts' long pleading with him, and he was removed from the Twelve and became estranged from the Church. Late in his life Elder Roberts described the paradox he had faced in the terms in which he saw it *after* he had successfully transcended it: "Will I give up my pride or will I be taken out of this glorious work?"[8]

Earlier in Church history there was a similar case of what I would call heroic though painful transcendence of the paradox. It is fairly easy now to know something of the differences, the apparent long-standing feud, between Brigham Young and Orson Pratt.[9] Brigham respected Elder Pratt's intelligence, literary power, and vigorous faith, and he used him to excellent effect at such times as the public announcement and defense of polygamy in 1852. But by early 1860 President Young felt their differences were so serious as to require formal action; he called the Apostles together on January 27, 1860, "to consider the doctrines that Orson Pratt had advanced in his last Sermon," and they decided Orson was wrong and all signed (except Orson) a unique bill of particulars.[10] Elder Pratt called on the President the next day and "admitted he was excited; and for the future would omit such points of doctrine in his discourses that related to the Plurality of Gods, etc., but would confine himself to the first principles of the Gospel."[11] President Young asked Orson why he was not as careful to observe the revelations given to preach in plainness and simplicity as to so strenuously observe the doctrines in other revelations. The following day, a Sunday, Orson acknowledged in a public sermon that there had been differences and he was yielding to the President. A few days later he again called at the President's office and admitted "he had a selfwilled determination in him." According to the office journal, kept by President Young's secretary:

> *The President said he had never differed with him, only on points of doctrine, and he never had any personal feelings, but he was anxious that correct doctrines should be taught for the benefit of the Church and the Nations of the earth. . . . President observed the brethren would have made it a matter of fellowship* [*but*] *he did not have it in his heart to disfellowship but merely to correct men in their views.*
>
> *Prest. also remarked to Orson he had been willing to go on a Mission to any place at the drop of the Hat, and observed you might as well question my authority to send you on a Mission as to dispute my views in doctrine. Bro. Orson said he had never felt unwillingness in the discharge of his practical duties.*[12]

President Young later that week directed the *Deseret News* not to print Orson's sermon because he found it too evasive and defensive in its retractions. By April there was some cause—whether because of continuing uncertainty in the Saints, or in Orson, or both—again to call the leaders together "to consider the Doctrines of Orson Pratt as taught in the *Seer* and other works." The Apostles concluded that Elder Pratt ought to retract in very specific terms—and to publish a sermon to that effect. As President Young expressed it, the earlier sermon of apology "represents me to the world as a tyrant trammelling them to believe as I do right or wrong; it is my calling . . . to see that right doctrines are taught."[13] Orson, a man of fierce integrity, said he believed Brother Brigham was called by God to preside but like other Prophets and leaders could be in error on some points; according to the office journal,

[*Elder Pratt*] *hardly felt he was competent to be an apostle and he left himself entirely in their hands, but he could not be hypocrite enough to retract his doctrines when he believed them, neither could he say he could receive doctrines that he could not believe; and if he was disfellowshipped he could not help it.* However, during twenty-four hours of the most painful confrontation between his deepest loyalties, Elder Pratt apparently decided that his truest integrity lay in his commitment to the Lord's kingdom rather than to the speculations of his own philosophy. He came to a meeting of the Apostles the next night with a sermon of recantation prepared, which President Young added a few remarks to and accepted:

Brother Orson Pratt asked if the subject was to be dropped; or was it to be resuscitated again. President Young observed he never wanted the subject to be mouthed again, and wished those in the room, not to mention it, and asked O. Pratt if he ever wanted to open new ground to preach about to submit such subjects to him first, remarking also that Bro. Orson was a sweet preacher, and he took great pleasure in hearing him, and had always admired his willingness to perform what labors had been required of him.[14]

Brother Brigham continued to admire Orson's preaching and chose him to represent the Church in answering the celebrated challenge of the Chaplain of the U.S. Congress, Dr. John P. Newman, to debate the biblical authority for polygamy in the Salt Lake Tabernacle in 1870–a debate Pratt carried with what Newman discovered to be astounding erudition and style. And just six months after that April 5, 1860, meeting, when it was reported to Brigham Young that Orson was still apparently being twitted by some for his public humiliation but bearing it well, a clerk reported, "The President remarked . . . if Bro. Orson was chopped up in inch pieces each piece would cry out Mormonism was true."[15] But in a page of minutes from the April meeting we get perhaps the best glimpse of President Young's feelings and understanding of the paradox, in his own words as taken down by the secretary:

This day I have seen the best spirit manifested. I have heard 15 or 16 men all running in the same stream. I was delighted. Tomorrow the Church will be 30 years old, about the age that Jesus was when he commenced his mission. We are improving and I just know it, my path is like the noon day sun, and I could cry out hallelujah Hallelujah Praise to God who has been merciful to us and conferred on us his Holy Spirit. . . . Bro. Orson I want you to do just as you have done in your Apostleship, but when you want to teach new doctrine, to write those ideas, and submit them to me, and if they are correct, I will tell you–there is not a man's sermons that I [*more*] *like to read, when you understand your subject–but you are not perfect, neither am I.*[16]

Once more, the story does not end that simply; after a while, Orson again published views on various matters that Brigham saw as undermining to his authority as Prophet and to the gospel tradition from Joseph Smith he felt responsible to preserve untainted, especially in the face of influential advocates like Orson Pratt. He was particularly concerned to keep the options open on matters such as the plurality of gods and God's progression in knowledge and power, and also about the natural processes affecting Adam's origin and status, rather than to let Orson Pratt's absolutism about God's perfection and his biblical literalism become standard by default. On August 23, 1865, the general authorities felt it necessary to publish in the *Deseret News* a summary of Orson Pratt's errors and their reasons for opposing them, along with a reprint of Elder Pratt's earlier recantation, and again Elder Pratt followed up with a public confession and apology. But in the summer of 1868 he *again* found himself in opposition to President Young in discussions in the School of the Prophets about Joseph Smith's translation of the Bible, and this apparently broadened out to bring up the old doctrinal differences. Then a surprising thing happened; with no apparent coercion or pressure, and right after these discussions, on July 1 Orson Pratt wrote the following letter to President Young:

Since the last two meetings at the school, I have, at times, reflected much and very seriously, upon the feelings which I have suffered myself for years to occasionally entertain respecting certain doctrines . . . now believed by the Church, and have tried to justify myself in taking an opposite view, on the supposition that I was supported by the letter of the word of God: but as often as I have yielded to this influence I have felt an indescribable wretchedness which fully convinces me that I am wrong; I wish to repent of these wrongs for I fully realize that my sins, in this respect, have been very great, and of long continuance, and that it has been only through your great forbearance and long suffering, and the patience of my quorum, that I have been continued in the high and responsible calling of the Apostleship to this day.

I am deeply sensible that I have greatly sinned against you, and against my brethren of the school, and against God, in foolishly trying to justify myself in advocating ideas, opposed to those which have been introduced by the highest authorities of the Church, and adopted by the Saints. I humbly ask you and the school to forgive me. Hereafter, through the grace of God assisting me, I am determined to be one with you, and never be found opposing anything that comes through the legitimate order of the Priesthood, knowing that it is perfectly right for me to humbly submit, in all matters of doctrine and principle, my judgment to those whose right it is, by divine appointment, to receive revelation and guide the Church.

There is no one thing in this world, or in that which is to come, which I do more earnestly desire, than to honor my calling, and be permitted to retain the same, and with my brethren the Twelve, enter the Celestial kingdom, with a full preparation to enjoy the glory thereof for ever. . . .

With feelings of great sorrow, and deep regret for all my past sins I subscribe myself your humble brother in Christ. Orson Pratt, Sen.[17]

Here we find none of the stubborn defensiveness and evasiveness of the earlier so-called recantations. The confession seems to come truly from Elder Pratt's deepest convictions. A few days later he spoke before the School of the Prophets, apologizing for "opposing doctrine revealed" and confessing that "whenever he had done so and excused himself because of what was written [by literally interpreting the scriptures] his mind became darkened and he felt bad."[18] We find no further examples of his opposing Brigham on doctrine. Wilford Woodruff later maintained that it was only President Young's "firmness" in resisting Orson Pratt's "unyielding stubbornness" in offering to resign the Apostleship rather than change his opinions that kept Elder Pratt in the Church.

My third example is not, as I believe the first two were, transcendent. It is more tragic than heroic, but it is thus a reminder of the truly tragic dimensions of the paradox of selfhood. Despite the meticulous work of Juanita Brooks concerning the Mountain Meadows Massacre and the illuminating exploration of her contribution by Levi Peterson in his fine essay, "The Mormon Historian as Tragedian,"[19] it is possible to go away from that work, as I suspect most do, with the impression that the only tragedy was that which occurred to the massacred men, women, and children–or perhaps to those who suffered the guilt of their horrifying deed. And we can distance ourselves, certain that we would never make such a mistake as those deluded fanatics did. I wish to explore briefly another tragedy, that of John D. Lee as he faced the paradox of integrity and obedience; I wish to honor his memory by insisting that he was not a mere deluded fanatic, that his was not a simple and simply wrong decision, and with the suggestion that, though I trust we could have done better, if it would have been a simple decision for us we have something to learn from him.

John D. Lee was a loyal and tried Saint, an intrepid builder of the Kingdom whose uninhibited diaries are an important part of our literary heritage. He was made a part of Brigham Young's own family through the sacred early Mormon ceremony of "adoption" by temple sealing and was a sincere priesthood holder who believed in keeping his covenants. After the massacre he continued for a while in positions of trust in southern Utah that could not have been possible without President Young's approval, but then the support was withdrawn. I believe that was because Brigham gradually became convinced that Lee had participated in violence–something Brigham intensely, almost irrationally, abhorred–and that Lee had lied about it, actions which threatened the Mormon community from within and without.

Brigham made his own tragic choice; he chose the welfare of the community over full candor and then over personal loyalty. Blame was increasingly focused on Lee by those who broke silence, and he was summarily excommunicated by the Church in 1870 and executed by civil authorities on the massacre site in 1877, twenty years after the event. He comported himself with remarkable, articulate dignity to the end, and near the end he wrote what he called a "confession," which was taken by a non-Mormon agent, altered in crucial ways Lee would not, I believe, have allowed, and then made the heart of an anti-Mormon sensation called *Mormonism Unveiled*. Despite the textual alterations it is possible, I think, to detect John D. Lee's authentic voice at important points. This is his description of his feelings upon entering the besieged encampment of emigrants he is about to betray to their deaths, they gathering about him in "wild consternation," some convinced "their happy deliverance had come," others looking on him "with doubt, distrust, and terror":

God knows my suffering was great. . . . I knew that I was acting a cruel part and doing a damnable deed. Yet my faith in the godliness of my leaders was such that it forced me to think that I was not sufficiently spiritual to act the important part I was commanded to perform. My hesitation was only momentary. Then feeling that duty compelled obedience to orders, *I laid aside my weakness and my humanity and became an instrument in the hands of my superiors and leaders.*[20]

The echoes of Eichmann are so strong they almost drown out the unintentionally ironic phrasing of the paradox we are discussing: Lee felt it was his "weakness and humanity"–his human compassion–that he must give up to be obedient. The struggle had not been easy or simple; after the council meeting a few days before, at which the final plans for the Massacre had been made, Lee tells us,

I . . . went away to myself, and bowed myself in prayer before God, and asked Him to overrule the decision of the Council. I shed many bitter tears, and my

tortured soul was wrung nearly from the body by my great suffering. I will here say, calling upon Heaven, angels, and the spirits of just men to witness what I say, that if I could then have had a thousand worlds to command, I would have given them freely to save that company from death.[21]

Of course, when he wrote this he knew the irony that that "thousand worlds" was indeed what he and the others had given up by proceeding–that is, their exaltation in the eternal, progressive realms of God. But at that earlier time, all he received, in the midst of his anguish, was a visit from a friend he trusted who assured him that to go ahead was all right, "for the brethren in the Priesthood were all united in the thing, and it would not be well for me to oppose them."

When he returned to the council they prayed together in a circle for divine instruction. After the prayer Major Higbee, commander of the Iron County Militia said, according to Lee, "I have the evidence of God's approval of our mission. It is God's will that we carry out our instructions to the letter." But for Lee this particular evil spirit would not come out with fasting and prayer. There had been preliminary discussions, a few days earlier, about possible action against the emigrants, after which Lee claims he found universal willingness among the Mormons, enraged over the real and rumored boasts and threats and actions of the emigrants, to launch an attack. Lee reported, in what is for me the most painful moment of his personal tragedy:

I spent one of the most miserable nights there that I ever in the history of my faith passed in my life. I spent much of the night in tears and at prayer. I wrestled with God for wisdom to guide me. I asked for some sign, some evidence that would satisfy me that my mission was of Heaven, but I got no satisfaction from my God.[22]

It seems that not only *after* the massacre did the heavens turn to brass for the Iron County Militia, as Levi Peterson notes in his essay, but the heavens did so as soon as murder conceived in the men's hearts.

Nevertheless, it will just not do to dismiss John D. Lee as a religious fanatic, victimized by the conditioning of his Mormon faith toward blind obedience. To do so is to demean the genuine paradox, the tragic complexity, of his situation; it is to come down too easily on the side of integrity to self, of inner conviction of moral right, over obedience to those one firmly believes–*also* on the basis of inner conviction–are his leaders on the path of salvation; it is to enthrone preservation of life as the ultimate value and thus bring into question all revealed religion and all civilized values that call for individual conformity and sacrifice.

Just as John D. Lee is an apparent example of a clearly *wrong* choice for blind obedience, but one which, I believe, on examination turns out to be somewhat more complex, so Levi Savage, of the Willie handcart tragedy of 1856, is an apparent example of a clearly *right* choice for individual integrity, but one which, I believe, is also somewhat more complex. Elder Savage was captain of the second hundred, one of only four among that company of 400 emigrants who had been West before, and the only one of them all who raised his voice in opposition at the meeting in Florence, Nebraska, in August when the company considered whether or not to go on to Utah that late. According to the narrative of John Chislett, who was in the company and left the Church after barely surviving the ordeal and before writing his account, the other leaders, including G. D. Grant and William Kimball, Church agents at Florence, favored their going on. They prophesied in the name of God the company would get through in safety, even that the weather would be arranged for their good.

But Levi Savage used his common sense and his knowledge of the country. He declared positively that to his certain knowledge we could not cross the mountains with a mixed company of aged people, women, and little children, so late in the season without much suffering, sickness, and death, . . . but he was rebuked by the other elders for want of faith, one elder even declaring that he would guarantee to eat all the snow that fell on us between Florence and Salt Lake City.[23]

Brother Savage's counsel was ignored and, indeed, a few weeks later, when the apostle, Franklin Richards, who had optimistically advocated the handcart plan in England, passed them on his way to Salt Lake, he stopped for a night and, being advised of Brother Savage's earlier opposition, "rebuked him very severely in open meeting for his lack of faith in God." According to Chislett, Elder Richards

gave us plenty of counsel to be faithful, prayerful, obedient to our leaders, etc., and wound up by prophesying in the name of Israel's God that "though it might storm on our right and on our left, the Lord would keep open our way before us and we should get to Zion in safety."[24]

More than fifty (one in eight) of the Willie Company died in the storms that overtook them in Wyoming, over 150 (one in four) of the Martin Company that was two weeks behind them. Chislett points up the painful irony that, according to all the old settlers in Utah, "the fall storms of 1856 were earlier and more severe than were ever known before or since. Instead of the Mormons' prophecies being fulfilled and their prayers answered, it would almost seem that the elements were unusually severe that season, as a rebuke to their presumption."[25]

According to Chislett, "It was the stout hearts and strong hands of the noble fellows who came to our relief, the good teams, the flour, beef, potatoes, the warm clothing and bedding, and not prayers nor prophecies, that saved us from death." He, of course, had forgotten that it was prayers and prophecies that had saved these English millworkers from Europe, from Babylon, and would make them into Saints, despite the costs, that it was the love and conviction built on prayers and prophecies that moved those he called "noble fellows" to risk their lives in the rescue, including G. D. Grant and William Kimball. These two, who in their zeal had been partially responsible for the plight of the handcart pioneers, had traveled to Salt Lake with Elder Richards, Chislett notes, and immediately, at Brigham Young's direction, turned around to come to their aid: "May God ever bless them for their generous, unselfish kindness and their manly fortitude. . . . How nobly, how faithfully, how bravely they wanted to bring us safely to the Valley–to the Zion of our hopes."[26] Indeed, William Kimball, who spent an entire day carrying women and children through floating ice on a crossing of the Sweetwater, according to the journal of one of the survivors, "staid so long in the water that he had to be taken out and packed to camp and he was a long time before he recovered as he was chil[le]d through and in after life he was allways afflicted with rheumatism."[27]

These originally overzealous and now bravely selfsacrificial rescuers, I believe, understood the paradox of integrity and obedience better than the apostate Chislett did, and Brigham Young understood it better than Chislett *or* Elder Richards: He severely and publicly chastised the apostle for not having had the common sense to stop the rear companies in Florence and for encouraging the emigrants to rely on miraculous intervention to protect them from needless folly in a practical decision that could be made rationally–something Brother Brigham would never do.[28] And Brigham Young, better than Chislett, understood that other paradox, of faith and works: When he was informed that some of the Martin company were arriving on Sunday, November 30, he dismissed the day's meetings and sent the Saints home to prepare to feed and nurse the survivors rather than stay there and pray. "Prayer is good," he said, "but when baked potatoes and milk are needed, prayer will not supply their place."[29] But perhaps Levi Savage understood better than any of them the paradox of integrity and obedience. According to Chislett's narrative, after Savage was defeated in his lone opposition at the Florence meeting, he said to his fellow Saints:

"Brethren and sisters, what I have said I know to be true; but, seeing you are to go forward, I will go with you, will help you all I can, will work with you, will rest with you, will suffer with you, and if necessary, I will die with you. May God in His mercy bless and preserve us. Amen."

[*Chislett continues*] *Brother Savage was true to his word; no man worked harder than he to alleviate the suffering which he had foreseen, when he had to endure it.*[30]

These images I have recalled of the perennial struggle between obedience and integrity, together with those of Abraham and Isaac, of Heber Kimball and Vilate,[31] must remain before us, not forgotten or rationalized away. They are images that, if they had been remembered and imaginatively perceived, may have helped us deal better than we did with the modern Abrahamic test for Mormons, the denial of priesthood to the blacks. In that test God, through his servants, asked us not only to sacrifice our political and social ideals and the understanding and the good will of our colleagues and friends, but he seemed to ask us to sacrifice the very essence of his own teachings to us. It appeared necessary to deny our understanding of the divine potential, based in an eternal existence coequal with God and each other, of all God's children, and the higher ethical vision of possible exaltation for all people through progression after death, concepts that are among the most attractive and vital features of our Mormon faith.

Those who failed the test, I believe, are those who thoughtlessly obeyed, even rationalizing the mystery away by finding some way to blame the *blacks* because of their supposed lineage or pre-existent mistakes. On the other hand, those also failed who emotionally opted for their own personal vision, rejected the authority of the Church and loyalty to their community, and blamed Brigham Young or the current Prophet or other supposedly racist Mormons, never themselves. My personal hero from that time is President Hugh B. Brown, who wrote the First Presidency message of 1969 that urged all Mormons to pray, and thus prepare, "that all of the blessings of the Gospel . . . become available to men of faith everywhere,"[32] which could only mean when blacks would be given the priesthood. Neither of the groups I mentioned that failed the test—whether conservatives or liberals—took that suggestion seriously, and thus they did not find a resolution of the paradox of obedience and integrity through their personal preparation nor did they help God prepare us to live the higher law of priesthood for all.

If, in our consideration of these examples of a central paradox from our heritage, we suppose there were simple solutions, if we imagine that we could have chosen easily and more wisely, I think we dishonor the great men and women who took part in these dramas and the full anguish with which they touched, and we must touch, the tragic heart of human experience. And, if we thus suppose there are easy solutions to the dilemma of personal integrity and social responsibility, we diminish drastically the potentiality of Mormon literature, and, I think, ultimately endanger our own salvation.

Much of the greatest literature in our Western tradition has derived its power from retaining the tension in this tragic paradox of individual and group values. Let me mention Antigone, whose admirable and absolute loyalty–even unto death–to her own conscience, over against the absolute demands of the state in the form of the equally unyielding Creon, led to immense tragedy. Or Cordelia, who insisted on integrity in the face of her father's need for public, ceremonial obedience and pursued that integrity to a disastrous, though ultimately redemptive, extreme. Or Billy Budd, at whose "unjust" execution we stand appalled, especially when it seems carried out by officers and crew who are impelled by some mysterious force, though none of them wants it to happen. Yet in the end, we are able to affirm that force though we recognize its cost; we stand with Captain Vere on the tragic rack of the paradox of individual integrity versus obedience to absolutely necessary civilized forms and admit that "we all wear the buttons of the King."

And, of course, there are cautionary tales. Thoreau, who maintained the paradox in *Walden* by using symbolic images of growth that transcended mere individualism, turned toward onesided polemic, however powerful, in *Civil Disobedience*, a onesidedness which grew until it emerged in his own life as such blind allegiance to John Brown that he could impressively defend him with the notion that the end justifies the means. Brown, you remember, was the abolitionist who, at Harpers Ferry, killed not only slaveholders but their children, with a rationale that especially chills Mormons because they remember that exact phrase issuing from lips of the child-murderers at the Haun's Mill Massacre: "Nits make lice." Those who, like Thoreau or Brown, would exalt the isolated individual conscience into an absolute and also those who, like

Creon or our Mormon ancester Major Higbee, would exalt obedience to society's judgment into an absolute, all need to learn to honor Oliver Cromwell's famous plea, "I beseech you, in the bowels of Christ, consider that you may be wrong."

Our own Mormon literature, it seems to me, has achieved its greatest heights when it has been able to preserve and transcend the paradox, rather than needing to oversimplify it into a battle and to choose a side. Our first generation writers (1830-1880) usually tended to exalt obedience and group values, but their best work comes when they intuitively assert their individualism in tension against or beyond those values—as in Parley P. Pratt's *Autobiography* or Eliza R. Snow's "Trail Diary." Our "second generation writers" (about 1930-1960) tended to exalt individualism against the values of what they saw as a declining culture and a deficient religion, but in their best work, such as Virginia Sorensen's *The Evening and the Morning* and Maurine Whipple's *The Giant Joshua*, they intuitively create the power of those traditional group values and covenants as a judgment on the excesses of individualism. In our own generation our best writers, in their best work, struggle with the same paradox, with no simple compromises or side-choosing: Clinton Larson's "Homestead in Idaho" and "Advent," Douglas Thayer's "Under the Cottonwoods" and "The Redtail Hawk," Eileen Kump's "The Willows" and "Sayso or Sense," Don Marshall's "A Sound of Drums" and "Fugues and Improvisations," Dian Saderup's story published in 1979 in *Sunstone*, which captures the painful paradox and its transcendence, without irony I believe, even in her title, "A Blessing of Duty."

Here I have tried to highlight the seriousness and centrality of the paradox of obedience and integrity in the search for selfhood. There is certainly a constant danger that individual integrity faces in any kind of powerful group—whether family, church, political party, or academic community. I worry about the tendency to *simplify* that danger, which is, I think, profoundly paradoxical, into a mere dichotomy. But perhaps one image of dichotomy that Richard Cummings used in his challenging address provides us, somewhat ironically, with a way toward genuine resolution. He described what he called "the theological and ecclesiastical dichotomy which has produced the identity crisis" in terms of a polarity we should all recognize, that is, those who lose themselves in the Church and those who seek to find themselves there. The former are those who "refer their problems and worries to the 'sure voice of authority,' " who renounce "their autonomous identity through blind obedience and mindless activism," and the latter are those who "think for ourselves in working out our own individual salvation as we each separately see fit and according to our own lights."[33] Notice the pronouns: *they* and *we*. Cummings, as I think we all would do given only those alternatives, clearly identifies with those who seek to *find* themselves in the Church and thus "reach their own thoughtful conclusions, however painful, and forge their individual testimonies in the crucible of private doubt and personal despair." But difficult and painful as that seems, it is still, I think, too easy, too simple. Perhaps it would be well for any of us who would seek to find ourselves rather than lose ourselves in the Church to remember Christ's ultimate statement of the paradox: He who would find his life, who *seeks* it, shall lose it, but he who will lose it shall find it. We all are startled a bit by the mystery in that, but I think we can respond to the imaginative and imaginable resolution there of the dilemma of the individual and the group–one that will prevent us from being gored on either horn of the dilemma.

But what is that resolution–in literal terms. Can we be less mystical? William Blake, considered by many a true mystic, nevertheless gave us a powerful articulation as well as moving imaginative representations of that resolution. He taught that "without contraries is no progression" and warned that "whoever tries to reconcile [the contraries] seeks to destroy existence"[34]–an interesting parallel to the Mormon idea that without opposition there is no existence and to Joseph Smith's intriguing notion that "by proving contraries truth is made manifest."[35] Blake rejected either compromise or choice as a solution–both poles have values which must be preserved. Blake used the image of marriage to convey his sense of a redemptive *fusion* of the various sets of conflicting values as opposed to compromise–or suppression or victory of one or the other poles. In the true marriage, neither individual is destroyed, but their individual loneliness and limitation is transcended in their mutual creative acts and the fruit they bear–which they could not bear alone. This image of marriage is for Blake mainly an imaginative resolution, but there is a literal one, I believe, in *literal* marriage and in what we can learn from one of its essential features.

The general resolution of the paradox of individual and group, of integrity to conscience and obedience to law or commandment, is, I believe, found in covenants, of which eternal marriage is one form. A covenant is not, contrary to popular cliche, merely a *contract* between individuals, or between God and the individual, with mutual benefits. It is, in the words of the fine Bible scholar, George Mendenhall, "[a] free, voluntary acceptance of ethical obligation on the basis of and as response to past experience."[36] A covenant is a free, conscientious binding of the individual will to God, to an eternal partner, to a community and its land and history and sacred texts. It is not made blindly but out of gratitude and hope based in real experience. It turns neither the individual will nor the community into an idol that holds ultimate authority but reserves that ultimate authority to God, who is known and served both through the self and the community. One remains perfectly free to break the covenant but is bound in conscience to the reality of his experience with the divine, both as an individual and through the experiences made possible to him only in the community. And paradoxically, this *binding* brings greater *freedom* than does individual autonomy. This is how Michael Novak, speaking specifically of the bonds of marriage, describes the paradox and its transcendence:

> *Marriage* is *an assault upon the lonely, atomic ego. Marriage* is *a threat to the solitary individual. Marriage does impose grueling, humbling, baffling, and frustrating responsibilities. Yet if one supposes that precisely such things are the preconditions for all true liberation, marriage is not the enemy of moral development in adults. Quite the opposite. . . .*[37]
>
> *Being married and having children has impressed on my mind certain lessons, for whose learning I cannot help being grateful. Most are lessons of difficulty and duress. Most of what I am forced to learn about myself is not pleasant. . . .*
>
> *Seeing myself through the unblinking eyes of an intimate, intelligent other, an honest spouse, is humiliating beyond anticipation. Maintaining a familial steadiness whatever the state of my own emotions is a standard by which I stand daily condemned. A rational man, acting as I act? . . .*
>
> *My dignity as a human being depends perhaps more on what sort of husband and parent I am, than on any professional work I am called upon to do. My bonds to them hold me back (and my wife even more) from many sorts of opportunities. And yet these do not feel like bonds. They are, I know, my liberation. They force me to be a different sort of human being, in a way in which I want and need to be forced.*[38]

As Martin Luther put it, "Marriage is the school of love." I would add that, for many of the same reasons which Novak articulates, that is, those liberating confrontations with self and others which a covenant demands, the Church also is the school of love.

To end where we began, this is how B. F. Cummings, in his fine book on the individual, which he had to publish himself, describes the paradox and its transcendence: "The self is insubordinate, wandering, imperially aloof, solitary, lonely, withdrawn, unvisited, impenetrable"; it "cannot escape from existence nor can it escape from the awareness of its existence" nor from the "inevitable sense of solitude" that is "born of the very fact of individuality," of "being an eternally identical one."[39] But Cummings continues elsewhere:

The Mormon view of an individual's progress through the eternities is first of all dependent upon his exercise of his free agency in conforming to all the conditions. We must not lose sight of the fact that ultimately exaltation rests in his hands and depends upon his decisions and actions. One of the conditions of his own progress is his affiliation with others whose goal is the same as his own. Nothing that he can do is of avail to him without these affiliations. Through all eternity he remains an individual but through eternity he will remain a social individual. His aim, then, becomes one of affiliation in the highest social circles for which he can qualify. This aspect of the doctrine could well be called affiliationism. It marks the fact of individuality and also that of association. These very affiliations augment the individual's stature as an individual. The whole concept of progress becomes one of associative progress, but this doctrine of affiliation opens up the way for each individual to develop to the fullest his individual powers. . . .[40]

I would suggest that the Association for Mormon Letters can fulfill the high hope Richard Cummings, as its President, articulated for it, that is, to provide "a partial but salutary resolution" of the Mormon identity crisis; but it can do that only if its members perceive that crisis not as a battle but as a paradox, a potentially fruitful one for Mormon life and Mormon letters. The Association can indeed, and *does* I think, provide what Richard called "an appropriate setting in which to maintain one's integrity as an individual in a Mormon context."[41] I would suggest that it will achieve its full potential only if it can find ways not only to "serve the Church's best interests," as Richard suggested it does, by helping individual members maintain, explore, and express their individuality but also by imaginatively challenging and helping them to endure in the struggle required to find their true selves in relationships, in the challenge of covenant-making, in the true marriage of the contraries of obedience and integrity.

NOTES

1. Richard J. Cummings, "Some Reflections on the Mormon Identity Crisis," Presidential Address to the Association for Mormon Letters, given 13 October 1979, printed in *Sunstone* 4 (December 1979). The quotation is from page 27.
2. Cummings, p. 29.
3. Truman G. Madsen, *Defender of the Faith* (Salt Lake City, Utah: Bookcraft, 1980), pp. 221-229
4. Madsen, p. 222.
5. Madsen, p. 223.
6. Madsen, p. 225.
7. Madsen, p. 226.
8. Madsen, p. 229.
9. See the discussion in Eugene England, *Brother Brigham* (Salt Lake City, Utah: Bookcraft, 1980), p. 87, and the extended analysis in Gary James Bergera, "The Orson Pratt–Brigham Young Controversy," *Dialogue: A Journal of Mormon Thought* 13 (Summer 1980): 7–49.
10. Minutes, 27 January 1860, *MS*, Brigham Young Papers, LDS Church Archives.
11. Secretary's Journal, 28 January 1860. LDS Church Archives.
12. Secretary's Journal, 31 January 1860.
13. Secretary's Journal, 4 April 1860.
14. Secretary's Journal, 5 April 1860.
15. Secretary's Journal, 1 October 1860.
16. Miscellaneous Papers, 5 April 1860, *MS*, Brigham Young Papers, LDS Church Archives.
17. Letter Book of Brigham Young, 1867-68, pp. 920-921, LDS Church Archives.
18. Church Historical Office Journal, 4 July 1868, LDS Church Archives.
19. Juanita Brooks, *The Mountain Meadows Massacre* (Stanford, Calif: Stanford University Press, 1950), and *John Doyle Lee; Zealot-Pioneer Builder-Scapegoat* (Glendale, Calif.: Arthur H. Clark Co, 1963 and [corrected new edition] 1972); Levi Peterson, "Juanita Brooks: The Mormon Historian as Tragedian," *Journal of Mormon History* 3 (1976): 47–54.
20. John D. Lee, *Mormonism Unveiled* (St. Louis: Bryan Brand and Co., 1878), pp. 239–240.
21. Lee, p. 234.
22. Lee, p. 228.
23. The Chislett narrative is quoted in Thomas B. Stenhouse, *The Rocky Mountain Saints* (New York: D. Appleton, 1873), p. 317.
24. Chislett, p. 319
25. Chislett, p. 332.
26. Chislett, p. 326.
27. The Journal of Patience Loader Archer, typescript of original, Harold B. Lee Library, Brigham Young University, p. 87.
28. See President Young's Sermon, 2 November 1856, *Journal of Discourses,* 26 vols. (London: Latter-day Saints Book Depot, 1854–86), 4:69.
29. Sermon printed in *Deseret News,* 10 December 1856.
30. Chislett, p. 317.
31. Stanley B. Kimball, *Heber C. Kimball: Mormon Patriarch and Pioneer* (Urbana: University of Illinois Press, 1981), p. 93. See my discussion of this modern version of the Abraham-Isaac story in "Joseph Smith and the Tragic Quest," reprinted above.
32. Issued December 15, 1969, and published in *Church News,* January 10, 1970, p. 12, and in *Dialogue* 4 (Winter 1969): 102–103.
33. Richard Cummings, p. 29
34. Quoted in *The Norton Anthology of English Literature: Major Authors Edition*, Abrams, et al., eds. (New York: W. W. Norton, 1975), p. 1323.
35. Joseph Smith Jr.,*History of the Church of Jesus Christ of Latter-day Saints*, B.H. Roberts, ed., 7 vols., 2nd ed. rev. (Salt Lake City: Deseret Book Co., 1951), 6:428.
36. George E. Mendenhall, in "Covenant," an article in *Encyclopedia Brittanica* (Chicago: Encyclopedia Brittanica Inc., 1979), 5:230.
37. Michael Novak, "The Family Out of Favor," *Harper's* 252 (April 1976): 39.

38. Novak, p. 42.
39. B. F. Cummings, *The Eternal Individual Self* (Salt Lake City: Utah Printing Co., 1968), pp. 7, 69, 70.
40. B. F. Cummings, p. 121.
41. Richard Cummings, p. 32.

Early 1966;
editorial for the first issue
of *Dialogue: A Journal of Mormon Thought.*

C H A P T E R 3

THE POSSIBILITY OF DIALOGUE

Prove all things; hold fast that which is good.
–Paul the Apostle

The paradoxical words of Paul quoted above are an obvious place to begin to consider the possibilities of dialogue about a Christian religion and its cultural heritage. The words are familiar to our time. "Examine. Test. Prove." The demand for reevaluation and for proof and the pressure toward thoroughgoing skepticism continue in our universities and mount in our society generally. The voices against dogmatism (especially religious dogmatism) grow in the land. And here is Paul, who brought Christianity to the Western world, speaking the same words. "Prove all things": consider all things; look at all possibilities; examine your inherited prejudices and evaluate again even your cherished beliefs; be open to what might be a new understanding–a new faith.

But, of course, Paul was no mere skeptic. The Christian apostle would have us give our searching a meaning, not allow it to serve as an easy posture. He also said, "Hold fast that which is good": respect certitude as well as doubt; commit yourself to the good you find; give yourself to the possibilities that begin to prove out; live the faith that is given you in your seeking–however deeply you continue to test that faith and examine others.

A Book of Mormon prophet named Alma understood this paradox. He knew that "faith is not to have a perfect knowledge" but is a willingness to "experiment" in new realms, to give place in our hearts for new words and not cast them out prematurely with our unbelief. He knew what it is to prove and also hold—to be open to seeds of potential meaning and being, continually both to test and to nourish them (because they can only be properly tested if nourished) until the good seeds produce fruit that is "most precious" (See Alma 32:27-42).

Paul's challenge and Alma's experiment have been deeply significant to my own experience of the possibilities of life and to my faith in the process of dialogue as a way to discover life's possibilities. I have tasted the precious fruit of faith in specific things; I have been able, in all my proving, to discover and to continue to hold some things fast as certainties—faith in the divinity of Christ and in the saving power of his teachings and Atonement, faith in the divine mission of his Church and his modern prophets—and the deep hunger of my soul has been fed as I have given myself to this faith. At the same time, I have sensed the risk of choice, the limitation of commitment to a defined context in this world that is full of richly complex possibilities and allows us only finite vision into their worth. Yet I have found that my very specific faith does not cut me off from this rich complexity; it actually intensifies and informs with meaning my involvement in it.

I am motivated, in my relationship to Christ and my desire to build his Kingdom, by both the questing openness and the loving authority exhibited in his life and in his revelations to his prophets. I think and act within a specific context of Mormon faith that defines my life and shapes my soul. I relate to my wife and children and friends and use my time in terms of the counsel of the Church and the heritage of Mormon experience. But my very grasp on this specific direction, this "iron rod," turns me out to all people and their experience in desire for dialogue with them. The very principles I accept as definitive of my life warn me to be continually open to the revelation of new possibilities for my life from both God and man.

My faith encourages my curiosity and awe; it thrusts me out into relationship with all the creation. The Christ I have come to know through my Mormon faith affirms the world as good and each of its people as eternally precious; he insists that my words and actions be integrated with each other and relevant to that world—that they not just speak *to* it but really make the connection. My faith in him encourages me to enter into dialogue.

Such a dialogue seems to me to depend on some initial commitment to values, to some beliefs that give a person a place from which to speak and a purpose for speaking. It can be engaged in best by those who hold fast that which is good. But such a dialogue depends also on willingness to prove all things. We must be willing to consider that anything we believe or base our lives upon may be a partial truth–at best something seen (as Saint Paul also said) "through a glass darkly"–or even may be dead wrong. We must take seriously the jovial words of the distinguished Mormon chemist, Henry Eyring, "In this Church we don't have to believe anything that isn't true."

A dialogue is possible if we can avoid looking upon doubt as a sin–or as a virtue–but can see it as a condition, a condition that can be productive if it leads one to seek and knock and ask and if the doubter is approached with sympathetic listening and thoughtful response or that can be destructive if it is used as an escape from responsibility or the doubter is approached with condemnation.

A dialogue is possible if, in trying to describe our findings and convictions, we can be honest with ourselves and each other, if we can use traditional forms and conventions without letting them become lies or idols. We must be witnesses for all that is real to us and no more, recognizing the eternal dignity of truth which gives it claim finally over expediency and even perhaps charity.

But a dialogue can realize its full possibilities only if there is charity, if we can speak with sensitivity to each other's framework or ability to hear and speak in order to communicate for each other's welfare, not to justify or exalt ourselves at each other's expense. We must truly listen to each other, respecting our essential brotherhood and the courage of those who try to speak, however they may differ from us in professional standing or religious belief or moral vision. We must speak and listen patiently, with good humor, with real expectation, and then our dialogue can serve both truth and charity.

Joseph Smith, one of the prophets to whom I give my faith, has recorded the voice of the Lord urging men to be "anxiously engaged in a good cause . . . and bring to pass much righteousness; for the power is in them, wherein they are agents unto themselves" (Doctrine and Covenants 58:27-28). I am motivated by my belief in that power and agency to test the possibilities that the journal we here begin can be successful in fostering many kinds of valuable dialogue. I am also motivated by partial agreement with Episcopal Bishop James A. Pike that "The church should be a launching pad and not a comfort station." (It should be both.) And I am motivated by the challenges to intelligent and creative discipleship made again and again by the leaders of the Church.

The faith I hold fast impels me to speak and to listen; it impels me to express honestly and fully and as gracefully as possible the convictions that shape my life, to try to demonstrate the things I find as I think and do research and experience the holy. It impels me to listen carefully and always. My faith as a Mormon encourages by specific doctrines my feeling that each man is eternally unique and god-like in potential, that each man deserves a hearing and that we have something important to learn from each man if we can hear him–if he can speak and we can listen well. Dialogue is possible to those who can. Such a dialogue will not solve all of our intellectual and spiritual problems–and it will not save us; but it can bring us joy and new vision and help us toward that dialogue with our deepest selves and with our God which can save us.

Minnesota, 1972, in response to a troubled returned missionary
I had known at Stanford;
published in *Dialogue*, Autumn/Winter 1973.

C H A P T E R 4

LETTER TO A COLLEGE STUDENT

Your letter caught me by surprise, not because your particular form of unhappiness and your objections to the Church are unique—and not only because I remember you as a person living in quite a different universe than the one of sharp criticism and disillusionment which you now project with such vividness. No, my surprise was due mainly I think to the distance that I have moved in my own spiritual life from constant attention to those kinds of problems. Just a few years ago, as an LDS Institute teacher, a member of the bishopric of a student ward, and a managing editor of *Dialogue*, I was confronted daily with the kinds of concerns you express, and I tended to think of them as central to the Gospel experience—to the struggle to know God and Christ and to love others. Now I am seldom involved with those particular problems—although overwhelmed with a whole set of other problems equally as mysterious and difficult and important. That is one measure of the distance between the Stanford Ward and the Faribault Branch.

You talk about your disillusionment with your mission, how, after committing yourself to "offer people peace and kindness and hope," you found among your companions much "pettiness, narrowness, deceit and childishness, not to mention the obnoxious piety that only those who have the One And Only Way of Truth can possess." Yes, I've seen those things, still do sometimes—in fact find them in myself. And you talk about "bewilderment," your sense of having been betrayed because your idealism and devotion to the Church have led you to give service to it, but that very service has paradoxically revealed to you "dangerous tendencies in our bureaucratic, businessman's organization which are spiritually emasculating–namely, commercialism, exploitation of the gullible, statistics, and the self-righteous refusal to admit blunder and consider change where necessary." Yes, those things are there too. Again, I find them in myself, in my own stumbling attempts to serve the Lord and the Church. And I am sure that you are right in your observation that "maybe it wasn't so hot in the 'good old days' either"–that these problems have been present whenever the Lord's Kingdom was organized among human beings.

Your letter brings back voices from the past, memories of precious friends and of other words spoken in anguish and tears:

Since I've stopped going through the formal motions of meetings and statistics-oriented assignments, prayer and service have become more spontaneous, joyful and personal. And valuable. Am I going to hell? Yet at times I feel alone, like I'm drifting from something which is supposed to be true and good, which may be just another cosmic hoax.

No, I don't think it's a cosmic hoax. And I don't think, as you suggest for a possibility, that the reason for the problems is that people have been taken in, like the congregations of Elmer Gantry and Marjoe, but by more clever and smoother operators. No, I find incredible sincerity and great dedication in the Church at all levels. I think that the problems you mention arise not from some group or individual's lack of sincerity or honesty but because of the same kinds of ignorance and sin that beset us all. The special problem in the Church is that our high level of general satisfaction with the Gospel life style and our genuine spiritual experiences and resulting strong commitments tend to make us willing to let sincerity be enough, without requiring of *ourselves* what missionaries are always requiring of other people whose beliefs they are challenging–that one must be (as completely as possible) *right* as well as *sincere*. If we take the whole Gospel seriously it challenges us to be thoughtful, to test, to be sensitive, to be balanced in our use of faith and reason, of experiential evidence and the witness of the Spirit. If more Church members did these things most of the excesses that bother you so much wouldn't happen–but none of us does them very consistently, not even you and me!

Your comment about how your life seems to have changed since you stopped struggling directly with the gospel in Church activity reminds me of a good friend who made a similar decision some years ago. He is possibly the most morally honest and sensitive person I have known, and after struggling for some years he found that he just could not cope with the various forms of bigotry, self-righteousness, etc., that he encountered weekly in Church meetings. It became an unbearable experience for him–psychologically and spiritually–and he and his wife finally decided there was nothing left but to take their family into inactivity. He continues to live the basic moral principles of the Gospel, but he and his family and the Church have suffered a great loss, I think. Though I can *understand* his decision (and, in fact, approve that kind of "vacation" for a short time for some people when things become unbearable and all attempts to do something about it apparently are unfruitful), I think such a decision as a permanent "solution" is a tragic cop-out. I pray with all my heart that you won't take that route.

I think I know what you and my friend have felt. I've been through some of the pain you describe myself, and I have my own battle ribbons (including a "purple heart" or two) from combat with particular brands of Mormon arrogance and provincialism, the "spiritual imperialism" that you speak of, various forms of fanaticism, racism, militarism, authoritarianism, that I have found in Church circles–and am convinced are deeply contrary to the Gospel and the ideals of the Church. My own missionary experience was no picnic, either. Charlotte and I (who went together as a married couple to Samoa) had experiences on our mission like those you were so appalled by in your own–encountering the invincible ignorance and insensitivity of some young missionaries just off an Idaho farm or Salt Lake's East Bench (I qualified on both counts) as we tried to relate to an alien culture, the smugness and self-righteousness of people presuming to take the truth to other people, though they were unable to comprehend either the strengths of those people or their own weaknesses.

You were right in your comment about appreciating the good people you found native to the country where you did your missionary work and your thinking that *they* should perhaps send missionaries to Zion. We felt that way ourselves many times. And yet you seem not yet to have learned some crucial lessons that, after a good deal of pain, we at least *began* to learn there: Mainly that *we* were as guilty of bigotry and insensitivity, of lack of love, in our judgment of some other missionaries as they were in their judgment of the native people; and that despite the mistakes, the bumbling, the blindness in many dimensions of the missionaries, most of them were serving the Lord faithfully in taking, however haltingly and inefficiently, his Gospel of faith and repentance and loving service to people who, in spite of their many great qualities, needed it and were made better by it.

At one point in our mission I wrote a letter to Elder Marion D. Hanks, then of the First Council of Seventy, much like the one you sent me. After letting me cool off for awhile, he wrote back probably the most helpful letter I have received from another human being in my life; he taught me to see the danger of riding off by myself on a white horse, to realize that just as one must not only be sincere but also right, so one must not only be right but also *effective*, and it wasn't very effective to go around self-righteously condemning my fellow missionaries or harboring resentments against them when I should be facing up to my own failings and weaknesses, and showing them increased love along with the right example.

I also began to see in Samoa how *important* the Gospel itself is–more important than my impatience with the weak vessels the Lord must choose to carry it to the world. Before we left for our mission Charlotte and I had been exposed somewhat to the social action idealism of the University of Utah and there was some vague questioning in our minds about whether really the best way to relate to and serve other societies was to go with a challenge to them to take on a new faith; shouldn't we rather be trying to help them with their medical needs, farming needs, educational needs, in short, to *develop* them since they were an "underdeveloped" country? We actually did make contact with many varieties of human pain and need in that still rather primitive society in Samoa but found that, despite the reality of their suffering from things like lack of good medicine, lack of good farming techniques, even their suffering from the oppression of colonial British society based in New Zealand, the Samoans suffered most deeply and most damagingly from directly personal and family problems–lack of ability to control anger, insensitivity to certain dimensions of loyalty in their relations with each other, simple ignorance about how to fulfill some of their capacities and yearnings for intelligence and understanding and expression. In short, they *most* needed the Gospel, with its individually liberating idealism, explicit moral and spiritual instruction, and opportunities for practical development. We saw that the cultural relativists that we had studied in college were wrong, that adultery for instance was not harmful to people in our society merely because they had been *taught* it was wrong and therefore felt guilty. It was clearly harmful to people in Samoa for intrinsic reasons; even though some of them had *not* been taught adultery was wrong, they suffered the natural results of such action–the breakdown of human relations and of crucial family strength, of the sense of individual worth and self-control and of fidelity to another person that lies at the heart of a good marriage. As a result, in the graphic words of Jacob in The Book of Mormon, "Many hearts died, pierced with deep wounds." But when such people joined or became active in the Church they found the support the Gospel provides for family unity and trust, for loyalty between husband and wife, through teaching and helping people to live the commandments of God–and they were incredibly happier, more liberated, though still "underdeveloped."

The Gospel is so overwhelmingly valuable that it crowds out the temptation to be overwhelmed by the mistakes people make trying to translate its ideals into specific Church expression and action–the real intellectual problems and puzzles that such human expression of the Gospel can get us involved in. This awareness has come to me most powerfully here in Minnesota, trying to serve as branch president to a group of about 100 saints scattered over seventy-five miles. We range from hard core, Utah-born, inactive to new, bright-eyed, convert student. All of us are guilty at various times of most of the forms of bigotry and hyprocrisy and of the various dangerous tendencies in bureaucracy and self-righteousness that have repulsed you, but at the same time there is closeness, communication, self-development and moving, penetrating spiritual experience available to us through our association and service in the Church–and I mean feelings and experiences crucial to our joy and progression that we just wouldn't have without the Church.

We see families united when one or both parents join the Church and take seriously the covenants of baptism. We see a young man, long devastated by drug experience and divorce and plagued by continual despair, gradually respond to the challenge to return to activity in the Church and regular use of his priesthood and thus begin to grow spiritually and in self-confidence and become a new person.

At our Easter service last month our visitors included a large family of Spanish Americans from Texas whom the missionaries had contacted. The family had with them a grandmother visiting from Mexico, who spoke no English. It happened that our main speaker, Frank Odd, was a recent addition to our branch who teaches Spanish at St. Olaf College. After a moving personal witness of the meaning of Christ and the new life our Savior brought us, Brother Odd asked us to excuse him while he spoke to a person there who had not been able to understand any of the service to that point. Then he gave the grandmother a special message in Spanish and bore his testimony to her. And though we did not understand much of what was being said then, we felt deeply a spirit of love and conviction witnessed by the Holy Ghost. Tears are shed often at our meetings, not "potato love" tears of gullible self-congratulation, but tears of joy and recognition of goodness and truth–such as those we shed recently while a man who had been inactive forty years passed the sacrament to us as a new deacon, beginning to prepare to baptize his wife and children. Or when a young man spoke last week with marvelous, miraculous effectiveness about his conversion to the Gospel and the value of the Church to him while standing before us as a living witness to what he was saying, because we were aware that through his involvement and service in the Church he has grown in just a few years from a totally withdrawn and inarticulate, even vocally and socially crippled person, to the dynamic young husband and father we saw before us.

Well, perhaps the awareness you expressed–that your own perspective may be faulty–is your saving grace. I believe that is the key for you, as it has been for me, and hope that I can help you see that feelingly, as some others have helped me. I continue to believe that the burden of change is on the persons, like yourself and me, who see the problems, who are pained by the failings of the Church. Since we are the only ones who see what we think is "wrong," we are the ones who must do something constructive about it, because the people who are committing the errors can't see them. What we can do about these problems is not leave, desert, turn the Church over to those who may be perverting it, nor is it to remain within but to withdraw spiritually through our own self-righteousness; we must reach out in love, trying to help–and also trying to learn, through our cooperation and common service, from the perspective and commitments of other people. We must learn to see our *own* faults–lack of courage, perhaps, or lack of whole-souled commitment, failings which may be, in the long run, more destructive than the ones we are condemning.

I love the Church with all my heart and mind, but it's a love that has to be developed, renewed–one which I know can lapse, can ebb and flow. I hope you'll give the Church a chance–again and again. It needs you–and you need it, because it is the means that the Lord has given us to struggle with the great moral and spiritual imperatives from God for attaining the possible Godhood within us. I think the Church is by far the best place to do that and the only place we really can, partly because of the very challenges that human association in the Church context provides and which have been so upsetting to you.

Written in 1975
and published in the *Ensign*, official magazine of the LDS Church,
April 1976.

C H A P T E R 5

SPEAKING THE TRUTH IN LOVE

One of my favorite stories, perhaps the one that best conveys to my ear the spirit of priesthood leadership, concerns John Taylor, who was President of the Church from 1877 to 1890. Earlier, while he was President of the Council of the Twelve, two men came to him for resolution of a bitter quarrel that had alienated them from each other. President Taylor was an exceptionally good singer, with emotional power tempered in such experiences as singing for the Prophet Joseph in the final hour at Carthage Jail; he told the two, "Brethren, before I hear your case, I would like very much to sing one of the songs of Zion for you." When he had finished, he commented that he never heard one of the Church's hymns without wanting to hear another and so sang one more–and then another, and another. Finally the two men were moved to tears and left, fully reconciled, without any discussion of their problem (see *Improvement Era* 43:522).

An example of singing may seem a strange beginning to a discussion of how to tame our tongues toward more effective speaking, but that singing by John Taylor, it seems to me, is a perfect illustration of my main point: What we say is important, but even more significant is how we speak, with what emotional and spiritual effect. The example gives the extreme case where the power for reconciliation lies entirely in the feelings communicated–the manner rather than the specific content. Most of us must–and can, I believe–learn to improve the quality of both what we say and how we say it.

Christ was concerned about our tongues. He knew, as his apostle James taught, that the tongue, like the bridle of a horse or the helm of a ship, has power to steer—potential to determine good or ill—greatly out of proportion to its size. James emphasized the harmful results, calling the tongue "a fire, a world of iniquity ... an unruly evil, full of deadly poison" (James 3:6, 8). And Christ warned his disciples in former times, "Those things which proceed out of the mouth come forth from the heart; and they defile the man" (Matt. 15:18).

But Christ also knew the power of the tongue for good, if properly tamed and trained: He has said to Latter-day Saints, "Take upon you the name of Christ, and speak the truth in soberness" (D&C 18:21), and he has promised us, "First seek to obtain my word, and then shall your tongue be loosed; then, if you desire, you shall have my Spirit and my word, yea, the power of God unto the convincing of men" (D&C 11:21).

A familiar missionary scripture ("And he gave some, apostles; and some, prophets ... for the perfecting of the saints. . . .") is followed by an explanation from the apostle Paul to the little branch at Ephesus of the reason we must have Christ's true Church—properly organized and led—to guide us toward perfection in the image of Christ:

> *That we henceforth be no more children, tossed to and fro, and carried about with every wind of doctrine, by the sleight of men, and cunning craftiness, whereby they lie in wait to deceive;*
>
> *But* speaking the truth in love, *may grow up into him in all things, which is the head, even Christ. (Eph. 4:14-15; my emphasis)*

One major source of the power of Christ, not only to save mankind from death but to redeem us from sin and ignorance, is that he spoke the truth in love and soberness. But how can we, the Saints (which means merely that we are trying to follow Christ), learn to speak the truth in love, that we might, rather than defile ourselves, bless and redeem others with words? Our examples, of course, should be Christ and his apostles, both those former ones, who wrote his words and their own in the Standard Works, and those who speak to us today. The Savior's language is spare, without the vain repetitions he warned against, absolutely sincere to the point of vigor, and courageous, near outspokenness, but always motivated by love and aimed at redemption, even when he scolded the Pharisees: "Ye blind guides, which strain at a gnat, and swallow a camel. . . .Cleanse first that which is within the cup and platter, that the outside of them may be clean also" (Matt. 23:24, 26).

We could do nothing better to help "tame our tongues" that they might speak the truth in love than to read often and carefully the words of Christ, in the Gospels, Third Nephi, and the Doctrine and Covenants (which consists mainly of the Lord's words to Joseph Smith). Next in value as models are the speeches and writing of the prophets and apostles, both those in the scriptures and those from the special witnesses today who know Christ best and are often called to speak directly for him. Especially would we do well to read and listen to President Spencer W. Kimball, the literal mouthpiece of the Lord Jesus Christ for our own time, whose plain-spoken vigor combined with incisive imagery and humbly recounted personal experience can, if we will have ears to hear, convey the quality of redemptive love in the truth he speaks.

Let me make a few suggestions that might help us do specific things to translate such examples into our own ways of speaking and writing:

First, it would seem obvious that we must be sincere in order to speak sincerely, that we must deeply value truth and care about people to be able to speak with redemptive integrity. As the Lord expressed it, "Out of the abundance of the heart the mouth speaketh" (Matt. 12:34); we must "cleanse first that which is within . . . that the outside . . . may be clean also." The apostle Paul came to a similar realization:

> *Though I speak with the tongues of men and of angels and have not charity I am become as sounding brass, or a tinkling cymbal.*
>
> *And though I have the gift of prophecy, and understand all mysteries, and all knowledge; and though I have all faith, so that I could remove mountains, and have not charity, I am nothing. (I Cor. 13:1-2)* [*Charity is defined in The Book of Mormon, Moroni 7:47, as "the pure love of Christ."*]

But this becomes a chicken and egg problem (which comes first?), because consciously cultivating sincere, loving speech will help us become more loving and sincere. As Lowell Bennion reminds us in his fine lesson on this subject (Gospel Doctrine class manual, *Teachings of the New Testament*, 1953, p. 84), "Speech not only mirrors the man, it also molds the man."

I find that my children–like most young people in our time–are especially sensitive to the danger of being hypocritical; they sometimes find it difficult, for instance, to respond right away to the exercises suggested in our family home evening lessons, such as going around the table with a word of praise from each for each family member or setting a goal to try consciously to respond with a patient loving word when offended during the week ("But, Dad, what if I don't *feel* patient?" or "Mom, you wouldn't want me to just make up something, would you?").

Obviously we must work on both our inner nature and our outer expression at the same time, possibly beginning with some thoughtful reflection about what we really do care most about and then making some conscious efforts to see that our speech accurately reflects those central values, rather than our temporary moods ("But, Becky, you *do* sincerely *want* to become more patient and constructive, don't you?"). We all need to learn the value of trying to speak the way we want to be—that is, not as a substitute or mask for our sincere feelings (which is hypocrisy) but as a means of helping us develop those feelings.

Sometimes we are blasphemous or profane or sarcastic because we seek attention or too much let our associates influence us, or are merely lazy and careless. Some reflection about whose opinion we really care most about—God's or our peers'—and how much it matters to find and be our own true selves would, I believe, help us begin to change. We sometimes flatter—and encourage flattery in others—because we forget that our first loyalty must be to Christ and the truth, that excessive praise for ourselves or the shallow regard of those we give it to are ultimately ashes in the mouth and that to be eternally happy we must care about eternal values more than the honors of men, position, comfort, security, or even safety. Christ rejected flattery, and scathingly warned: "Woe unto you, when all men shall speak well of you! For so did their fathers to the false prophets" (Luke 6:26). That example and consciousness of our own priorities can help us begin to be more courageous in speaking and requiring the truth.

And that suggests a second way to develop our ability to speak with integrity and love: We need to cultivate moral courage. It seems clear that most forms of insincere and unloving speech arise from fear: fear of serious reflection on what we most care about and want to be, fear of exposing our limited selves, fear of the opinion or power of others, fear of demonstrating a whole-souled commitment to Christ when it might be unpopular or even dangerous to do so. We need to read often Paul's farewell to the Ephesian saints, in which he reminds them he has served the Lord "with all humility of mind and many tears" and has "kept back nothing that was profitable unto you":

And now, behold, I go bound in the spirit unto Jerusalem, not knowing the things that shall befall me there:

Save that the Holy Ghost witnesseth in every city, saying that bonds and afflictions abide me.

But none of these things move me, neither count I my life dear unto myself, so that I might finish my course with joy, and the ministry, which I have received of the Lord Jesus, to testify the gospel of the grace of God. (Acts 20:22-24)

But how can we develop such courage? John has told us that "perfect love casteth out fear" (I John 4:18), which love is the fruit of the Spirit when we try to live the gospel fully, relying on the Lord. It's something of a chicken and egg problem again, but again we can start by reflecting on what we at least *want* our true values to be. Can we, for instance, really say with the apostle Paul, "The Lord is my helper, and I will not fear what man shall do unto me" (Heb. 13:6)? Can we have the confidence of Nephi: "I will go and do the things which the Lord hath commanded, for I know that the Lord giveth no commandments unto the children of men, save he shall prepare a way for them that they may accomplish the thing which he commandeth them" (I Nephi 3:7)? God has commanded us not only to tell the truth but to actively speak out the truth in order to bring redemption, assuring us that we can succeed because he is our helper. If we will only begin to take some risks, speaking the truth lovingly and boldly even though we feel inept or weak or exposed, the Lord will keep his promises, and we will be surprised at the response in others and in ourselves.

Let me give some examples, one personal, if I may. Not long after becoming the first Mormon on the staff of a Lutheran college, I was invited to speak at the daily chapel service. My first inclination was to talk on some general Christian principle; but I had recently heard some comments on campus about Mormons not being Christians. As I thought and prayed about what to do, I felt that I should meet the prejudice head on and finally, with what I admit was much uneasiness and fear, I spoke forthrightly in defense of the central and unique principles of the restored gospel of Christ and bore personal testimony concerning them. There were some raised eyebrows and cold shoulders, but the response from the students and most of the faculty was very positive, and I was often called upon or found opportunity thereafter to preach the gospel directly in that academic community. Such exposure quite likely offended some of my colleagues, but on the other hand some students joined the Church and many others more carefully examined their own beliefs and values.

Another example: A new member of our ward spoke in sacrament meeting some years ago on how gospel principles might be translated into politically liberal social and economic action in our nation. The next week, a politically conservative brother used testimony meeting to rebut the newcomer and to question by implication his faith and religious orthodoxy. Offended, the first man was tempted to lash back or retreat into haughty silence, but as he reflected he remembered times when such reactions by others had led to extended feuds, inactivity, and even apostasy. He finally decided, though with little confidence, to try the Lord's counsel: He made an appointment and went to the brother who had criticized him, asked forgiveness for alarming him, and bore his testimony concerning the fundamentals of the gospel. The brother responded in like spirit, sharing his testimony and asking forgiveness. They became good friends, continuing to differ and sometimes openly disagree, but serving as a powerful example to all of us in the ward of brotherhood and the value of open, sincere, but loving, expression.

If we can develop the courage to take some personal risks and can learn to rely on the Spirit as we break out of old inhibitions and prejudices, we can be more effective in both vigorously defending our faith in the world and in lovingly challenging people in the Church to live the gospel better. From Christ himself, his disciples from early times have learned to "speak the word of God with boldness" and thus to bring redemption to mankind. It may seem a contradiction to encourage boldness when we've been talking about speaking in love, but true love is redemptive and redemption may require boldness, pain, suffering, even–as the Atonement itself manifests–unto death. Of course, in all our boldness, we must be true to the great principle of giving milk before meat and to Paul's great lesson (when he advised the Corinthians not to eat food previously offered to idols if only because it might offend a brother trained in orthodox Judaism) that we consider the harm we might do to the faith of others with a truth or action, however harmless to ourselves. These too are part of speaking the truth in love.

All priesthood leaders and parents need to develop this ability to speak the truth boldly yet in a way that will bring those in their stewardship to salvation. We can err in both directions: I have had the experience of speaking in a sacrament meeting, or to my own wife or children, with a self-righteous zeal that made my words, though true, not only ineffective to bring about the change I sought, but offensive and, to my bitter regret, destructive of the spirit of the meeting or of my home. On the other hand, I have, in counseling situations, or in interviewing those responsible to me in my Church leadership positions, sometimes been too nondirective, too timidly vague, or merely supportive when I should have called to repentance or account. The Lord, through the Prophet Joseph, has taught us the proper balance:

Reproving betimes with sharpness, when moved upon by the Holy Ghost; and then showing forth afterwards an increase of love toward him whom thou hast reproved, lest he esteem thee to be his enemy;

That he may know that thy faithfulness is stronger than the cords of death. (D&C 121:43-44)

If we can follow that counsel, each of us can learn more fully to speak the truth with a kind of love that changes and redeems ourselves and others. In my experience (and this is a third suggestion), we can help prepare to do this by learning to be more open about our own opinions, convictions, experiences, our mistakes, even our shortcomings. When President Kimball, at the close of last October Conference, shared with us his feeling that his life could be improved and that he intended to do so by applying principles he had jotted down during the conference, we were moved to increased trust and desire to follow his example rather than any lack of confidence. We must gain trust and understanding through sharing our whole selves before we can be in a position to move others with our words. The Church community is blessed, not fractured, by those who express themselves sincerely and openly–even their disagreements and their vulnerability–rather than those who keep silent in public but criticize in private or harbor resentment or guilt or gnaw alone on the bones of their failures and hurts.

One of our family's finest home evening experiences occurred when our teenage son, Mark, took what I'm sure seemed an enormous risk and called the family to repentance for a spirit of bickering and uncooperative self-concern that had been increasing over a few weeks–but only after first gaining our hearts by confessing in tears his own failures and his sorrow at what we had lost.

Christ told his former-day disciples (Matt. 5:23-24) to go and be reconciled to their brethren before offering their gifts at the altar (the equivalent, I would think, of taking the sacrament); he told us latter-day disciples: "On this, the Lord's day, thou shalt offer thine oblations and thy sacraments unto the Most High, confessing thy sins unto thy brethren, and before the Lord" (D&C 59:12).

We *can* do some things, then, to tame our tongues in a positive way–to learn to speak the truth in love and thus "grow up into Christ in all things." I have made three interrelated suggestions to guide our efforts:

1. Be sincere; reflect on what we truly care most about–or want to–and then consciously work, even with specific exercises, to make our expressions true to those values.

2. Especially cultivate moral courage, the ability to be loyal, *despite the costs*, to our ultimate values, having confidence that the Lord is our helper; as a specific effort consciously work more forthrightly (but with the spirit of understanding and love that will make us effective) to preach repentance to this generation, both outside and within the Church.

3. In the strength of that courage strive to gain the confidence of others, so they truly can hear us, particularly by sharing more openly our defeats and our uncertainties–but also our victories, our spiritual experiences, and our deepest convictions–that they may be open to our words (even when we "reprove betimes with sharpness") because they know that "our faithfulness is stronger than the cords of death."

Finally, it would seem that sincerity in speech and life depends on the nature and strength of our ultimate convictions and that the most powerful sincerity, the only kind sufficient to bring redemption, is that based on a whole-souled commitment to Christ. It is really only his example and the truth revealed in his gospel of salvation that will move us to tame our tongues until we can speak the truth in love.

The Phi Kappa Phi Honors Address at Brigham Young University, March 1975;
published as a pamphlet by Phi Kappa Phi
and then by *Dialogue*, Autumn 1975.

CHAPTER 6

GREAT BOOKS OR TRUE RELIGION? DEFINING THE MORMON SCHOLAR

I propose to explore what it might mean in these last days to be a Mormon scholar, a Latter-day Saint intellectual. Perhaps some of you flinch at the label, "intellectual"; it isn't always a complimentary term in our society—or even in the Church. I use it in an essentially neutral way, as descriptive of your gift from the Lord that makes you delight in ideas, alive to the life that goes on in your mind as well as outside it, that makes you question set forms and conventional wisdom to see if they really are truth or only habit, whether they endure because right or merely because of fear or sloth; I use the term intellectual to refer to the gift from the Lord that makes you curious about why as well as how, anxious to serve him by being creative as well as obedient. You, more than most people, have it in you to exemplify Sir Thomas More's phrase in Robert Bolt's play, *A Man For All Seasons*, when he says God made animals for innocence and plants for their simplicity, but humans he made "to serve him wittily, in the tangle of our minds."

The Restoration has been characterized from the first by such people as you, by intellectuals, though our histories have so far tended to slight them as such. Take Joseph Smith, founder of the School of the Prophets, student of Hebrew in frontier Ohio in the midst of desperate struggles of the fledgling Church to survive. Read his King Follett funeral sermon, where he proposes the most intellectually exciting as well as spiritually satisfying vision of man's nature and destiny in human history. Then he says:

This is good doctrine. It tastes good. I can taste the principles of eternal life, and so can you. They are given to me by the revelation of Jesus Christ; and I know that when I tell you these words of eternal life as they are given to me, you taste them, and I know that you believe them. You say that honey is sweet, and so do I. I can also taste the spirit of eternal life. I know that it is good, and when I tell you of these things which were given me by the inspiration of the Holy Spirit, you are bound to receive them as sweet, and rejoice more and more.

That is the perspective and language of an intellectual, one to whom ideas taste sweet. Or read Section 88 of the Doctrine and Covenants, which Joseph Smith gave a special name, "The Olive Leaf." It is an intriguing revelation of how God relates to the physical universe, how physical light relates to intelligence. Think of the kinds of questions Joseph must have asked to move the Lord to give it. Surely that man was an intellectual, as well as a charismatic leader, a fine husband and father, a city-planner, and a Prophet of God. Think of the Pratt brothers, Parley P. and Orson, one a marvelously creative theologian and writer, the other a first-rate mathematician and astronomer. Many of you, I hope, have seen the calendar published by the Sunstone Foundation, a group of your peers, young LDS intellectuals who are selling the calendars to raise money to publish a journal in which to explore and express their gifts; the cover picture is of Temple Square in 1875, with the temple walls just starting up, and in the corner of the Square is Orson's observatory, a witness of the amazing intellectual vitality of that pioneer community still struggling to survive in a desert frontier. Think of Eliza R. Snow, accomplished poet, fine thinker, energetic leader in the late nineteenth-century women's movement, or her niece, Louisa Green, first editor of the *Women's Exponent,* or Eliza's brother Lorenzo Snow, an early graduate of the experimental Oberlin College and himself a poet and writer of skill as well as a courageous and inspiring President of the Church during some of its most difficult hours. Think of Orson Spencer, appointed first president of the University of Deseret by Brigham Young, and Emmeline B. Wells, and Brigham Young himself (whose lesser known qualities as a thinker and writer are well revealed in his letters, such as those to his sons recently published), or of B. H. Roberts or James Talmage–or of Juanita Brooks. (I recently heard Sister Brooks praised in a totally non-Mormon group as a supreme example of the historians' ideal because she was able, in her book on the Mountain Meadows Massacre, to attain a remarkable degree of objectivity despite a clear continued loyalty to her own people and faith.) These are our intellectual heroes–or ought to be.

But let me remind you of something about all of them. Juanita Brooks served the Church devotedly, as a stake Relief Society president among other things, for many years, and she then remained an unembittered and faithful Latter-day Saint wife and mother despite the almost total rejection of her and her husband by her own people because of that book on Mountain Meadows. Not only Joseph Smith gave his life for the Church; Parley Pratt bled to death after being stabbed by an assassin while serving a mission for the Church, dying, as he said in his last testimony, "a martyr to the faith." Orson Spencer was a cultivated, sensitive intellectual, whose equally cultivated and sensitive wife died in a tent in Iowa when the Saints were driven from Nauvoo; after teaching for a time in the new University of Deseret, he humbly accepted a mission call from Brigham Young in 1856 and died of tuberculosis while serving in St. Louis. And B. H. Roberts, whose combination of commitment to historical truth with a clear sense of ultimate values and a conviction of the divinity of the Restoration shines out from his *Comprehensive History of the Church* in a way that remains a standard for all LDS historians. This B. H. Roberts, man of conscience and integrity, after real struggle humbled himself to the authority of the presidency of the Church when that authority came into conflict with his political convictions and ambitions. What is my point? These intellectual heroes I hold up to you were also spiritual and moral heroes; these men and women pursued the truth with courage, and new ideas and creative expression with delight, but they finally put their faith in the Lord and loyalty to his Church over everything–over their pride, their comfort, health, lives–even their gift itself, when it came to that. So I propose to you *the Mormon scholar*, the Latter-day Saint intellectual of the last generation before the year 2000: a person whose standards and mission will of course best be formed and expressed by your generation itself–perhaps with some little help from what report I can give you here of the past and of the stir and struggle in myself and in my own generation. My call to your generation is that you help establish a new tradition of intellectual service to God and his Kingdom, a new style founded in part on the great tradition of the pioneer intellectuals and with the benefit of the example of the successes and an understanding of the failures of some in this past generation or two. I call you to affirm your gift with courageous integrity and fullness of heart and to develop and manifest your loyalty to the gospel and the restored Church in such a whole-souled and creative way that you can have that measure of acceptance you need: It will never be total, of course, given the critical edge characteristic of the intellectual enterprise, but you must earn enough to allow you to serve the Lord as he intends with a minimum of apology, of being on guard. I call you to be loyal to true religion, not merely great books, especially when it comes to a choice, as sometimes it does. Of course, what I'm really doing is trying to chart a new course for myself, because I span these two periods. I have been part of the growing pains and mistakes of the recent past, of improperly resolved loyalties and defensiveness and uncertain role in the Kingdom, but I have also had some experiences, especially these past few years, including a reacquaintance with the pioneer intellectual tradition, that are changing me and make me want to be part of what I hope your generation will define and exemplify–the new Latter-day Saint intellectual life.

Since early in my teens I have loved the gospel with my mind–rejoicing in the great concepts of God and man, of our uncreated, eternal existence, our divine parentage, and our endless journey of increased knowledge and power and joy that lies ahead. But I have in recent years, while serving as a branch president in Minnesota, learned again to love the Church, as well as the gospel, and with both mind and heart: I have both a broadly based intellectual conviction and a deep spiritual witness that the Church structure, informed by restored gospel principles, is the means that the Lord has given us to bring us to Christ–to involve us in a saving struggle with the great moral and spiritual imperatives from God for attaining the possible godhood within us. I am convinced that the Church is the only place we can really do that, partly because of the very challenges that human association in the Church context provides and which are sometimes so upsetting to us intellectuals.

One of Martin Luther's great statements is helpful here. He said, "Marriage is the school of love." I believe that is true (in even more ways than Luther meant, of course, if we consider eternal marriage), but the statement is also true of the Church. The Church also is the school of love–the place where, through being given assignments to serve, while being taught true principles by which to understand and act in the world, we are continually confronted with the personal and social challenges that can teach us how to love in that unique, unqualified way Christ showed us and taught us was the only way to salvation.

One reason I can quote Luther is that I have been teaching at a Lutheran college, and that has also helped change my perspective on the Mormon intellectual in the past five years. St. Olaf College encourages its teachers, just as Brigham Young did the teachers here at BYU, to deal openly and continually with the religious and moral implications of their subject matter. I didn't need any particular encouragement for that, but I did find at St. Olaf, compared to Stanford or California State University, much greater freedom–from legal and professional as well as social pressure–to be forthright about my convictions. Incidentally, some of you may have felt or imagined that being at a Church school decreases your freedom and that of your teachers–and it may in some ways. But you have a much greater amount, at Brigham Young University, of what is the most important academic freedom, in my opinion–the freedom to express and discuss openly your positive religious and moral views and convictions rather than merely your negative ones or your criticism.

In this process of exploring openly with my students the religious and moral dimensions of literature, the principal subject I teach, I have been forced to consider certain things much more directly than ever before–the intellectual perspective and moral vision of the authors and the qualities of the societies they describe or from which their writing emerges. I have also been more forcefully confronted with the effect on my students' thinking and life decisions of all those things I expose them to. And I have come to be increasingly uneasy with the perspectives of formalist literary criticism in which I was trained under some of the great masters of such criticism. Over the past few years I have become increasingly uneasy about the inadequacy of formalist criteria (I mean those concerned with aesthetic qualities–structure, style, organization, etc.) to account for the experiences of my students–and myself–with certain literature, especially some which powerfully affected us despite its obvious lack of formal or aesthetic perfection.

Some of these rather vague concerns were brought into focus last fall by Robert Scholes, the fine critic from Brown Unversity. He spoke at St. Olaf in a symposium honoring Ole Rolvaag (who wrote his famous novel, *Giants In The Earth*, fifty years ago, while a member of our St. Olaf faculty). Scholes traced, in the work of Midwestern writers Rolvaag, Willa Cather, Sinclair Lewis, and William Gass, the building of one "great" tradition of literature on a pioneer vision that he characterized, in both its social and religious dimensions, as "deeply and tragically wrong" because it was "too limited, too material, too rapacious."

Scholes calls the basic flaw in that vision "prairie consciousness": The Midwestern pioneers had the illusion, facing those ever-receding plains, of a world that was limitless and which they could never use up. Worse, they rested in the arrogant assumption that they had the right, nay, even the religious duty, to exploit it as quickly and fully as they could. We know the moral consequences of such a vision in our polluted, tacky, alienated modern world, which derives directly from a frontier past in which a natural balance was destroyed and materialistic concerns took precedence over solving problems of human relationships. Much of the literature in that great Midwestern tradition derives its power from its brilliant satirizing of the quality of life that resulted.

In a private conversation after his address, Professor Scholes and I discussed other pioneer visions. I mentioned the Mormons and he generalized to other mountain peoples. He pointed out that most of these groups had avoided the arrogance of "prairie consciousness." Why? Partly because they were forced to humility by more stringent physical circumstances in desert and mountain country. But the Mormons, I reflected, were saved from arrogance mainly by a sense of religious consecration and the prophetic leadership that *took* them to the mountains, rather than to the gold of California, and *kept* them there, continually facing new struggles and challenges. We then talked about the lack of a "great" literature among such mountain peoples, including the Mormons, a lack, that is, in terms of general fame and by traditional formalist standards. And Scholes risked a rather astounding conjecture: It might have been because their social vision was *more* successful that the literature of such people has been less successful than, say, that of the Midwest–at least less successful by those orthodox literary criteria.

Suddenly some things clicked together for me, and I began to consider some new directions for defining a Mormon aesthetic, a set of principles upon which to assess and encourage our own literary tradition. I thought how often I had heard similar explanations for the lack of a great Mormon literature, though they were offered condescendingly by Gentiles and apologetically by Mormons, including myself. Many have said that Mormonism answers so well so many basic questions and provides such a satisfying way of life for most of its people that there is not sufficient tension or tragedy. What I have finally clearly realized is that there is no need to apologize: Religious success is certainly preferable to literary success.

Of course, we may not have to choose, and I'm certainly not advocating that we intentionally neglect the formal and other values of great literature, just because we rejoice in our religion and the comparative greatness of the societies it has produced. But we must more clearly and intelligently face the fact that there are values, even in religion itself, other than purely literary or aesthetic ones; there are social and religious and moral values, and they are not always intrinsically bound up in the formal perfections. In fact, it is somewhat sobering to reflect that, at least in America, Robert Scholes' conjecture seems all too accurate: The "great" literature of the past has almost invariably grown out of the religious failure of a group (e.g., *The Scarlet Letter*) or the religious despair of an individual (e.g., *Moby Dick*), and, at least in the twentieth century, the so-called "great" literature has mainly been content to describe a morally barren or depraved contemporary landscape or has been based on a vision that has itself been shot through with moral or philosophical error. To the extent we have to choose between great books and true religion–and you will discover increasingly, I believe, that the choice must sometimes be made–we should rejoice that we can choose true religion, and without apology.

But let me be more optimistic and back off a bit from the offensive (and perhaps false) dilemma that I posed in the title of these remarks–"Great Books or True Religion?" Of course there is value in great literature, in great books of all kinds that you have studied and will, I trust, continue to study. My point is that they are not the most important things in your lives–not even within the exercise of your special intellectual gifts–and that you have near at hand some great literature, great books and ideas of all kinds in your own tradition, that you perhaps have neglected and for which you may even need to develop some special insights and criteria in order to appreciate them properly. And these are things you should be less defensive, less apologetic about, should more anxiously pursue in the future than my generation has.

Part of the reason for this defensiveness is that Mormons and Mormonism have had from the beginning a bad press, both at the popular and at the more sophisticated or academic levels. Our unusual history of physical persecution has carried over into various forms of misunderstanding and prejudice in the world of print and scholarship. It has been assumed, even by those like Wallace Stegner who have been able to praise some aspects of our achievement, that our beliefs are absurd and our perspective essentially anti-intellectual. This has been partly because of our superficial similarity to groups that developed on the American frontier that were rabidly anti-intellectual and partly because in some ways we *have* been anti-intellectual, or have at least stressed other values more. But some of this rejection has been outright prejudice based on intentional ignorance and unscholarly assumptions by gentile thinkers; and perhaps some of it is even a semi-conscious shying away from our truth-claims which, if they proved convincing, could not be dismissed as merely interesting ideas—as the ideas of most other churches and groups can. In contrast, the gospel assertions about history and about physical, moral, and spiritual reality make absolute claims on the action and thinking of those who seriously entertain them. How else explain, for instance, the continued avoidance of serious consideration of the Book of Mormon by scholars of American history and literature? In its very existence, and the response of millions to it, it is a powerful and incontrovertible fact about America, no matter what initial assumptions one makes about its origin. Or how explain the general avoidance in theological circles of Mormon ideas about the nature of God? Those ideas both precede and in important ways move far beyond the thinking of Alfred North Whitehead and the "process theologians," which thinking has been hailed by many in America as perhaps the most exciting new development in twentieth-century theology.

Take Christopher Lasch, for instance, a fine historian, who, in a review of some literature on the Mormon experience in the *New York Review of Books* back in 1967, finds much to praise in our early ideals and achievements. He puts his finger squarely on what made the Mormon pioneer vision different from the Midwestern one that Scholes, you remember, characterized as materialistic, even rapacious: "In Utah, under Young's leadership the Mormons created a self-sufficient, cooperative, egalitarian, and authoritarian economy devoted not to individual enrichment but to the collective well-being of the flock." He cites our present Church Historian, Leonard Arrington, who in his landmark study of the Mormon economy, *Great Basin Kingdom*,

. . . shows how the Mormons accomplished, through a system of cooperative and compulsory labor, impressive feats of planning and development—irrigation, roads, canals, sugar beet factories, iron works—without generating the institutions or the inequalities elsewhere associated with industrial progress; indeed, without even developing a money economy.

Lasch concludes: "Cooperation and planning caused the desert to bloom, in marked contrast to the exploitive patterns of agriculture which on other frontiers exhausted natural resources and left the land a smoking waste." But though Lasch recognizes that those practices of our ancestors were uniquely successful from a human and ecological point of view, like other gentile intellectuals he fails to see the connection of those successes to our religious truth and consequent heroic devotion to correct principles; in fact, in obvious ignorance of its content, he characterizes our theology, surely the most comprehensively rational theology in existence, as inconsistent, even "grotesque." And, like a number of recent commentators, including some of our own intellectuals who have left the Church and turned around to criticize, he sees no continuance in the twentieth century of those remarkable but for him inexplicable pioneer virtues. He claims that our accelerating growth rate is only possible because we have gradually sacrificed the utopian, communitarian commitments, the very ideals which in the nineteenth century posed a challenge to the American way of life, that especially threatened exploitive, laissez-faire capitalism so much that the Church was hounded and driven and almost destroyed. Some of that charge is close enough to the truth to make me uncomfortable–the claim that we are no longer persecuted, are even courted by politicians and the popular press, simply because many of us are no longer a challenge but have become rather a defense of some of the most reactionary elements in American life: racism, individualistic economic conservatism, middle-class conspicuous suburbanism.

Nevertheless Lasch is essentially wrong: That original inspiriting vision that produced almost utopian success in our early societies was the direct result of a true and (in modern times) unique religious vision, an egalitarian, communal ideal in which all of life–including the social order–is integrated together and is motivated by religious faith rather than economic sanctions, etc. And that same ideal remains vital with us today, called to our minds and hearts each time we make our covenants of consecration in the temple, motivating much that we do as the Church expands in the third world, especially South America, where we are building–cooperatively–schools, churches, even whole colonies; it is lived out explicitly right here in capitalist America, even in East Bench Salt Lake City or Provo, by individuals who without coercion or even being asked give all beyond their basic needs to building up the Kingdom. In fact, it is maintained by all of us in the Church who see life whole, not divided between sacred and secular, as almost all other twentieth-century religion has done.

Our own literature has intuited this well. Take Maurine Whipple's *The Giant Joshua*, which is, despite its flaws and the way its vision and artistic force weaken toward the end, probably our best piece of Mormon fiction to date. In writing about the colonization of St. George, Whipple examines the most crucial elements of our pioneer experience–the building of communities under prophetic direction, against private inclination, with the aid and challenge of the United Order and of polygamy. And she shows, undergirding all, the search for effective group religious life and individual redemption. This passage gets at the heart of the struggle and achievement:

> . . .[*After one year of the United Order, Apostle Snow*] *surveyed his community and was not ashamed to uphold its accomplishments even to Brigham, whose face these days seemed more than ever like parchment, whose eyes could not hide their longing for proof that this work of his lifetime would stand.*
>
> *"Enoch hats* [*i.e., hats produced in the United Order*]*, a half-finished Temple, brush grubbed from the sidewalks and the square," inventoried Erastus, "and above all, something you can't see but is worth much more to a man–a sense of responsibility toward his neighbor, an armor against selfishness and greed. . . ."*

But let me make my point more clear by discussing briefly a piece of Mormon literature that it is quite certain none of you has read. I do this in part because there has been some reaction among Church members against *The Giant Joshua*, because of its frankness about such things as polygamy and Mountain Meadows, that may color your response to it. This other example is a better one also because it, even more clearly than that novel, helps make another point that must be considered in our Mormon aesthetic–that a literature such as ours, which I have suggested may be inferior in form to that conventionally recognized as great but which is superior in content and vision, shows to best advantage in certain genres–those characterized by personal witness to faith and experience, ones in which the truth of actual living and of direct confession is at least as important as aesthetic or metaphorical truth. I mean journals and diaries, letters, sermons, lyric poetry (especially hymns), autobiography and autobiographical fiction, and the personal essay. We should look more closely at our rich heritage in these genres.

The diary of Joseph Millett, which I came across last year in the Church Historical Department, is to me a prime example, a major exhibit in the reevaluation I am suggesting. Joseph Millett's father was converted by Brigham Young and called to take charge of the masonry work on the Kirtland Temple, where he invented an extraordinarily hard exterior plaster that glittered with the pieces of china dishes that the women sacrificed to be broken up in it. (That plaster, by the way, is a perfect symbol for our religion and literature because it is rooted in real experience and expresses concisely and precisely the difference between Mormon colonists and, say, Rolvaag's Midwesterners. Rather than accumulating and clinging to the material objects of civilization, the Saints gave their treasured china dishes and precious porcelain ware to be crushed up in the plaster used to adorn the walls of their temple to God.) After the Saints were driven from Nauvoo, the Millett family stayed at Winter Quarters in Iowa helping others move on until they went to Salt Lake in 1850 and settled, under Brigham Young's direction, in Manti. In August of 1852 Brigham Young convened a special conference that was an unprecedented occasion on the American Frontier. Only three years into a colonization effort that had barely escaped disaster and which still existed on the bare edge of survival, he called together 2,000 of the Elders of Israel and reminded them of their greater task–to take the gospel to all nations. And he sent ninety-eight of them, including a number of general authorities, and also Joseph Millett, then eighteen years old, on missions to literally the four quarters of the earth, including Europe, Africa, the West Indies, China, Siam, India–young Joseph to Nova Scotia. Elder Millett's diary tells of his father's blessing, the setting apart by Apostle Jedediah Grant, and then his journey, essentially alone and literally penniless–without purse or scrip–across a continuent that was still mainly a wilderness frontier, to his field of labor. But now listen to his own voice, certainly unsophisticated and lacking the formal graces but with some of that intuitive sense of significant detail and forthright revelation of self that are at least as important to good literature as those other qualities–and more important to true religion:

Apr. 13, 1853 I went to Cranberry Head, near to Yarmouth. Here I found Brother John Robinson and Brother Benjamin T. Mitchell at Mr. Moses Shaw's. The Brethren (Robinson and Mitchell) said that they were going to travel together. The Brethren both said I was too young and inexperienced to travel with either of them. They said I had better go to Halifax and see Brother A. D. L. Buckland and get counsel from him. Apr. 14 I went in to Yarmouth. Came back to Mr. Grace's. He treated me kindly. I stayed until Saturday. Started for Halifax. Left Cape Sable to my right hand. Traveled two hundred ten miles around the coast capes and bays to get to Halifax. I had to rely upon Him whose business I was on. I felt my weakness. A poor ill-clothed ignorant boy in my teens, thousand of miles from home, amongst strangers. The promise in my Blessings, the encouraging words of President Young to me, with the faith I had in the Gospel, kept me up. Many a time I would turn in to the woods and brush in some desolate place, with a full heart, wet eyes and face, to call on my Master for strength and aid. I believed the Gospel of Christ. I never had preached it. I knew not where to find it in the scriptures. I had to give my Bible to the boatman [*at the channel*] *for passage across.*

From that low point of loneliness and rejection and lack of confidence in his ability, the journal records a growing self-confidence as Elder Millett obtains books and tracts at the branch in Halifax and studies the gospel. He decides, because a prophet has called him to Nova Scotia, not to return to the states with the other missionaries (who had become discouraged at their lack of success), crosses over to nearby Cape Breton Island and, after being joined by a locally called missionary from Halifax, begins to teach and baptize. He organizes a branch and starts to have extraordinary experiences such as the following (notice the simple but effective narrative skill and sense of drama, combined with sincere, almost humorously direct reliance on the Lord):

June 30, 1853 At the brothers Bagnal's they were starting out to fish. I said, "Success to you; you must catch a whale," just in a foolish, joking way, and thought no more about it until I went down to Brother John McGilvery's. After a while one of the girls came down and said that Brother Millett had promised that Uncle Joseph's folks would get a whale and the Gentiles said that now you see he is a false prophet, for any fool would know that they can't get a whale. I overheard the girls talking about the whale. It then came to my mind what I had said. I then ran to the woods and thought how foolish I was to say such a thing. I prayed the Lord to forgive [*me*]*, that I desired to do right. I felt the position we were in. I couldn't keep back the tears. I called on the Lord to help me in his cause. About one o'clock P.M. the people noticed six boats coming in the Bay towing something. Some said is was the hull of a schooner; others said no, that is was the whale that the Mormon promised* *about. The brothers Bagnal's was the first boat going out of the Bay. They heard the report of a cannon and saw the flag and topmast of the packet steamer circling around, [which] fired their third gun as soon as they saw that the fishermen were coming; the steamer went on and Brother Bagnal was the first to the prize. And it was a lucky day for all of them that assisted in getting the prize in. The whale I believe was above seventy feet long, the biggest fish I ever saw. . . . I never have ceased to thank the Lord for his goodness.*

Notice the well-controlled humor and the sense of effective diction in this later passage:

July 27, 1853 Elder Adamson and myself went to Mr. Gibbons, a rich infidel. He said he was an astronomer and philosopher. Said that Mormonism was more reasonable than the rest of the religions and as for polygamy it was the only thing to regenerate the human family.

Or witness the self-effacing but clearly communicated sense of a life lived in great spiritual beauty in these passages:

July 31, 1853 Brother Allen Adamson says he must go to Halifax and perhaps on in to the States. Wants to make fitout for the Valley. Anxious to gather with the Saints. He was from Dundee, Scotland. So I will be left alone with almost every door closed against me. Elder Adamson has been with me pretty near 2 months. . . . Some was ready to be baptised at Gabarouse when Brother Adamson came to me but I had never baptised. So when he came we were ready to commence. After I saw him baptize, I could then baptize. Oh, must I part with a good companion in him.

August 1 Elder Allen Adamson left me for Gabarouse after I blessed him and he blessed me. I went about 3 miles with him. Then we parted not to meet again in this land. In the last two weeks I have held two meetings in private houses. I have to depend on the Lord, not on Brother Adamson. I have felt rather shy about asking favors of people; had rather go into the woods, pick blueberries, bless them and eat, and felt myself welcome. I find myself in rather straitened circumstances, although I have some friends.

Despite those few friends, opposition from the Protestant clergy was very severe: Elder Millett's handbills were torn down; schools and halls were closed to him. Finally a Reverend McLeod comes directly to a home where he is staying and confronts him. Notice the sense of well-paced dialogue and of dramatic timing, which conveys both humor and the steady seriousness of conviction:

"Are you that imposter that has come to lead the people astray?" "No sir, I am a servant of the living God and I am preaching His Gospel." Says he,

"Brother McArthy, what does the scriptures say? 'Though we or an angel from Heaven preach any other gospel than we have preached, let him be accursed.' " Says Brother McArthy, "This young man has preached the same gospel that Paul did. But you are preaching another gospel."

The dinner was just ready. . . . As he went to sit down he said, "There is a sick woman in the other room and you people profess to do miracles. Heal that woman; then I will believe in your doctrine." Just then the door opened and the woman came out and said, "I am healed." He said, "Yes, the devil can do miracles."

Believe me, these are only a few samples of the quality of this record of the life of a Latter-day Saint. Near the end of his journal, when he is looking back over his life as an old man, Joseph Millett shows what seems to me extraordinary ability to summarize a life in one anecdote, to capture the central moral vision and sense of self acquired by one who has lived a true religion. He concludes with an experience recalled from many years before, in 1871. He and his wife had been called in 1856 to that same constantly struggling Dixie Mission that Maurine Whipple tells about, and then later to the even more harsh life in the Mormon settlement in Spring Valley, Nevada, where their oldest daughter died of typhoid and many suffered great sickness and hunger. This lifelong servant of the Lord, who learned on his mission, and never forgot, what it is like to be in need and how to give, leaves us with this final picture of himself:

. . .one of my children came in, said that Brother Newton Hall's folks were out of bread. Had none that day. I put . . . our flour in sack to send up to Brother Hall's. Just then Brother Hall came in. Says I, "Brother Hall, how are you out for flour." "Brother Millett, we have none." "Well, Brother Hall, there is some in that sack. I have divided and was going to send it to you. Your children told mine that you were out." Brother Hall began to cry. Said he had tried others. Could not get any. Went to the cedars and prayed to the Lord and the Lord told him to go to Joseph Millett. "Well, Brother Hall, you needn't bring this back if the Lord sent you for it. You don't owe me for it." You can't tell how good it made me feel to know that the Lord knew that there was such a person as Joseph Millett.

I have to call that great literature, though, as I've suggested, to do so offends to some degree my formalist training and convictions; so, I have to come up with some new criteria and a new ranking of the old, some means of judgment and appreciation that will recognize that the power of Joseph Millett's journal derives in large part from the true religion that he and his people knew and lived, that will factor in the moral and social truth of the author's vision and his effect on our own vision as we put ourselves in his hands as readers.

Now, don't misunderstand me. I am not suggesting didacticism as an adequate or even good criterion for literature. I'm not advocating a return to the pious moralizing that plagued Victorian literature. In fact, it could well be argued that the decline in quality of the content–the moral and philosophical vision–in most recent literature, especially poetry, is a direct result of intentional neglect of form. What we must remember is that, all other things being equal, the more skilled and effective the formal elements the better and more powerful the literature. But if the moral goodness or intellectual truth of the author's vision is flawed, the formal beauty and power will only make the writing more effective for evil–more able to take possession of the reader. Moreover, the truth and goodness of the author's vision must be weighed into our assessment and will sometimes compensate for formal inadequacy or even give rise intuitively to finer formal achievements. Especially will this latter happen in unsophisticated and confessional forms like letters and journals, where the writer is able to project the fundamental and ultimately exemplary quality of life lived day by day–as Joseph Millett does.

What, then, about you, whom I have characterized, at least potentially, as the new Latter-day Saint intellectuals? How might you generalize what I have said about literature to other great books and ideas that you are and will be dealing with, in a variety of fields? You must develop your own vision of what, as an intellectual, your contribution to the Kingdom might be, of how you might love the Lord as he commanded–with all your mind, as well as your heart, might, and strength. You must develop your own style and your own standards, not with arrogant indifference to the standards and resources of the Western intellectual tradition which has helped form you, but with the courage to go creatively beyond that tradition in finding a way to be properly loyal to your special gifts and to the Church and the restored gospel.

Let me give you one remarkable manifesto for Mormon intellectuals, one with which some of you are familiar and which I think ought to inspire and give some direction to us all. This is B. H. Roberts, member of the First Council of Seventy, writing in 1906 in an interesting context: In creating a course of study for the Church's seventies, he had proposed a new and more naturalistic understanding of the manner in which Joseph Smith may have used divine instruments in translating the Book of Mormon. He received many letters challenging or agreeing with his theory, and a lively exchange with his critics was printed in the *Improvement Era.* The following appears near the end of one of his responses:

I believe "Mormonism" affords opportunity . . . for thoughtful disciples who will not be content with merely repeating some of its truths, but will develop its truths; and enlarge it by that development. Not half—not one-hundredth part—not a thousandth part of that which Joseph Smith revealed to the Church has yet been unfolded, either to the Church or to the world. The work of the expounder has scarcely begun. The Prophet planted by teaching the germ-truths of the great dispensation of the fullness of times. The watering and the weeding is going on, and God is giving the increase, and will give it more abundantly in the future as more intelligent discipleship shall obtain. The disciples of "Mormonism," growing discontented with the necessarily primitive methods which have hitherto prevailed in sustaining the doctrine, will yet take profounder and broader views of the great doctrines committed to the Church; and, departing from mere repetition, will cast them in new formulas; cooperating in the works of the Spirit, until they help to give to the truths received a more forceful expression, and carry it beyond the earlier and cruder stages of its development.

President Roberts, of course, is not suggesting that the intellectual's task is to create new doctrine, but rather it is to take revealed doctrine and give it new formulations that will relate to the changing world we live in, that will enable us, for instance, to more effectively criticize our flawed social, political, artistic and intellectual environment by using the great germ-truths of the gospel. We need to respond, affirming where we can, denying where we must, to such things as the women's liberation movement, which is significantly altering our perspectives and lives in this country, or to the twentieth-century sense of the challenge of evil, focused in the holocaust in which six million Jews were destroyed, an event which has destroyed much faith in our world because for many it calls into serious question the intentions and nature of a supposedly good and all-powerful God. We have the resources in the gospel to respond profoundly to these challenges, both for our own people and for others.

What am I saying? As a first principle for Mormon intellectuals, you should know and use your own great intellectual traditions and the resources of your own true religion, before you get too impressed with the great books and great ideas from other sources. Know and use them both, in constant dialogue.

As a second principle, I call you to a proper sense of self-consciousness as intellectuals and a loyalty to each other and to your own loose community within the Church, but only as part of, and ultimately second to, your commitment to full communion with the full Church. Consider a young Mormon intellectual, a college teacher in a small ward that badly needs leadership. He has been in the ward a number of years but has had no significant effect on it, because his career is apparently more important to him. He once agreed to serve as bishop, but insisted in advance on limiting his service to a certain period, served efficiently and well enough to show how much difference he really could make, and then returned to his scholarship and teaching and to semiactivity. He will likely succeed fairly well in his academic career, but he has failed to serve the Lord with his gift–and he may truly have lost his soul, and his family's future, for that mess of honors and publications. Many of you will be called into similar situations where you might strengthen a branch or ward–by the natural opportunities all over the world that will come to you, in academic life, business, government, etc., because of your intellectual and other gifts, or perhaps by the whisperings of the Spirit in your heart, as I have felt, or even by direct call from the Lord's servants. May you meet the challenge–the opportunity provided by the Lord–better than this young intellectual I have described.

My generation and the previous one have in many ways failed to meet the standard I am setting for you. I call you to join us in going beyond our failures and even our few successes. As one measure of our failure, I ask you to notice how few thinkers and writers are now willing and able to appear in all four of our periodicals for expression of ideas, *Exponent II, Dialogue: A Journal of Mormon Thought, BYU Studies,* and the *Ensign.* I ask you to reject the labels of this previous generation that have fragmented our intellectual community and to some extent the larger Church–I mean labels like "orthodox" and "unorthodox," "liberal" and "conservative." These are gentile terms and have no place in a community of the Saints, if used to hold oneself apart and reject others from fellowship, love, and forgiveness. And as one measure of a danger for failure that you may already be slipping into, evidence of your own degree of loyalty to the Mormon intellectual tradition and community and your awareness, I ask how many of your have read Juanita Brooks and Leonard Arrington as well as Bruce Catton and Samuel Eliot Morison; Parley Pratt's *Key to the Science of Theology* and Sterling McMurrin's *Theological Foundations of the Mormon Religion* as well as Karl Barth and C. S. Lewis and Nels Ferre; Joseph Smith's *Lectures on Faith* as well as Paul Tillich's *Dynamics of Faith*; Lowell Bennion as well as Martin Buber; *The Giant Joshua* as well as *Giants in the Earth* or *Main Street; A Believing People: The Literature of the Latter-day Saints*, edited by Professors Cracroft and Lambert of BYU's English department, as well as the Norton anthologies of literature? Do you subscribe to *Dialogue, Exponent II* and *BYU Studies* as well as *Encounter*, the *New York Review of Books* and *Scientific American*? Will you read *Sunstone* as well as *Harper's* or *Psychology Today?* The past generations have been a time of seed planting, of struggle and mistakes and losses. You can nurture and harvest what we have planted if you will and can profit from our experience. You can be more Christian, better Saints than we have been, both helping and sustaining each other in the inevitable clashes you will have with uncomprehending or unsympathetic authority and with what you might consider ignorance or low-browism, in the Church as well as outside it. You can also act to reduce those clashes and their consequences by working loyally within the Church, both serving humbly in all its functions and moving wisely and courageously to increase understanding and acceptance of the role and contribution of the intellectual.

Since the intellectual endeavor is always easy to misunderstand and tends by its very nature–its emphasis on analysis, criticism, on ventures into the unknown–to threaten and alienate, you must find ways to show that, in the great phrase from the 121st section of the Doctrine and Covenants, "your faithfulness is stronger than the cords of death." Your gift will make you inescapably aware of problems in the Church, and thus the burden of change will be on you, because others, often those committing the errors, can't see what is "wrong." What you can do about such problems is not leave, desert, turn the Church over to those who in your point of view are perverting it, nor to remain within, only to withdraw spiritually through self-righteousness. You must reach out in love, trying to help–and also trying to learn, through your cooperation and common service, from the perspective and commitment of others with different gifts than your intellectual gift, and learning to see your own faults and failings, which may be, in the long run, more destructive than the ones you easily see in others.

Be true to your special gift. Read the great books and learn to be critical of them. Learn to do without the agreement or approval of everyone in the world or even in the Church. Another great speech from *A Man for All Seasons* is More's response to Richard Rich, an ambitious young intellectual who ultimately betrays More (and loses his soul) by selling out to his ambition. More, who intuits Rich's problem and probable future, has told him to be satisfied with being a teacher; he can be a fine one. Rich asks who would know if he were, and More replies, "You, your students, your friends, God. Not a bad public that." Be satisfied with such a public. Be loyal to your peers; learn to help them and yourself find your place in the Church. Be courageous and honest. God does not need your lies, even your shading of the truth, to build up his Kingdom. Our history, our theology, our present selves do not need to be censored or dressed up in false clothes or cosmetics. Remember your own inclination to sin, to arrogance, to lack of proper appreciation of the different but equally valuable gifts of those who aren't intellectuals. Remember the scriptural warnings about milk before meat and not leading the innocent astray; remember the Apostle Paul's humble example of not eating the food offered to idols, not wanting to do anything that might offend his brother who might not understand, even though he knew it was something harmless for himself. And remember the simplest, clearest, and most effective formula for balancing faith and reason, given by Elder Marion D. Hanks, an intellectual who knows from experience: Search the scriptures, seek the Lord in mighty prayer, and serve faithfully in whatever Church calling comes to you.

With what power I have, my power as your brother in Christ and the power of the priesthood we share, I bless you. May you succeed where too many of us have not and even go beyond where we have succeeded. May you be more self-confident, more accepting of the gift God has given you. At the same time may you be more loyal, both to your own intellectual tradition as Latter-day Saints and also to the true revealed principles and practices that have informed the lives of those who have built that tradition. And may you be, above all, committed to living such lives, loving and blessing your brothers and sisters with your gift, acting bravely to communicate its values to them and freely forgiving and asking forgiveness when your exercise of your gift is misunderstood or mistaken. In these ways, and in others that he may help us discover, I ask the Lord to bless us all, in order that we might use his gift of intelligence as he would want us to.

One of a series given in 1966, when I was in the Stanford Ward Bishopric, to introduce Mormonism to friends of LDS students; published in *Dialogue*, Autumn 1967.

CHAPTER 7

THAT THEY MIGHT NOT SUFFER: THE GIFT OF ATONEMENT

A deep feeling of estrangement haunts modern life and literature and thought. The feeling is not at all new to human experience, but in our time we seem especially conscious of it. More of us seem caught up by the divisions in our lives to a terrible anguish or a numbed resignation.

We find ourselves cut off from *others*, relating to each other as things, not as personal images of the eternal God, unable to say our truest thoughts and feelings to each other, exterminating each other in the gas ovens of Auschwitz and the firestorms of Berlin, fighting unjust wars to satisfy our greed or pride, responding to the color we reflect to each other's eyes and not to our sense of each other's being.

We find ourselves cut off from *God*, without a deep sense of joyful relation to him, witnessing him die in us and our civilization through the dead forms of our concepts of him and the inflexible forms of our response to him in the world, unable to let our confidence wax strong in his presence through the feeling that our lives are in harmony with his will.

And we find ourselves cut off from *ourselves*. We sin. We act contrary to our image of ourselves and break our deepest integrity. We do not just make mistakes through lack of knowledge or judgment but consciously go contrary to our sense of right. Therefore we not only suffer the natural consequences of all wrong action (however innocently done), but we also suffer the inner estrangement of guilt—that supreme human suffering which gives us our images of hell. This is an important distinction, made very clearly in Christian thought: "To him that knoweth to do good, and doeth it not, to him it is sin" is James's definition (James 4:17). Christ had said, "If ye were blind, ye should have no sin, but now ye say, We see; therefore your sin remaineth" (John 9:41). We all know sin. We are inescapably moral by nature in that we cannot evade the question that finally comes into all reflection: "Am I justified?" We have eaten of the tree of knowledge of good and evil and find the self of action tragically divided against the self of belief.

These are things we all know about. And if we are Christians we also know something about a claim which is incredible to most people—the claim that these estrangements can uniquely be healed through the Atonement of Christ. Atonement—a word whose pronunciation disguises its meaning, which is literally *at one ment*, a bringing to unity, a reconciliation of that which is estranged: me and you, me and God, or me and myself. The Atonement remains, as Paul described it, "unto the Jews a stumbling block, and unto the Greeks foolishness." We have no greater need than that there be a force of healing in all our public and inner strife; that there be some source of forgiveness and change for the oppressor as well as help for the oppressed; that there be something large enough in love to reach past the wrongs we have done and can never fully make restitution for; that there be hope in the possibility that anyone can be renewed by specific means to a life of greater justice and mercy toward others. But for most of us the claim that such a possibility truly exists is scandalous.

The scandal to humanistic people is the idea that they cannot make it alone—that their reason will not save them. Knowing what is right is not enough; there must be power to *do* what is right, and humans (as the appalling organized evil of this century has reminded us), no matter how sophisticated or civilized they become, continue to act against what they know is right—their additional knowledge and merely efficient reason capable of becoming, in fact, more powerful means of doing *evil* rather than increased good. The scandal to the non-Christian is that God would take the necessary reconciliation upon himself but is unable to do it except by descending below all of us into particular events in the history of the Jews and finally into the particular body and life of one human, Jesus of Nazareth—and that thereby he would enter the full range of human experience. The scandal to the non-Mormon is the claim by a contemporary church of special insight into the meaning and means of the Atonement and of special authority in making it efficacious in the lives of men.

In his letter about Mormon beliefs to Chicago editor John Wentworth in 1842, Joseph Smith said, "We believe that through the Atonement of Christ, all mankind may be saved, by obedience to the laws and ordinances of the Gospel." The Atonement makes it possible that *all* of us *may* be saved–by obedience. God's concern is for the salvation of everyone and he expresses that concern in the free gift of Atonement, which, as we shall see, is directly related to our actual growth through obedience–in fact, *makes such obedience possible*. The understanding that Joseph Smith had come to through a long process of revelation and study finds succinct expression in this Article of Faith. It embodies a unique understanding of the harmonious relationship of grace and works and of the resulting effect of the Atonement on the moral nature of us all, and it implies a unique role of the properly authorized Church in bringing to all people the full power of that effect through the teachings and ordinances of the Gospel.

In traditional Christian thought, the Atonement of Christ has always been related directly to the Fall of Adam. For some, it has seemed a direct and relatively simple answer, a solution to the estrangement of God from mortals which was caused by God's rejection of Adam after Adam's rebellion had spoiled God's plan. But most Christians (and Jews) have been able to see that it is inconsistent with their understanding of the nature of God to imagine him turning his back on us, to suppose that we must propitiate God and win back his favor in the process of Atonement. Clearly any rejection involved is the rejection of God by us and any reconciliation must be the reconciliation of us to God. As Paul said to the Corinthians, "[God] has reconciled us to himself by Jesus Christ, and hath given to us the ministry of reconciliation; to wit, God was in Christ, reconciling the world unto himself, not imputing their trespasses unto them. . . ." (II Cor. 5:18-19). But in too much Christian theology, as well as folk religion, the Atonement has remained an event remote from the common life of mortals, somehow involving Adam and God and mysterious supernatural realms such as the spirit prison or strange metaphysical structures such as absolute justice. For many, the Atonement is something crucial, no doubt, and to be deeply grateful for, but has nothing very clear to do with redeeming the daily round of studying differential equations and commuting to work and waking up in the night in the deep loneliness and pain of our regret.

Mormons are certainly not immune to this tendency to miss the immediate relevance of the Atonement to their day-to-day lives, but there are dramatically unorthodox resources in Mormon theology with which to involve us in that relevance. In Mormon scriptures Adam's action did in no way spoil God's plan but was, in fact, *part* of the plan–a preordained action, necessary to our eternal development, which he and Eve entered into knowingly. Mormons do not look upon them as depraved, willful sinners caught up in a pride of their own being and a desire to know which led them to rebel against God, but rather Mormons see them as great, courageous figures who chose a difficult path necessary to their and our progression–the way of estrangement and reconciliation, of sin and resultant openness to redeeming love.

Mormon scriptures tell of Adam and Eve becoming, as it were, Christians. Sometime after their expulsion from the Garden, in the time of separation from God and extreme consciousness of the threat of death, they are taught by an angel of the Lord about Christ's mission, which would come to fruition on the earth in the far distant future. Christ's Atonement would include a Resurrection which would eventually reunite each person's spirit and body in a condition of *everlasting* life; and it would also include a Redemption that could immediately give to each of us *who chose to respond to it* power to be reunited to ourself and to God in a condition of *eternal* (or increasingly God-like) life. These scriptures, given in vision to Joseph Smith from the writings of Moses, unabashedly imply a notion heretical to most traditional Christian thought–*felix culpa*, the fortunate fall. Adam's response to the great message of the angel about the forthcoming Atonement is, "Blessed be the name of God, for because of my transgression my eyes are opened, and in this life I shall have joy, and again in the flesh I shall see God" (Moses 5:10).

A Book of Mormon prophet makes the point in these words:

Adam fell that men might be; and men are, that they might have joy.

And the Messiah cometh in the fulness of time that he may redeem the children of men from the fall. And because that they are redeemed from the fall they have become free forever, knowing good from evil; to act for themselves and not to be acted upon. . . . (II Nephi 2:25-26).

The clear implication is that the process of estrangement and reconciliation, of sin and atonement, is not a flaw, an accidental thwarting of

God's plan, but an essential part of it, a necessary ingredient of our eternal realization of our possibilities as children of God. Through this process, and apparently no other, we are able to reach the depths and thereby the heights of our soul's capacity–to know fully our capacity for evil but also then to know the full freedom and strength of soul that come uniquely through being caught up in response to the "pure love of Christ."

There is an additional important implication of this account of Adam, which is reinforced by many experiences in the Book of Mormon. It is clear that long before Christ had actually performed the central acts of the Atonement– the suffering in Gethsemane, the death on the cross, the Resurrection–mortals were able to be affected by those acts through the prophetic knowledge that God *intended* to perform them in the future. What this means is that the mechanics of the mission itself did not need to occur at a certain point in time as a *precursor* to their effect on people, as some theories of the Atonement would require; Christ's mission was not to straighten out some metaphysical warp in the universe that Adam's taking of the fruit had created. The effects of the Atonement were not metaphysical but moral and spiritual: They reach people living at any time and place through their *knowledge* of the spirit and events of the Atonement.

About 600 years before Christ was born, a young man living in Jerusalem, seeking confirmation of his father's spiritual experiences, was given a remarkable vision:

. . .I looked and beheld the great city of Jerusalem, and also other cities. And I beheld the city of Nazareth; and in the city of Nazareth I beheld a virgin. . . . And it came to pass that I saw the heavens open; and an angel came down and stood before me; and said unto me; Nephi, what beholdst thou? And I said unto him: a virgin most beautiful and fair above all other virgins. And he said unto me: knowest thou the condescension of God? And I said unto him: I know that he loveth his children; nevertheless, I do not kow the meaning of all things. And he said unto me: behold the virgin whom thou seest is the mother of the Son of God, after the manner of the flesh. . . . And I looked and beheld the virgin again, bearing a child in her arms. And the angel said unto me: behold the Lamb of God, yea, even the Son of the Eternal Father. (I Nephi 11:13-21)

After further explanation by the Angel, Nephi continues,

And the angel said unto me again: Look and behold the condescension of God! And I looked and beheld the Redeemer of the world, of whom my Father had spoken. (I Nephi 11:26-27)

We have here an important insight into the Atonement of Christ, an insight preserved by this young man and his people in their religious history as they journeyed to America and until their descendants 600 years later welcomed Christ there after his death and resurrection. The word chosen by Joseph Smith in his translation is crucial: *condescension*—descending with. Christ is the descending of God with us into all that we experience, including our estrangement, and this is the heart of the power of the Atonement.

Many years after this group of people had arrived in America, one of their great prophet-kings named Benjamin, approaching old age and death, gathered his people together to declare to them a great revelation of understanding that had come to him. After reminding them in very colorful terms of the implication of their human tendency to sin and the effects of guilt upon a sinner—"which doth cause him to shrink from the presence of God, and to fill his breast with guilt, pain, and anguish, which is like an unquenchable fire, whose flame ascendeth up forever and ever"—King Benjamin tells them of a vision that had come to him of an event still 125 years *in the future*:

For behold, the time cometh, and is not far distant, that with power, the Lord Omnipotent who reigneth, who was, and is from all eternity to all eternity, shall come down from heaven among the children of men, and shall dwell in a tabernacle of clay. . . .

And lo, he shall suffer temptations, and pain of body, hunger, thirst, fatigue, even more than man can suffer, except it be unto death: for behold blood cometh from every pore, so great shall be his anguish for the wickedness and the abominations of his people. And he shall be called Jesus Christ, the Son of God, the Father of Heaven and earth, the Creator of all things from the beginning; and his mother shall be called Mary. And lo, he cometh unto his own, that salvation might come unto the children of men even through faith on his name. . . . (Mosiah 3:5, 7-9)

Here for the first time chronologically in all known scripture we have a clear reference to what seems to be the central experience of the part of Christ's Atonement that concerns our individual sins: "Behold, blood cometh from every pore, so great shall be his anguish for the wickedness and the abominations of his people." This is not a description of what occurred on the cross but of what occurred in the Garden of Gethsemane in that night when Christ participated fully in the fearful loneliness that lies at the extremity of human experience–participated even in the anguish of estrangement. Christ descended, through capabilities which only he had as the literal Son of God, into the fullness, both in depth and breadth, of human guilt. We begin to get clearer insight into what occurred in that Garden through a revelation given by the Lord Jesus Christ to Joseph Smith in 1830:

Therefore I command you to repent–repent, lest . . . your sufferings be sore–how sore you know not, how exquisite you know not, yea, how hard to bear you know not. For behold, I, God, have suffered these things for all, that they might not suffer if they would repent; but if they would not repent they must suffer even as I; which suffering caused myself, even God, the greatest of all, to tremble because of pain, and to bleed at every pore, and to suffer both body and spirit–and would that I might not drink the bitter cup, and shrink–Nevertheless, glory be to the Father, and I partook and finished my preparations *unto the children of men. (Doctrine and Covenants 19:15-19; my emphasis)*

Although we certainly can't begin to understand all that happened in Gethsemane, especially *how* it happened, we can begin to feel the impact in our hearts of the divine love expressed there. Jesus Christ has created the greatest possibility we can imagine: that our common lot of meaninglessness and alienation can be redeemed, that we need not suffer if we would repent. The God who planned and created and who directs our earth experience, who sent us here into tragic risk and suffering because only here could we experience further growth in his likeness, has sent his son, not only to guide and teach us through his revelations and his life, but to enter willingly into the depths of man's life. He takes upon him human "temptations," "sicknesses" and "infirmities" that he might be "filled with mercy" and thus come to "know according to the flesh how to succor his people" (see Alma 7:11-13)–not offering solutions without knowing the pain of the problem and not setting prior conditions, but taking into himself the fullness of pain in all human estrangement by gaining some awful awareness of the full force of human evil. Because the love is unconditionally offered and comes freely from the same person who gives us our standard of right and who will eventually judge us, it has the power to release us from the barrier of our own guilt and give us the strength to repent.

The effect of King Benjamin's revelation on his people was immediate and dramatic. After hearing his words,

. . .they all cried with one voice, saying: Yea, we believe all the words which thou hast spoken unto us; and also, we know of their surety and truth, because of the Spirit of the Lord Omnipotent, which has wrought a mighty change in us, or in our hearts, that we have no more disposition to do evil, but to do good continually. And we, ourselves, also, through the infinite goodness of God, and the manifestations of his Spirit, have great views of that which is to come. . . . And it is the faith which we have had on the things which our king has spoken unto us that has brought us to this great knowledge, whereby we rejoice with such exceeding great joy. And we are willing to enter into a covenant with our God to do his will, and to be obedient to his commandments and all things that he shall command us, all the remainder of our days. . . . (Mosiah 5:2-5)

King Benjamin responded,

Ye have spoken the words that I desired; and, now, because of the covenant which ye have made ye shall be called the children of Christ, his sons, and his daughters; for behold, this day he hath spiritually begotten you; for ye say that your hearts are changed through faith on his name. . . . And under this head ye are made free, and there is no other head whereby ye can be made free. There is no other name given whereby salvation cometh; therefore, I would that ye should take upon you the name of Christ, all you that have entered into the covenant with God that ye shall be obedient unto the end of your lives. (Mosiah 5:6-8)

A great thing is occurring here—the formation of a Christian community *125 years before Christ* as a group of people respond in faith to the possibility that they can be at one with themselves through means provided by Christ. Struck to the heart by the meaning of God's love extended to them in the midst of their estrangement from him and themselves, they experience a mighty change which leads them into a covenant, and the covenant sustains a process of development through continual repentance toward the image of Christ.

Fifty years later, another prophet among these people, clearly influenced by the prophecies and experiences which had been part of his people's history, discoursed on the sacrifice of Christ and made even clearer what had happened to King Benjamin's people:

. . . it is expedient that there should be a great and last sacrifice, and then shall there be . . . a stop to the shedding of blood, then shall the law of Moses be fulfilled. . . .

And behold, this is the whole meaning of the law, every whit pointing to that great and last sacrifice; and that great and last sacrifice will be the Son of God, yea, infinite and eternal.

And thus he shall bring salvation to all those who shall believe on his name; this being the intent of this last sacrifice, to bring about the bowels of mercy, which overpowereth justice and bringeth about means unto men that they may have faith unto repentance.

And thus mercy can satisfy the demands of justice, and encircles them in the arms of safety, while he that exercises no faith unto repentance is exposed to the whole law of the demands of justice; therefore only unto him that has faith unto repentance is brought about the great and eternal plan of redemption. (Alma 34:13-16; my emphasis)

This prophet, named Amulek, seems to be saying that Christ's sacrifice–his suffering–is uniquely capable of striking through the barrier in our nature which prevents me from overcoming my estrangement from myself enough to move on to achieve the exalting power to act as I believe. Here we must remind ourselves of an amazing aspect of the eternal human personality. Paradoxically, our moral sense of justice both brings me to the awareness of sin that must begin all repentance and yet interferes with my attempts to repent. I feel that every action must bear its consequences and that I must justify my actions to myself; since there is a gap between belief and action I am in a state which brings into my heart and mind a sense of guilt, of unbearable division within myself. As Alma taught his sinful son Corianton, "There was a punishment affixed, and a just law given, which brought remorse of conscience unto man" (Alma 42:18). This same moral nature, this sense of justice that demands satisfaction, causes me to want to improve my life but also to insist that I pay the penalty in some way for my sin. But of course there is no way I can finally do this. As Paul knew from his own experience and expressed so poignantly in his epistles, the law which Jews looked to for salvation in the Pharisaic tradition can inculcate great moral seriousness and indicate direction for change, but it can also be a terrible burden because humans always fail to some degree in living it fully; it therefore stands as a continual reminder of our failure–a failure that the law's framework of justice demands be paid for, but which we are incapable of paying for. God pierces to the heart of this paradox through the Atonement, and it becomes possible for us personally to experience both alienation and reconciliation, which opens us to the full meaning of both evil and good, bringing us to a condition of meekness and lowliness of heart where we can freely accept from God the power to be a god. And Alma also taught his son this other essential role God plays in the Atonement. Besides giving mortals "remorse of conscience" by giving the law and *judging* us, "God himself atoneth for the sins of the world, to bring about the plan of mercy, to appease the demands of justice . . ." (Alma 42:15).

Christ is the unique manifestation in human experience of the fullness of that unconditional love from God which Paul chose to represent with the Greek term *agape*. As Paul expressed it, "While we were yet sinners, Christ died for us" (Romans 5:8). Christ's sacrificial love was not conditional upon our qualities, our repentance, anything; he expressed his love to us while we were yet in our sins—not *completing* the process of forgiveness, which depends on our response, but *initiating* it in a free act of mercy. This is a kind of love quite independent from the notion of justice. There is no *quid-pro-quo* about it. It is entirely unbalanced, unmerited, unrelated to the specific worthiness of the object (except in that each of us has intrinsic worth through our eternal existence and God-like potential), and that is precisely why it is redemptive. It takes a risk, without calculation, on the possibility that we can realize our infinite worth. It gets directly at that barrier in us, our sense of justice, which makes me incapable of having unconditional love *for myself*—unable to respond positively to my own potential, because I am unable to forgive myself, unable to be at peace with myself until I have somehow "made up" in suffering for my sins, something I am utterly incapable of doing. The demands of justice that Amulek and Alma are talking about, which must be overpowered, are from *our own sense of justice*, not some abstract eternal principle but our own demands on ourselves; those demands which bring us into estrangement with ourselves (as we gain new knowledge of right but do not live up to it) and thus begin the process of growth through repentance, but we cannot complete that process. An awareness of the true meaning and source of that last sacrifice and its intent has the power, as Amulek says, "to bring about the bowels of mercy, which overpowereth justice, and bringeth about means unto men that they may have faith unto repentance."

That the Atonement is performed by *Christ,* the son and revelation of God, is, of course, crucial. He represents to us the ultimate source of justice and is the one whose teachings and example bring us directly to face our need for repentance; he awakens our own sense of justice and stands as a judge over all our actions and thus *only he* can fully release us from what becomes the immobilizing burden of that judgment, through the power of mercy extended unconditionally in his Atonement. It is possible, as King Benjamin's people found, to be moved to sufficient faith in the divine being, by his unique redemptive act, that there comes into the soul a power which can bring us to repentance as no other power can. I stand all amazed at this love–and that is precisely the point: This love can move us with sufficient amazement through our knowledge of it to change our minds and our hearts, to release us from self-inflicted suffering as it creates in us the possibility of new being through repentance.

The question "Why is man's salvation dependent on Christ and the events surrounding his death?" is the most central and the most difficult question in Christian theology. The answers (and there are many) are, as I have said, the chief scandal of Christianity to the non-believer. Attempts to define logical theories of the Atonement based on New Testament scriptures have been largely contradictory and ultimately futile–mainly because the New Testament is not a book of theology, a logical treatise, but rather gives us the reaction, the varied emotional responses, to the Atonement as people experienced it and tried to find images for their joy. Some clearly felt released from the powers of evil and darkness which they believed, much more literally than any of us today, were all around them. Some believed that their souls had been bought from the devil. Some felt that Christ had taken their place in suffering the just and necessary punishment under the law for their sins. The explanation I have tried to develop, based largely on Book of Mormon scriptures, is at significant variance with most of these theories, especially on one major point: The redemptive effect of the Atonement depends on how *an individual* responds to it rather than on some independent effect on the universe or God, which theories such as the ransom theory, the substitution theory, the satisfaction theory, etc., all tend to imply. Of course, the rich reality of the Atonement lies beyond any theory or explanation, including the one I am suggesting here, and people can bring themselves into redeeming relationship with God from within the framework of each of these theories as they reach through to that rich reality. But the needs for powerful personal response and for a release from the immobilizing demands of justice within each of us seem to me crucial and best served by an explanation different from the traditional theories.

The ransom theory, which was prominent in Christian thought into the Middle Ages, seems very crude to us today. The idea was that because of Adam's sin man deserved to die and go to hell, but God bought the souls of mortals from the devil with the sacrifice of Christ. Satan was deceived into believing that he could keep Christ's soul in exchange, but once the bargain was completed, the devil could not hold the soul of the divine, sinless Christ. Of course, this seems to require a concept of a God with whom the devil can make bargains and who in turn is capable of practicing a shabby trick on Satan. The more sophisticated "satisfaction" theory was put forth in the twelfth century by Saint Anselm. In Anselm's view, God's nature, which includes absolute justice and mercy, demands satisfaction for our sins even though God *wants* to forgive us. We ourselves are incapable of providing that satisfaction because our sin is infinite, being rebellion against an infinite being. Therefore, to retain his honor and position, God himself, in the person of Christ, becomes a substitute for us all in paying for sin through suffering. This view of the Atonement prevails in various forms down to the present day.

The popular image associated with the theory is that of the traffic court: We have broken the law; justice must be satisfied, but we haven't enough money; Christ steps forward to pay the fine and release mortals while still upholding the law. An immediate objection to this view is that it seems on the face of things to be a legalistic formula clearly influenced by the feudal times in which it grew up. It implies that God is in a position much like a feudal lord: If he allows offenses against his justice to go unanswered, if he allows people to get off easy, his position will be questioned in the minds of his subjects, which will lead to disrespect and rebellion. Of course, this is carried even further in the notion some have that there is some absolute principle of *retributive* justice (as opposed to natural law of cause and effect), which God himself is bound by despite his own desires. Thus a certain amount of sin must be balanced in the scheme of things, sometime and by someone, with equivalent punishment and suffering–in addition to the natural consequences of actions. But it is a very disquieting notion that God should be bound to an unfortunate situation and in a way that we clearly are not. In human experience, we continually are able to forgive each other without satisfaction and yet with some redemptive effect.

Anselm's contemporary, Abelard, was convinced that God *could* forgive us without conditions and that the problem lies in our nature not God's. He denied the whole legalistic framework, believing that Christ's sacrifice exercises its power by moving us to an awareness of guilt and a change of life: "The purpose and cause of the incarnation was that He might illuminate the world by His wisdom and excite it to the love of Himself." The danger of this unusual position, which places the *moral influence* of Christ at the center of the Atonement, was immediately seen–and Abelard's work was rewarded by his denunciation as a heretic. The main problem is that his theory seems to leave the Atonement without a foundation of absolute necessity. In other words, if someone drowns trying to save me after I've fallen in a stream, it is one thing, but if he walks along a stream with me and suddenly jumps in and drowns, crying, "Look how much I love you; I'm giving my life for you," it's hard to see some kind of essential sacrifice taking place.

The Mormon concept of the Atonement which I have suggested seems to me close to Abelard's–with the important addition of an understanding of *why the atonement is absolutely necessary*. It is not necessary because of some eternal structure of justice in the universe outside us which demands payment from us for our sins, nor of some similar structure within the nature of God. The Atonement is absolutely necessary because of the nature of *intelligences,* a nature that is self-existent, not the creation of God, and therefore uniquely impervious to metaphysical coercion. The problem is not that God's justice must be satisfied (or the universe's) but that *our* own sense of justice demands satisfaction. When it creates a barrier to repentance, that barrier must be broken through, and it cannot be broken by metaphysical tinkering with our nature; it can only be broken through by the powerful persuasion of a kind of love which transcends our sense of justice without denying it–the kind of love that Christ was uniquely able to manifest in the Atonement.

The Atonement is a necessary, but not sufficient, factor in salvation from sin–necessary because only Christ can fully motivate the process in free agents, and insufficient because an agent must respond and complete the process. There is no condition in which we can imagine God being *unable* to forgive. The question is what effect will the forgiveness have; the forgiveness is meaningless unless it leads to repentance. The forgiveness extended in the dramatic events of the Atonement is that kind of forgiveness uniquely capable of bringing "means unto men that they may have faith unto repentance." In other words, the forgiveness must be *accepted* in order to be efficacious: "For what doth it profit a man if a gift is bestowed upon him, and he receive not the gift" (Doctrine and Covenants 88:33).

As Paul Tillich has pointed out, the most difficult thing for us to do is accept our acceptance, to accept the fact that God accepts us, loves us–freely–even in our sins. Our practice in our dealings with other people and, most important to my point here, in our dealings with ourselves, is to demand satisfaction before we can accept, to demand justice before we can forgive. This is not Christ's way, and *therefore* his love (and the love which he tells us we can develop in response to that love) is redemptive. It has a quality of mercy which allows us to be at one with ourselves and thus gain the strength to be the new person that our sense of justice in the first place demanded that we be. We do not repent in order that God will forgive us and atone for our sins, but rather God atones for our sins and begins the process of forgiveness, by extending unconditional love to us, in order that we might repent and thus bring to conclusion the process of forgiveness. And the center of the experience is Christ's ability to break through the barrier of justice, in those who can freely respond, with the shock of eternal love expressed in Gethsemane. It comes to us only through our deep knowledge of that event and our involvement in the process of sustaining that knowledge in our lives, through the continual reminding of ourselves of the event and our recommitment to the implications of it which occurs in the ordinances of the gospel. The process is a complex one, an ongoing one. It may be triggered by particular events and have climaxes, but essentially it is a lifelong process–one beautifully described toward the end of the Book of Mormon in these words from the prophet Mormon to his son Moroni:

> *. . .repentance is unto them that are under condemnation and under the curse of a broken law. And the first fruits of repentance is baptism; and baptism cometh by faith unto the fulfilling the commandments; and the fulfilling the commandments bringeth remission of sins; and the remission of sins bringeth meekness and lowliness of heart and because of meekness and lowliness of heart cometh the visitation of the Holy Ghost, which comforter filleth with hope and perfect love. . . . (Moroni 8:24-26)*

As a young missionary, I had not yet experienced the central drama of the Christian faith and of my Mormon faith in a decisive personal way. Towards the end of my mission experience in Hawaii, in a new assignment different from previous assignments that had meant mainly teaching primary school and administration, I was suddenly faced with a very real human situation involving the central principles of the gospel. A Southern sharecropper, who had lived a life of extreme brutality and self-indulgence, had jumped ship in Hawaii, married a Japanese girl, and under her influence and the influence of children coming into his life had softened and opened–to the point of hearing the gospel from previous missionaries. He had believed their message and came to me with a plea for help. He believed that certain principles were true but could not find the power to change his life to live in accordance with those principles and was suffering deeply. He was estranged from himself, his habits terribly opposed to his sense of God and what God hoped for him. As I tried to help him, searching again the scriptures and explanations of the scriptures having to do with the Atonement, as I gropingly expressed my growing sense of what the love of Christ meant to me and tried to express, along with my companion and the man's family, some of that same unconditional love to him, and as I watched him grow under that love and under his growing awareness that Christ was capable of loving and forgiving him in his present condition, he and I both came slowly and then suddenly to a deep sense of the kind of love, expressed in Gethsemane, that made Atonement possible. I saw him change dramatically as the power inherent in an understanding of that experience came into his life. The burden of sin was lifted and the healing, renewing process of repentance made possible as he said to himself, "If God can have this kind of love for me, who am I to withhold it from myself?" My life didn't change as dramatically, but the beginnings of change were laid there, and the understanding of atoning love that began there has been increasingly vindicated in all my experience.

Humans in our time have turned upon each other with incredible hate and cruelty. And the victims and dispossessed and their allies have turned back in kind. The ills of our time, which grow by escalation–blow for blow, hurt for hurt, raid for raid, riot for riot, all defended in the name of justice and personal or national rights–must eventually be subjected to more than justice.

Each of us must come to a kind of love that can be extended equally to victim and victimizer, dispossessed and dispossessor–and even to ourselves, a kind of love that moves us to demand justice in sociey and within ourselves and that then goes beyond justice to offer forgiveness and healing and beyond guilt to offer redemption and newness of life.

I am convinced by my thought and experience and the deepest whisperings in my soul that there is a source of that love—one that transcends all others and is therefore our salvation.

Written as a review of Harold Kushner's bestseller,
When Bad Things Happen to Good People;
published in *BYU Studies*, Fall 1983.

CHAPTER 8

HOW CAN GOD BE BOTH GOOD AND POWERFUL?

If you see a blind man, kick him; why should you be kinder than God?" That bit of folk wisdom from Iran seems cruel, but it captures a common response to evil and suffering by those who think God controls everything and does so with perfect justice: The victims must deserve it. It is less direct, but as cruel, that parents I know about could stand in a church meeting and give thanks that their son had "miraculously" survived an automobile accident because of his righteousness, in the presence of the parents of their son's friend, who did not survive that crash.

Harold Kushner, a rabbi whose own son's death radically changed his thinking about God, has written *When Bad Things Happen to Good People* "for all those people whose love for God and devotion to Him lead them to blame themselves for their suffering" and by implication for all those, like Job's "comforters," whose theology leads them to blame the victim—or those like Job, who blame God himself.

The book is written by a thoughtful and humane man, from the power of his own pain and the realism earned by much counseling of others in grief. It is designed to help victims and their families and pastors with specific examples and arguments which can help prevent the person who has been hurt by life from compounding the damage by also hurting himself or letting herself be hurt by others misguidedly trying to help. The book's success has been demonstrated by many months on the bestseller lists and by a growing volume of letters and calls of gratitude to Kushner, with many requests for more of the same kind of help. But the book's central thesis breaks new ground in a way that has put Kushner at odds with both traditional Christian theologians and his own Jewish colleagues. His answer to what he calls the only question that really matters, "Why do bad things happen to good people?" is that they happen in situations not within God's total control: God is good and fair but *not* omnipotent.

As a rabbi at the Jewish Theological Seminary of America points out, Kushner's idea is a "radical break" with the Judeo-Christian past: "All the traditional answers say that God is in some way responsible for suffering" (*Time*, July 19, 1982, p. 80). But much of the book's power comes from Kushner's effectiveness in showing just how unhelpful, even cruel, such "traditional answers" (however satisfying to theologians) have been to those actually suffering: 1. Pain and loss are God's punishment of the wicked. (Fine, if you are a normally sinful adult, or even a rabbi merely trying to live righteously, but what about the *innocent child* born with progeria or "rapid aging," as Kushner's son Aaron was, or struck with horribly painful bone cancer?) 2. The child (or mother) was needed on the other side; God has a more important mission for them. (A loving God would at least take them without pain. Besides, you mean God needs my wife more than I and my six small children do? And more than he needed the wonderful single woman down the street? That's like saying to my daughter, "It's your fault that your mother died. If you had needed her more, she would still be alive.") 3. She is happier there, freed from this world's sin and pain. (Then why keep any of us here so long. Are you saying that I should rejoice and thank God that my daughter was killed in an airplane collision? That it is just my own selfishness that makes my sorrow? That what looks like evil really isn't?) 4. God has some inscrutable purpose in doing this to you; if you could see the big picture, you'd understand. (But that's hypothetical; we *don't* see any such big picture in 250 randomly gathered lives snuffed out in an airliner disaster. Besides, if a human artist or employer made children suffer so that something immensely impressive or valuable could come to pass, we would put him in prison. Why then should we excuse God for causing such undeserved pain, no matter how wonderful the ultimate result might be?) 5. But suffering *can* be educational; it even ennobles us. To a primitive, doctors performing an operation might look like they are torturing the patient when they are really helping him. This accident that has made you a paraplegic will also make you more sensitive. (What right do *you*, who can walk out of this hospital and drive a car and play tennis, have to tell me it is in my best interest to be paralyzed? It's obvious that not all trouble and suffering improves people, and if it could, why doesn't your all-powerful God precisely control what he sends each person so that we *are* all improved, in fact, all made perfect? And if that's what we think he's doing, why should we interfere, why try to *prevent* suffering or do away with the pain?) 6. Well, God only let this happen to *you* because he knew you are strong enough to bear the loss of your son. (You mean, if only I were a weaker person, Aaron would still be alive? I have seen many people's faith and lives destroyed by such tragedies. If God is a perfect and all-powerful tester of us, why does he miscalculate so often?)

If none of the traditional answers are satisfying to the victims, what can we say then? Why *do* bad things happen to good people? Kushner finds the key in the book of Job, which he reads as a *rejection* of the traditional answers in favor of a tough but realistic alternative suggested by God himself as he sides with Job against his "comforters." Kushner claims that the Book of Job gives an unusual answer to the old problem of theodicy (How can we justify an all-powerful God, or believe in his justice, when he allows evil and innocent suffering in his creation?): The three statements, 1) God is all-powerful and causes all to happen, 2) God is perfectly just, and 3) Job is a good person, can all be accepted without contradiction only while Job is healthy and being blessed. The Book of Job is about which statement to reject when bad things happen to such a "perfect" man (and by implication, whenever they happen to children). Job's visitors (and all of us when we in some way blame the victim) reject number 3, but Job knows he is good and will not deny his own integrity in order to hold the world together theologically— "Though he destroy me, yet will I maintain my ways before Him" (Job 13:15).

Job rejects statement number 2; he affirms that God, being absolute, is not limited by our notions of goodness: "Behold he snatches away and who can hinder Him? Who can say to Him, What are you doing?"(Job 9:12). But Kushner wonders how we can genuinely love God if he is "too great" for human considerations of morality: "The problem with such an answer is that it tries to promote justice and fairness and at the same time tries to celebrate God for being so great that He is beyond the limitations of justice and fairness." Kushner thinks that the author of the Book of Job has God appear out of the whirlwind *not* to reinforce Job's position by asserting that he doesn't *have* to explain suffering to his ignorant and weak creation, man, but rather to teach Job that it is too difficult even for God to keep cruelty and chaos from claiming their innocent victims (Job 40 and 41). In other words, the author of Job gives up statement number 1, that God is omnipotent, the cause of everything–and Kushner agrees:

If God is a god of justice and not of power, then He can still be on our side when bad things happen to us. . . . Our misfortunes are none of His doing, and so we can turn to Him for help. . . . We will turn to God, not to be judged or forgiven, not to be rewarded or punished, but to be strengthened and comforted.

It is unfortunate that this resolution to the problem of evil should be seen as utterly new, because, of course, it is the one revealed nearly 150 years ago to Joseph Smith. In fact, Kushner has one passage that could have come almost directly out of the "King Follett Discourse": Like the Prophet, he analyzes the first verses of Genesis and finds that the original Hebrew describes God working with material already in existence. Then Kushner writes, "This is what it means to create: not to make something out of nothing, but to make order out of chaos." Joseph Smith understood that the elements, our core intelligences, and the laws that govern the development and interaction of intelligences and elements have all existed co-eternally with God. He did not create from nothing and cannot annihilate what exists; he can only shape and mold ("organize") the elements according to eternal laws and can only help intelligences to progress as they in their agency allow.

For Kushner, as for Mormons, the existence of evil is explained by the incompleteness of God's creation and thus his limited control of the universe: "Suppose that Creation, the process of replacing chaos with order, were still going on." Tragedies do not reflect God's choices; they occur because chaos still continues "in those corners of the universe where God's creative light has not yet penetrated." Evil is "that aspect of reality which stands independent of His will, and which angers and saddens God even as it angers and saddens us."

But Kushner's formulations lead him back toward an explanation for evil as least as old as Augustine: evil as "privation," the mere absence of good. Kushner is refreshingly straightforward about some of the logical implications of that position–and especially helpful in suggesting practical applications of the idea in counseling situations, but he really has no better answer than traditional theologians to the obvious next question: Why *didn't* God complete the universe? *Why* is it left less than perfect and thus shot through with evil?

Kushner makes a valiant try, pointing out that the Sunday School stories of miracles that imply a God willing and able to make exceptions to the laws of nature for nice people also imply a frighteningly imprecise universe: "A world in which good people suffer from the same natural dangers that others do causes problems. But a world in which good people were immune to those laws would cause even more problems." He confesses recognition of the logical trap he is approaching: "If God was designing a world for our maximum benefit, why could He not create unchanging laws of nature which would not do any harm to any of us, good or bad?"

Why not, indeed? And Kushner's attempt to answer, without a more complete theology like that revealed to Joseph Smith, leads him into serious trouble and a troubling cop-out. He tries to point out the beneficial aspects of pain. (It warns us to draw back from injury or overexertion, etc., is "the price we pay for being alive.") But, recognizing that he is *still* not answering the ultimate question of why God designed things that way, he confesses,

I don't have a good answer to why there is sickness and disease, why germs and viruses and malignant tumors in the first place. . . . I don't know why people are mortal and fated to die, and I don't know why people die at the time and in the way they do.

And finally, apparently because he does not have a sure faith in a life after death where justice can finally be done and the results of our sufferings become positive, Kushner succumbs to a kind of Stoic minimalism, asking us to be courageous and helpful to one another in the face of what remains a mystery:

Many of us . . . will come to the point where death will be the only healer for the pain which our lives have come to contain. . . . It is one thing to explain that mortality in general is good for people in general. It is something else again to try to tell someone who has lost a parent, a wife, or a child that death is good. . . . We can't explain it any more than we can explain life itself.

Kushner is more helpful than most Judeo-Christian theologians, then, in facing up to the evidence that God is limited by natural law, human nature, and human freedom. But he is really no better at explaining how things got that way, *why* God has created such a universe—or didn't create a better one. And therefore Kushner's speculations lead him to positions that, despite the practical values of his book, alarm me as much as they do the traditional theologians. He seems to have adopted a kind of wishfully sentimental Deism: "It may be that God finished His work of creating eons ago, and left the rest to us. . . . God has created a world in which many more good things than bad things happen." He restricts God's power much more than the Bible, or the needs of his basic position, would require: "God does not want you to be sick or crippled . . . but He can't make it go away. That is something which is too hard even for God."

Kushner recognizes the danger of meaninglessness in his removing God as a cause and cure of our suffering: "Have I made it harder for people to accept their illnesses, their misfortunes, their family tragedies by telling them that they are not sent by God as part of some master plan of His?" And he brings God back in as some kind of psychological aid, aid given not directly but merely through "the knowledge that we are not alone," through belief that God, though not obviously doing anything, is "at the side of the afflicted and downcast." But then Kushner seems to contradict his Deism by suggesting that God "helps by inspiring people to help," for instance, by becoming doctors and medical researchers (and rabbis?) and that in some way, though "God may not prevent calamity, He gives us the strength and perseverance to overcome it."

However, the greatest limitation of Kushner's position is revealed at the end of the book, when he reviews Archibald MacLeish's version of Job in the play *J.B.* and apparently approves its presumptuous existentialism:

J.B. cannot turn for help and comfort to a God who is described as making man imperfect and then punishing him for his imperfections. . . . He forgives God for not making a more just universe, and decides to take it as it is. He stops looking for justice . . . and looks for love instead.

Kushner then asks *us* "to forgive the world for not being perfect, to forgive God for not making a better world, to reach out to the people around us, and to go on living despite it all."

The advice to love and live instead of blaming is good, but such intellectual underpinnings are extremely weak. And modern man has been much more inclined to anger or indifference rather than forgiveness toward such a strange God: He cannot build a better universe or interfere in this one but is to be thanked and worshipped for providing in some mysterious way some only occasionally effective aid—"the ability to forgive and the ability to love" and thus (at least for those of us not maimed by God's strange universe) the ability "to live fully, bravely and meaningfully in this less-than-perfect world."

Mormon theology provides a crucial intellectual underpinning for Kushner's good practical counsel. It empowers a secure confidence and gratitude toward God instead of requiring us, as Kushner does, to "forgive" him or to belittle his power by merely hoping he is helping in some vague way. Mormon doctrine effectively answers the traditionally unanswered question, "Why did God make such a universe where natural laws, human nature, and human freedom limit him?" The crucial new understanding given to Joseph Smith was that natural laws and the essence of human nature contained in "intelligences," including their need and capacity for freedom, have existed co-eternally with God. He did not create them out of nothing and can only affect them within limits imposed by themselves. But he *can* act with great power within those limits to lift all intelligences–who will–to become like himself. And that in turn explains God's traditionally unexplained *purpose* in creation: to act in love to give other beings like himself more of the freedom and creative power he possesses.

Evil is indeed privation, the less than perfect condition of humans and the harmful effects which humans thus have on each other in their ignorance and sin and which inexorable natural laws have on them in their ignorance and lack of power. But that privation is a *given* in the cosmos, not something built in or intentionally left out by God, and it is something God is working with all his power to remove through his creative acts and through helping us progressively respond to those acts. God does all that Kushner recognizes him as doing in our mortal lives–and much more, including using his perfect understanding of natural law to bless us individually as we let him. That includes provision of a "mortal probation" that extends far beyond this life, beyond the accidents of death and condition that unfairly limit the opportunities for choice and growth of some. A long pre-mortal life and continued individual existence and growth after death are the guarantees, in Joseph Smith's theology, that there will be equal opportunity for *every person* to develop to his full potential. That revealed understanding is missing from traditional thought, which therefore must try to justify God in terms of the obviously unequal conditions of *this* life.

On the Mormon view, then, there is no rational or emotional need to *excuse* God. He can be trusted and worshipped in full confidence that he is at least as good and loving as our highest standards, the very ones he taught us, require. God is doing all that *can* be done, given the nature of things, to help us overcome evil as we progress in the struggle with it; he in no sense created evil in order to do that, but in choosing to help us progress God *had* to bring us into a condition where there were new things to learn and choices to be made. That condition, *unavoidably*, is one where evil results from our imperfections and imperfect choices. And God only takes on such a responsibility because he has the immense power to provide absolutely sufficient means, here and hereafter, so that he can assure each of us that the evil *can* be overcome, if we will.

Yes, there is remaining mystery, as there is in all attempts to explain the ultimate, but the troubling mystery in Mormon thought centers in the nature of the universe, not in the nature of God: How did such a universe, with its own basic, unchanging laws, and such beings as God and men, with their potential for "eternal increase," come to be? Joseph Smith's answer, that they didn't come to be, but always were, both thrills me and multiplies the mystery.

What value then is Kushner's book? It can be very useful to anyone who must try to help the suffering or grieving, which includes us all. Its basic message is that of the Book of Mormon prophet Alma: Rather than explaining or blaming, we should "mourn with those that mourn . . . and comfort those that stand in need of comfort" (Mosiah 18:9). And it gives many practical suggestions about how to do that. It also helps us see the advantages, if we do not want to be like Job's "miserable comforters," of holding the universe, not God or the victims, reponsible. And, with the additional strength of the Mormon understanding, it can, much better than traditional theology, help us see satisfactory reasons for not holding God responsible for the nature of that universe, while still acknowledging his powerful, pervasive efforts for good—his hand in all things.

Published in *Dialogue*, Autumn 1974;
for a less somber view of this contrary see Clifton Jolley's "Selling the Chevrolet," *Dialogue*, Fall 1983.

C H A P T E R 9

BLESSING THE CHEVROLET

For a moment Abijah felt stunned; in this, his first real emergency, he had almost forgotten God!

He turned to Brother Tuckett.

Clory, sitting on a boulder near-by, wondered at the sudden purpose in Brother Tuckett's movements. What were they going to do? And then she saw Brother Tuckett appear with the bottle of consecrated sweet oil. She heard Lon say, 'You be "Mouth," Brother Abijah,' and the full significance of the scene burst upon her. Why, they were preparing for 'the laying on of hands'! For Abijah would have to be 'Mouth' since he held the higher priesthood! She sat up in horror. Administering to an ox!

She saw Melancthon Tuckett rub the oil between the animal's red ears and then both he and Abijah rest their hands, one over the other, on its head.

'We unitedly lay our hands upon thy head, O ox . . . this oil which has been dedicated and consecrated and set apart for the healing of the sick in the household of faith. . . .'

Bewilderedly Clory grasped the fact that this prayer had all the earnest supplication of the ceremony performed for any ailing human being.

. . . .Clory watched him calmly speak to the ox. Opening its eyes, it stared at the men with its gentle, liquid gaze. She was not greatly surprised when it scrambled to its feet.

–Maurine Whipple, *The Giant Joshua*

At various times I have heard and read, with mild curiosity, of the anointing of animals by the power of the priesthood in pioneer times, but it wasn't until I found myself with my own hands placed in blessing on the hood of my Chevrolet that I really felt what that experience meant to those early Saints, who depended on their animals, as we do our cars, for quite crucial things.

One evening last fall, Charlotte and I drove about sixty miles to visit a young couple in the Mormon branch congregation of which I am president, converts of a few years who had slipped into inactivity and growing doubt but were now trying to rebuild their faith. We had supper and a good visit and gave a blessing to their new daughter, who had been ill for some time with a vague disorder that kept her crying severely for long stretches. When we tried to return home the car would not start. We managed to push it to the only garage in that small town just before it closed and were told that the trouble was apparently a broken timing gear, which would take about two days to order and install. Our young friends lent us their car to drive to our home and bring back when we came for ours. When I phoned to check two days later I was told that the timing gear was installed but for some reason the car would not start; I drove over anyway and tried to help, but as the afternoon wore on and we tried all kinds of variations of the timing apparatus, plugs, etc., we could only get an occasional rough chug and some backfiring. The mechanic finally said he was afraid he would have to tear out the new timing gear and check it, which would take well into the next day. But I had to be back home to conduct an important branch meeting that night, and when my anxiety reached a certain point, I found that it was quite natural, while the mechanic was helping at the gas pumps out front, to literally place my hands on the car and give it a blessing, explaining to the Lord that I was about his work, that my branch needed me, and I needed some extraordinary help to get there. The mechanic came back, made another adjustment, and halfheartedly tried the starter again for the hundredth time. So help me, I was not even surprised when, after a few mild growls, the engine started. The mechanic was incredulous and insisted on a test drive before he would let me go; after a few miles the engine was still running quite rough, but he agreed that I could probably get home and have it tuned up some more later—and I was off. It was only on the long ride back that I became properly aware of what had happened, was amazed, and gave thanks.

I have had many occasions to bless my wife and my children and have not been surprised to see them healed, against all the odds, or relax from pain into peace or sleep under my very hands. And on a couple of occasions when we had car trouble during our many trips back to Utah from California or Minnesota they have suggested that we pray for help and it has seemed to come. I now remember, while on a little-used Nevada back road in early spring, driving onto the shoulder to look at some flowers, finding myself stuck in hub deep mud, and, after a family prayer, inexplicably making it back up on the pavement. And a number of times, following such a prayer, we have limped across hundreds of miles of desert or a nighttime of closed stations with leaking radiators or worn bearings or something else that should have stopped us. But those things have occurred in fairly naturalistic ways that I sort of took for granted—as nice experiences for my children but nothing miraculous—and haven't thought much about until recently, when I started blessing my Chevrolet.

At Christmas this year we visited our folks in Utah and on our way home noticed there was a certain nagging mushiness when we tried to accelerate and also that a noisy muffler was getting louder. Crossing South Dakota on a Saturday afternoon we found few mechanics available, but finally one took time to look at the car and found a dirty fuel filter, which he replaced, and a loose tailpipe connection, which he tightened and wired together so it couldn't work loose again. When the car still had no pickup—in fact, seemed worse—he took a look at the mileage (84,000) and cheerfully declared that the transmission was probably going ($400), but I could probably make it home. We started again but found that now we couldn't get up over forty miles an hour on the level, could barely make it over those infinitesimal variations in the landscape they call hills in South Dakota, and were getting about three miles per gallon. I calculated that even if things didn't get worse it would take us well into Sunday to get home and we would probably run out of money for gas before then or stall on one of the (comparative) mountains of Minnesota. And if things *did* get worse, we could be marooned on the South Dakota prairie (fairly dangerous in January) or at best stuck in some motel until Monday when someone might be able to put in a new transmission—except that we couldn't pay for it.

Suddenly I found myself gripping the steering wheel with a special intensity and giving the car a blessing again. I told the Lord that my family was in danger and that our branch needed us the next day and it was time once more for some special help. I felt impressed to take the next exit, which led us to a town some distance from the freeway, and without any surprise felt directed to a certain station. The owner looked things over, disconnected a vacuum hose, and had me drive off for a test. There was no change and I went back disappointed and for the first time surprised. But the station owner greeted me with a grin and said, "I'll bet I know what the problem is; I heard it as you drove off." He put the car on the hoist and soon found out he was right. Disconnecting the tailpipe at the place the previous mechanic had wired it, he pushed a hose down it and found that the inner wall had collapsed almost shut. He explained that my Chevrolet was from one of those few years when they had experimented with double-walled tailpipes. Sometimes, in the extremes of heat and cold of the upper Midwest that inner wall collapses, shutting off the exhaust and producing symptoms much like a bad transmission or an engine that needs overhauling. In fact, the reason he recognized the problem was that a friend of his had, just the month before, wasted $500 on his engine before he discovered that he had this very problem. The only reason I had been getting any power was because the pressure had forced the tailpipe connection loose so that the exhaust could escape there; and when the previous mechanic had wired that so it couldn't force open, the engine's power was shut down. I found myself quite calm, without surprise, as he told me these things, without anxiety when he was at first unable to locate a new tailpipe at that late hour on Saturday but then barely caught one supply house in time to get a length of some flexible pipe and some clamps and then cut out the curved section where the collapse was and clamp in the flexpipe securely enough for us to get home.

I do not understand fully why or how the Lord does these things—though I know he does. In fact, if I think about it much, there are difficulties: How about our free agency and our need to learn to solve our own problems and be maturely independent—not like infants always asking for help? How fit all this with the Lord's assurances that he makes his sun and rain to come down equally on all his children—the just and the unjust? How about all that suffering, apparently uninterrupted by God, in the Sub-Sahara famine, Southeast Asia's constant bloodshed, the animal-like packs of deserted children in South American cities, the emotional destruction during slow death in American nursing homes? Couldn't God have veered the typhoon that killed thousands in Bangladesh or the earthquake that killed thousands in Iran, as well as guide the mechanic to straighten out the timing on my Chev or me to someone who could cure my car? I don't know. Perhaps it has something to do with God *guiding people* rather than interfering with nature; perhaps it has something to do with his being asked in faith and for reasons that have to do with his most important purposes, which aren't just keeping people alive but saving their souls. Yet he seems mysteriously selective about helping there as well. And of course, even when he does clearly respond it isn't always the way we want or expect. In that almost too painfully moving autobiographical account, "The Death of a Son" by Carole Hansen, that appeared in *Dialogue* (Autumn 1967), we were powerfully reminded that God, in response to a priesthood blessing, can give assurance and peace, even to the point of being misunderstood, and then eventually can give conviction of his care and the child's ultimate welfare—all *without* giving what parents emotionally want most, the child's life. Again, I don't know why or how.

All I really know is that I continue to ask blessings and to see them given. Last week our branch held a special fast and had a prayer session for the four-year-old daughter of some friends of one of our members. She had to come from Colorado for extremely dangerous heart surgery at the Mayo Clinic to correct a congenital defect. The parents had lived with the specter of losing this child as she grew into a poignantly frail elfin joy while they waited for her to be old enough to risk the operation, and they had fasted each week over the past months as the time grew close. They had been told the chances were about fifty-fifty, but somehow none of us was surprised when the last exploratory catheterization at the Clinic revealed the condition to be less serious than had been supposed and when (after an anointing by her father and a local Rochester Branch brother) the operation went extremely well and she was up and skittering around after only a few days in intensive care. Last fall I felt moved to give a special blessing to a dear and extremely capable friend who was suffering anxiety and self-reproach under the pressure of his professional responsibilities and the possibility of failing his family and himself by not meeting them, and I had no doubt that the Lord would bless him with the measure of self-confidence he needed to succeed, and he did. And yesterday a faithful, long-suffering father and I were suddenly called out of our Sunday School preparation meeting to find his child in the chapel having a severe seizure. (She has had a condition from birth that causes a reaction, at entirely unpredictable moments.) As the father took her in his arms and held her jaw so she wouldn't bite her tongue, I placed my hands on her head and through the power of the priesthood rebuked the uncontrolled shaking of her entire body. As I continued to stroke her head, the shaking quickly quieted. Then we carried her to the car to be taken home to rest, and I returned to explain to those who had been present what had happened and to ask their prayers for her.

The opportunities, the needs, come often, and the Lord's response forms a bright thread in the texture of gospel living. But I don't fully understand why or how. I only know that I continue to ask–and to acknowledge the Lord's hand in all things.

One version of a challenging, renewing pilgrimage we made each six months for five years; published in *Dialogue*, Summer 1973.

C H A P T E R 1 0

GOING TO CONFERENCE

KSL Radio reaches east barely twenty miles past Rock Springs, Wyoming. That's where we were first able to make out the words of Elder Spencer W. Kimball at 11:30 Friday morning, October 6, 1972. His voice roughened by static and the throat cancer he once barely survived, the new President of the Quorum of the Twelve Apostles was beginning the final address of the Solemn Assembly. It wasn't until that night on a rebroadcast that we knew the details of that unique ceremony where ten thousand priesthood leaders from all over the world, gathered in the Tabernacle, had sustained a new President of the Church and witnessed directly the prophetic mantle descending upon him. Elder Kimball was again, as he had done at the inauguration of President Joseph Fielding Smith, recounting firmly the process of succession to the presidency: calling by God to the apostleship, preparation by long training in that Quorum and divine preservation until, by strict seniority, the mantle passes to the Lord's Anointed; he was putting to an end (perhaps) that awful speculation many of us felt as we grew up in the Church, founded on the persistent rumor that the Lord might choose anyone in the Church for his new prophet, even someone we knew, even one of us. There will never again for us be anything like watching for the white smoke from the cardinals' mysterious meeting after the prolonged voting for a Pope. We know who the next Prophet will be—Elder Kimball, if he continues to be preserved, or else the next apostle in line.

We had been driving all night from Minnesota–members of our branch, including some young converts and two of my daughters (Charlotte, liberated by her position as district president, had flown ahead to Relief Society conference). We heard this last speech and later listened to the afternoon session as we drove down through the crescendo of fall colors from Echo Canyon through Coalville (plumed with orange-gold cottonwoods), past the mountain back-drop above Snyderville (still spectacular though scarred by new ski runs), into Parley's Canyon, with its subtle mottling of scrub oak, shading from deep purple and wine through rusts and browns to grass yellow, accented with bright gold aspens and a few remaining florescent red maples.

The unfolding mountains and canyons and colors, together with the persistent voice of counsel and conviction from persons they had very recently come to accept as Authorities, men of God, were almost overwhelming for our young friends raised in crowded Brooklyn and flat Minnesota and schooled on secular relativism and Protestant skepticism. The choir seemed in collusion with some master plan and built a Handel chorus to a grand climax as we made the last turn out on Foothill Boulevard above the Valley. But then we were greeted with smog so thick it even obscured the buildings which now hide the temple we were all so anxious to see. (Our embarrassment was relieved somewhat when the skies cleared by Sunday in time for a clear and satisfactorily impressive view of the Valley and circling mountains before we left.)

On Saturday and Sunday we were able to get most of us into at least one session at the Tabernacle and watched the other sessions on TV. For me, conference is an old song which brings a familiar spirit apart from the meaning of the words. For those with us the tune was not familiar and there were some struggles with the lyrics. A few of the more liberated females were appalled at some of the remarks on women and their place in the home (Charlotte counseled patience). Most of these first-timers found the setting too formal and impersonal–especially as it came over on TV–and in particular contrast with their limited Church experience in our small, personal, and generally very informal (not to say chaotic) branch. But they looked for and felt the power of the Prophet.

It was President Lee's conference. He was in charge from the first moment, conducting each session with a dignified assurance that paradoxically allowed him to be more spontaneous and personal than I remember President Smith or even President McKay. In four major addresses he set and modulated the tone and communicated a great range of specific direction and feeling. First there was the austerity of the formal voting at the beginning of the Solemn Assembly. President Tanner called each priesthood rank of the Church in order (First Presidency, Apostles, general authorities, high priests, etc., to Aaronic Priesthood and general assembly) to stand and sustain, if they would, the new Prophet, then each group again to stand in order and sustain the First Presidency, then the Quorum of the Twelve, with the new apostle, Bruce R. McConkie, then the other general authorities. This standing and voting, the repetition for each group of all the groups they were voting for, took nearly forty minutes, but it was not boring, even to us listening over the radio to the rebroadcast; it was like a long formal preparation, a chastening of the emotions, and, according to Charlotte, who had been there, the sense of building power was marvelously tangible even to a young non-member friend sitting with her. Then President Lee spoke, bearing direct witness to what had happened to him, almost standing aside from himself and describing with awe the new emotions and powers being released within him–a new sense of the reality of Christ, for the first time feeling what it means to love all mankind. The formality had stretched the united feelings of the assembly so that when President Lee's voice finally broke in an intense revelation of feeling, the hearts of thousands there responded. And Charlotte's bemused consciousness that almost all of those present were men was transcended by seeing so many of them in tears and, at the end of the session, by the way the general authorities and others expressed their joy by freely embracing each other.

Since I find in myself tendencies toward both conservatism and liberalism, depending upon the issue and the context, it has been both unsettling and satisfying to find President Lee impartially roasting extremes in both tendencies. A year ago last spring, in his "iron rod" speech he harshly exposed the temporizing indulged in by some "liberals" in the Church; in *this* conference, both in his address Saturday morning and in the priesthood session Saturday evening, he leveled on the conservatives. He condemned any use of evil means in apparently good causes, such as going beyond the law and the Constitution in combating pornography or using non-Church organizations or position in the Church in fighting against Communism in any way that turns brother against brother. Saturday evening he leaned over the pulpit and gave a prophetic tongue-lashing to the spiritualist gossips who spread rumors and write books on details concerning the last days that neither the Lord nor the Prophet (nor common sense) has been moved to reveal. He told us to come down to earth–not to pass on rumors no matter how attractive (like the one going the rounds in Utah and California that had apparently most disturbed him: that his patriarchal blessing had promised he would be President when the Savior came). And he held the priesthood leadership responsible for putting a stop to this kind of speculation and gossip.

That steely chastisement was one indication of the authority and strength of the new Prophet, of his freedom to assume full stature as President and call the Church to repentance. But the qualities revealed in him that impressed Charlotte and me most were quite different, though perhaps related, especially his humility and responsiveness. Throughout the conference his conducting was marked by warm and sensitive informality in his comments about individual speakers. There was the tone that should mark a good sacrament meeting, that reveals the kind of flexibility made possible through guidance by the Spirit. One example especially moving to me occurred Sunday morning when Elder LeGrand Richards spoke. He remains one of the general authorities who disdain the teleprompter (with its temptation to metronomic turning of the head and disconcertingly impassive recitation of everything, even personal experience and testimony). He gave a speech that was unprepared in the sense of not being written out or memorized, but prepared for by a lifetime of enthusiastic missionary work. He stumbled over words, occasionally fumbled in his pocket for quotes written on slips of paper, informed millions of our Christian brothers listening in that Christ had announced in 1820 that their creeds were an abomination in his sight and, after quoting some of their traditional creedal statements about the nature of God to them, allowed that that was one of the best descriptions of *nothing* he had ever heard. Elder Richards' voice rose in that characteristic crescendo that carried him beyond his denunciations to moving expression of his joy in the gospel and love for all men, transformed that stooped body and brought back the thrilling vibrancy I remember from twenty-five years ago. Then his testimony was completed and he shrank back into a rather bent and aged man helping himself with his cane down the steps. In the silence President Lee rose, expressed personal gratitude for the spirit and testimony of a grand old missionary, and asked the Lord to keep him long among us. I say Amen to that.

We had difficulty getting in the tabernacle even at 6:45 on Sunday morning, because high school and college students from Utah and Idaho had come in buses shortly after 5:00 that morning and filled the balconies where the only open seating was. They remained throughout the day, and again it was unusually difficult to get into the afternoon session. About five minutes before the session was to start, as President Lee came out from the rooms underneath the choir seats and was greeting general authorities' wives and regional representatives seated at the right of the stand, these young people, triggered by some small group of them, rose and sang, "We Thank Thee, Oh God, for a Prophet." The rest of us joined in, and I was able to see President Lee's response from where I stood near the front on the main floor. Rather than ascending the stand or turning to the audience to take the honor, he turned and faced at attention the place where all the Prophets who had preceded him, from Brigham Young, had sat and stood and preached. He then joined us in singing, honoring and teaching us to honor the role, not the man.

Conference is a time for feeling more than for ideas, as President Lee reminded us in his last address. Those who go looking for dramatic new doctrine or new policy are apt to continue to be disappointed (I too have gone yearning, hoping to hear that announcement about the priesthood being extended to all). Those things will come in statements from the First Presidency day by day as the revelations come. Conference will continue to be a kind of rite, a shoring up of faith and confidence, of feelings of unity and achievement. It is a place to feel what I felt when I met on the grounds a group of Saints from Samoa, whom I had known as rather inept, struggling new members in badly organized, barely functioning branches fifteen years ago and who are now stalwart stake presidents and bishops, Relief Society presidents and teachers–and have converted nearly half the population of their islands. I embraced one young man whom I had taught English when he was twelve (we had read Frost's "Stopping by Woods on a Snowy Evening" and there at the Equator tried to imagine together what snow could be); he is now a translator for the Church, and later I was able to sit in the section equipped with foreign language microphones and hear him translating into Samoan the words of President Lee.

This conference was a time for me to agree with the young soldier converted in Vietnam President Lee told about, who had come to feel, despite the great difficulties he would face on going home, "If the gospel's true, nothing else matters." At least not nearly as much. Going to conference made it possible for me to feel more strongly than ever that the great soul-satisfying truths of the gospel and my experiences of love and growth in the Church are much more important than the things that give me trouble.

A response to the Washington Temple dedication,
November 1974;
published in *Dialogue*, Summer 1974.

C H A P T E R 1 1

THE HOSANNA SHOUT IN WASHINGTON, D.C.

The first time I participated in the "Hosanna Shout" I felt the actual presence of beings from another world joining us in that cry of praise and the following "Hosanna Anthem." That was in the celestial room of the Oakland Temple in 1964, following President David O. McKay's dedicatory prayer. My heightened spiritual sensitivity was partly due, I am sure, to the power of that prayer and my special feelings about President McKay–but also to the way in which President Hugh B. Brown led us in that unique ceremony (apparently performed only at temple dedications and deriving in part from the jubilant waving of palm branches during Ancient Israel's Feast of the Tabernacles). The experience, especially that first time, could have seemed awkward or even bizarre–mature citizens of the down-to-earth twentieth century, in business suits and college tweed and stylish bouffant hairdos, waving handkerchiefs over our heads and actually shouting hosannas. But President Brown, in explaining the procedure to us and then leading us with his own special dignity, which is intellectual and moral as well as physical, helped invest the experience with a solemn joy that was overwhelming; it was a full-hearted and full-voiced response to the prophetic prayer we had just heard. And I do believe, strange as it perhaps seems for me, a skeptical, rationalistic, university-trained professor of English, to be saying this, that we were joined by spiritual beings–whether former prophets, angelic messengers, or repentant sinners–who had similar reasons to our own to rejoice.

Elder Brown was also present at the recent temple dedication in Washington, D.C., and he again gave our experience a special poignancy; though he did no officiating because he is no longer in the First Presidency and only spoke briefly in an early session we did not attend, friends reported the spirit and content of what he said, and it set the tone for that week in Washington for us. He merely told of his long involvement in the planning of the Washington Temple and its special, personal meaning to him. At the same time he spoke forthrightly about his long illness and more than once said, in effect, "This is a departing point for me. Perhaps a final preparation for an assignment to another field." That unusual emotional openness, even bluntness, on the part of general authorities who spoke in the various sessions was a characteristic of the dedication that my wife, Charlotte, and I most valued. We had traveled from one of the farthest outlying branches in the temple district (which includes most of the Midwest as well as the Eastern United States) and were able to stay most of the week with friends in Washington and enjoy some of the city's historical and cultural richness and see the lovely wooded reaches of the Potomac River. But it was our particular good fortune to be able to get some extra unclaimed tickets from one of those we stayed with who is a bishop and thus to attend two of the ten sessions. A dedicatory service for a temple is much like a session of general conference, but it is also profoundly different, and attending an extra session made us especially conscious of this.

Tuesday we traveled to Mount Vernon through the muted colors of Virginia's late fall countryside, and Wednesday we spent the morning and early afternoon with our friends Claudia and Richard Bushman from Boston; we briefly visited both houses of Congress (our representatives were disappointingly casual and inattentive to each other or to basic issues, in my untutored opinion), roamed the statuary halls in the Capitol Building to find Brigham Young (impressive in seated but prophetic grandeur, though at present pushed into a rather inconspicuous corner because of Bicentennial renovations), and watched with unfeigned awe the closing minutes of an argument before the Supreme Court (the only one of our institutions, Richard noted, which we can say, without reservation, has worked). At lunch we talked about the growing self-consciousness of Mormon women (Claudia is editor of the new independent journal for LDS women, *Exponent II*, and of a collection of essays on nineteenth century Mormon women soon to be published), and that led naturally to a brief consideration of the merits of polygamy in the hereafter (Richard seemed to be the only one in favor); but mainly we used that reunion to strengthen each other by reviewing the special joys and opportunities and challenges we are experiencing in raising our large families outside Mormon Country. We then dashed to the new Hirshhorn Museum of twentieth century art for a quick walk-through before the 4:30 dedication session. The Bushmans left early because Richard, as president of the Boston Stake, had been asked to give the closing prayer and was to be on the stand in the solemn assembly room well in advance of the fifteen-minute period before each session when we were to be seated and thoughtfully preparing ourselves for the service. Charlotte and I lingered a bit at the museum and then drove out the Baltimore Expressway to the northeast so that we could come back along the beltway from the east and enjoy that spectacular view of the temple rising directly out of a grove of trees and growing dramatically as you approach almost to its base and then turn with the beltway along its side.

After the turnoff from the beltway, the road to the temple passes through nearly a mile of richly wooded park. Our first closeup view dispelled some of our anxiety, aroused by early sketches we had seen and by some of the recent gentile appraisals of the temple's architecture ("reminiscent of Disneyworld"; "like a suburban hotel"), because it is a striking and successful conception, particularly in its setting, and we feel certain it will soon establish itself as "beautiful" in the hearts of Church members of all varieties of aesthetic training and preference, much as the Salt Lake and Hawaiian Temples have done. Of course, that is largely because of the emotional significance of what happens in temples, and we felt that immediately as we entered and took our places before one of the television sets in the annex (the solemn assembly room seats about 1000, and other thousands were gathered before closed circuit TV in other rooms and halls, from the celestial room to the foyer). We meditated for fifteen minutes, with the image before us of the First Presidency, all in white suits (that unusual attire at first somewhat startling but soon seeming quite apt and becoming), seated behind the highest level of the white tiers of triple pulpits that have characterized solemn assembly rooms since Kirtland. Then President Marion G. Romney, in the opening sermon of the session, sketched the history of temples ancient and modern and formed an expansive image of the temple as both a sacred enclosure, a place for Christ to dwell, and also a point of continuity, opening out to connect earth with heaven and the living with the dead–serving through the redemptive love expressed there to unite in one great family all generations as well as all nations of the children of God. I thought, yes, surely it is for us the center of things, the spiritual navel, the still point of the turning world.

As we listened we remembered again that purely architectural standards are secondary to some other things, and even our one criticism (the subtly delightful highlighting of the six towers with abstract stained glass columns at the corners is marred by rather harsh color combinations in the glass that seem to suggest an excessively "appropriate" red, white, and blue) faded quickly into the background as we heard President Romney recount the deeply moving stories of the dedication and sacrifices, the nearly rash idealism, of the early Saints who built the Kirtland and Nauvoo and early Utah temples. He reminded us how comparatively costly those temples were, given the frontier economy and the relative destitution of the Saints, told of their responsiveness to the Lord's commands for haste in preparing a place in Kirtland for him to send his messengers and in Nauvoo for them to perform sacred work for the salvation of their dead loved ones, of their immense care in crafting the buildings, even in their haste, and yet their marvelous nonchalance in leaving those mere buildings (in Nauvoo, immediately after a secret nighttime dedication under threat of mob interference) when they had to move on with the prophets. I remembered my own favorite story about temple building–of the Kirtland women who collected their few remaining pieces of china to be crushed into the mortar used on the temple face so that it would shine with the rays of the westering sun. And I thought of the fifty years of building the Salt Lake Temple and the seventeen days of celebration that marked its dedication–what it must have been like for those people, my actual and my spiritual ancestors, to shout hosanna in the House of God. Those rough and ready frontier people, living at first in sod huts, struggling in the Great Basin sand and dirt to stay alive, those people whose direct, pragmatic, even violent ways I know from reading their diaries and from my own early life; I think of them going up to the House of the Lord in St. George, or Logan or Manti–and finally in that loveliest of all buildings, in Salt Lake–and washing themselves and making themselves clean, looking on their own finest craftsmanship, which imaged for them the possibilities of gentleness and progress and perfection, seeing the religious history of the world acted out before them and themselves joining in that action in such a way as to give them a clear sense of their place in that history, having their hearts turned to their fathers and their children and to their wives and husbands in sacred covenants, being given, in short, a tremendous charge of idealism to work its slow transformation on the clay of their lives. I thought how the same thing was happening now, the gathering there of people, like ourselves, from far-flung, struggling mission branches and, like our East Coast friends, from the pressures of an increasingly secularized society, the blear and smear of trade and, yes, the soiling politics of Washington; and I thought of the moving, powerful idealism that was touching us all.

J. Willard Marriott spoke at that session. He is perhaps the most prominent of the growing enclave of extremely successful and powerful Washington Mormons, head of a growing empire of hotels, restaurants, and now catering services. He is best known, even in the Church, for his business success and his generous gifts to Brigham Young University, the University of Utah, and other institutions, but that quickly faded into the background as he spoke humbly and movingly, with great theological soundness, about the large painting of Christ's second coming in the temple foyer that he had been responsible for helping plan and arrange. The painting, which we were able to examine in detail on a tour of the temple after the session, is certainly impressive as it confronts you at the end of a long, bridged corridor from the annex to the main foyer where it covers one wall–though it escapes me why we sent Mormon artists to Paris to prepare to paint the scenes in the Salt Lake Temple and yet are now using non-Mormon artists. The figure of Christ, coming in his glory, is pleasant and commanding enough, though the face is too merely cheerful and Aryan for my taste, much like the one of Christ in the new mural in the Church office building (also by a non-Mormon); it is not nearly as penetratingly tragic as the one by Chambers that was President Harold B. Lee's favorite or as morally challenging as the one by Kim Whitesides that was on the cover of *Dialogue* several years ago. But again going beyond aesthetic considerations, the painting serves as an important, arresting reminder of the seriousness of what we are preparing for in our temples–of our literal faith in an end to secular history and of the joy and sorrow that will attend that literal separation of the sheep from the goats (yes, in case you have wondered, the one black in the painting–as well as a Polynesian, an Oriental, and a Lamanite–is on Christ's right hand with the righteous "sheep" who are being caught up to meet those of the First

Resurrection coming with Christ; the unrighteous "goats" on Christ's left hand are all white).

In discussing the spiritual challenge of that painting, and of the event it confronts us with, Brother Marriott quoted John the Revelator's report of the Lord's great command to us all in these latter days: "Babylon the great is fallen, is fallen. . . . Come out of her, my people, that ye be not partakers of her sins, and that ye receive not of her plagues" (Revelation 18:2,4). That must be a personally poignant challenge to Brother Marriott and to all other post-Watergate Washington Mormons, who are definitely in that world, though trying not to be of it–people like Jack and Renee Carlson, with whom we stayed (he is Assistant Secretary of the Interior for Energy and Minerals, and with the recent shift by President Ford towards reliance on the Interior Department to "handle" energy, is in an extremely important and exposed position), or Mark Cannon, executive assistant for the Supreme Court Justices, or the many serving in Congress or in less prominent but responsible positions in the National Archives, the Justice Department, Federal Trade Commission, etc. Mary Bradford, whose husband, Chick, is a prominent banker as well as a bishop in Washington, and who interviewed and wrote about Washington Mormons for a recent issue of the *Ensign*, thinks that they all face some special problems in the corridors of power. She feels that basic Mormon ideals and conditioning make them especially vulnerable, particularly naive and reticent, incapable of certain instincts and possibilities of action demanded in the heady infighting of the big government-big business complexes. Perhaps she is right; Christ talked of the Children of Darkness being wiser in some things than the Children of Light. The Byzantine depths revealed by Watergate are perhaps, and perhaps we can rejoice at it, beyond our fathoming; if indeed the Elders of Israel are to save the Constitution they may perhaps best do it indirectly, or at least at lower levels of power, by in some sense coming out of Babylon and avoiding both her sins and her plagues.

Certainly the temple will help, and the dedication was a great beginning. At the close of that first session, Richard Bushman, speaking with a moving clarity and forthrightness that resonated with the perspective gained from his deep and successful immersion in historical scholarship and teaching at a secular university, combined with humble, sometimes sorrowful service to the Lord as a bishop and stake president, asked that the young people there (those over twelve were invited, and many were there from all over the East, including his own son) might be inspired with strength to live purely in a difficult world and be moved to return to make their eternal marriage vows and to help bring salvation to children of God of other generations. His prayer is already being answered in the spiritual rejuvenation of those—young and old—who attended. Our hearts responded to that special directness of the general authorities, who took advantage of about the only occasion they have any more where they can feel free to talk directly to us as "Temple Saints," without the intrusion of the microphone and the television camera and the sense of responsibility to "the world listening in" that tends to make many of their general conference addresses comparatively cautious and impersonal. But at the dedication, two of those whom I remember as normally among the most reticent, Alvin R. Dyer and Loren Dunn (one speaking in each of the two sessions we attended), gave two of the most moving, because most direct and personal, talks we heard there or have heard any place else within memory.

Elder Dyer, who like Elder Brown has not spoken in conference recently because of illness, was helped to the pulpit by his brethren, and speaking in a voice still profoundly affected by his stroke from some years ago, one naturally breaking toward falsetto and pushed even more that way by bursts of emotion, was yet blessed with sufficient control to complete his remarks and move us to tears with a simple testimony of how his illness had chastened and benefited him, made him aware and appreciative of things he had not before seen. Elder Dunn, in a Thursday morning session we were able to attend in the solemn assembly room, put aside his prepared sermon and, in the first really personal expression I remember hearing from him, told a series of accounts by members of his own family who had had manifestations or visitations from their kindred dead and then bore one of the most directly touching testimonies of the existence of God and of his love expressed in salvation for the dead I have ever felt. That set the emotional tone for the session. After Elder Boyd K. Packer had spoken with a similar directness about the Oakland Temple dedication and a specially revealed message he had heard President Lee give there concerning turning the hearts of the fathers to their children *in this earth life* through building strong families, and after Patriarch Eldred G. Smith had given the most forthright talk I have heard on the doctrine of an Eternal Mother as an equal partner with our Father in that divine companionship which is our God and our direct model for the purpose of this life and future lives—after all this you can imagine how our hearts were softened and our necks, habitually stiff with the pride of the world, bent to hear the Prophet's dedicatory prayer. I leave you to read that in one of the Church publications, to see the unique dimension of that revelation of the heart and mind of Spencer W. Kimball in communion with God, the special diction, self-effacing but precise (speaking of himself as the "incumbent" prophet), combined with a stunning vision of the Latter-day work sweeping to its conclusion. We were truly then ready to shout hosannas—and we did. And then we joined in that unique expression of Mormon culture, not particularly aesthetic, perhaps, but serving much higher values than art, when we united with our leaders and a chorus of our peers in one great circle, our eyes wet with joy but our voices not choked, singing the Hosanna Anthem.

We stayed that night with Bishop Bradford and Mary, talking late into the night after he returned from helping arrange for the funeral of an elderly sister in his ward who had died the day before. Bishop Bradford arose the next morning with his son Steve, who was up at 5:30 to prepare for a long bike ride to his seminary class. The bishop, talking proudly of his son's dedication, drove Charlotte and me to the airport on his way to work, and we all parted there, Charlotte to get back home to prepare for the district Relief Society leadership meetings she was to lead the next day and I to spend a frantic day doing research at the Harvard Library before heading back to my own district meetings. As I relaxed after takeoff, I felt the special events of the week settling upon my spirit and strengthening me to meet the great needs of the people in my little branch—and great needs of my own; and as the plane abruptly banked toward the northeast I glanced down and saw under the wing the temple, its translucent white marble highlighted in the early sun against the green and grey of that great city.

A response to Lester Bush's crucial study,
"Mormonism's Negro Doctrine: An Historical Overview";
both published in *Dialogue*, Spring 1973.

C H A P T E R 1 2

THE MORMON CROSS

The story of God asking Abraham to offer his son, his only son, as a burnt offering offends me. I can find no way to be at peace with it. Yes, I know that it is a sign, a type, of God's sacrifice of his own son, his only begotten son, who would (in fact, through the lineage of Abraham and Isaac) come as a blessing to all the world. Yes, I've read Kierkegaard, and I know that faith in the living God makes ultimate demands–beyond experience, beyond emotion, beyond reason–and I have read the modern scriptures and know that a true witness comes only after a trial of faith. But for God, who had called Abraham out of idolatry, out of the way of sacrifice of human beings in order to appease and please the gods, for God to turn now and ask not only that Abraham give up the thing most dear to him, the miraculous blessing that God had given him in his old age, but to *kill* that son and thus to give up one of the chief sources of his vital relationship to God, the higher ethical and spiritual vision to which God had called him, by violating God's own teachings–that is beyond my comprehension or the power of my spirit to say yes to. It is a trial, a cross, a mystery. It is a cross Christians and Jews have borne, in one way or another, for centuries.

We Mormons have our own special cross–one which must weigh heavily on our hearts if we are truly trying to live our religion as Paul recommends: proving all things, holding fast that which is good. When God asks us, as we believe he does, not to give blacks of African descent the priesthood at this time [1973; policy changed in 1978], he asks us to sacrifice not only our political and social ideals and the understanding and good will of our colleagues and friends, but he seems to ask us to sacrifice the very essence of his own teachings about the divine potential of all his children and the higher ethical vision he has given us of possible exaltation for all people, concepts that are among the most attractive and vital features of our faith.

I have given myself with all my soul to that faith. I have felt a witness within the deepest core of my being that God lives, that his son Jesus Christ is truly our Savior and has restored his gospel through the Prophet Joseph Smith and maintained his true Church on earth down to his present Prophet, Harold B. Lee. As I go about my duties as a branch president, trying to be a true pastor of a small flock, to counsel precious souls in trouble and answer the questions of new converts and of my children as they seek to develop their faith, I find that, apart from my own sins and failings, this is, in its way, the heaviest cross I have to bear. The latest writing on the subject, "Mormonism's Negro Doctrine: An Historical Overview," by Lester Bush (*Dialogue*, Spring 1973) is amazingly thorough and dispassionate; it gives by far the most complete picture we have of how LDS Church policy with respect to blacks has developed to the present point. Yet it merely confirms a conviction I have had for some time–that the policy of denying blacks the priesthood is rationally untenable from a number of perspectives, historical, theological, ethical, social, psychological, in fact from all perspectives but one: ecclesiastical authority. But for me that perspective outweighs all the others because I am convinced that ecclesiastically the Church is doing what the Lord has directed, even though morally and spiritually its members may not be. I am certain that the Church is directed through revelation, that at least the most recent Prophets have prayed sincerely about this matter and that if the Lord thought it best to make a change at this time he could get through to his leaders and have a change made. However, as I will try to explain later, I also believe that the Lord does wish a change *could* be made and that we all bear responsibility for the fact that it hasn't been made yet. But first let me try to lay some groundwork.

Discussion about this issue has been damaged considerably, I believe, by heated and misleading arguments about whether what the Church is doing is a "policy" or a "doctrine." The reason for the heat has been the assumption of many that those words are synonymous, respectively, with "manmade" and "revealed," which fails to recognize that a policy can be revealed or not and so can a doctrine. It seems to me that a more useful distinction is the following: A policy is an administrative decision affecting the actions of Church members and usually made to meet the particular needs of the time. It may be revealed, inspired, or just plain common sense and may be changed as needs or times change. A doctrine on the other hand is a teaching, a description or reasonable consequence of a description of reality, usually ultimate reality. For instance, it is Church *policy*, revealed or at least inspired, that Church members are to have a family night together each Monday evening, with no interferences; this has not always been Church policy and it may change as conditions in society change. On the other hand, it is a revealed *doctrine* that family life is central to the plan of salvation, that only in families can individuals reach their full potential, and that therefore family relationships can and should be eternal. Of course, as is the case in these examples, a policy can be related to or derived from a doctrine, but the policy can be changed, even dramatically, while the doctrine can change only in the sense that our understanding of its underlying metaphysical reality can grow, through the process of continual revelation and individual study and practice.

A policy can be not revealed, though official, a practical decision for which no special inspiration is claimed, such as, I suspect, the recent decision to have temple recommends renewed on people's birthdays rather than at a set time, to avoid crowding up the schedules of interviewing officials. Doctrines also can be not revealed and not official, though accepted by many, for instance the idea that present-day blacks are cursed because of Cain's or Ham's wrong-doing; there is no basis in any scripture or claimed revelation for this teaching, even though it has been taught by many in the Church, and it contradicts basic and clearly revealed doctrines about the nature of God and his relationship to man and the process of salvation. (For instance, the second Article of Faith, "We believe that men will be punished for their own sins," and Alma 3:19: ". . . I would that ye should see that they brought upon themselves the curse; and even so doth every man bring upon himself his own condemnation.") Of course recognition of the basic truth of the scriptures just quoted, within the historical process that Bush documents, has led good Mormons, trained to expect a rational theology and seeking a way blacks could have brought a curse upon themselves, to develop another doctrine, for which no claim of revelation has been made that I am aware of and which is also not official and, I think, untrue–that blacks must have brought about their limitation with respect to the priesthood by conduct or choice in the pre-existence. This teaching contradicts the basic revealed gospel doctrines concerning repentance and its role in the plan of salvation: Blacks have no chance to repent or change in order to remove the restrictions, a provision our merciful God makes everywhere else; in fact, blacks have no opportunity even to *know* what their supposed mistake or wrong choice was!

The psychological and spiritual damage done by the implication of an inherited curse or the allegation of an unspecified act or choice in the pre-existence which blacks cannot know about or repent of is precisely delineated by the Prophet Joseph Smith in the *Lectures on Faith* (along with the clear teaching that God's character is such that he does not operate that way):

. . . it is also necessary that men should have an idea that [God] is no respecter of persons, for with the idea of all the other excellencies in his character, and this one wanting, men could not exercise faith in him; because if he were a respecter of persons, they could not tell what their privileges were, nor how far they were authorized to exercise faith in him, or whether they were authorized to do it at all, but all must be confusion; but no sooner are the minds of men made acquainted with the truth on this point, that he is no respecter of persons, than they see that they have authority by faith to lay hold on eternal life, the richest boon of heaven, because God is no respecter of persons, and that every man in every nation has an equal privilege. (Lecture Third, paragraph 23)

The "pre-existent mistake" rationale contradicts itself because, while based on a spurious connection between actions in the pre-mortal life and opportunities in this life, it implies there is no genuine relationship between spiritual and moral attainments there and here: It implies that all blacks are unworthy of something all whites can have, and thus it essentially states that the most noble black man who has ever lived (choose your own example: Elijah Abel, Martin Luther King, Ralph Bunche) is in some crucial sense not up to the level of–is, in a word, inferior to–the most depraved white man (Hitler, Stalin, Charles Manson). It strikes at the heart of a unique and emotionally and intellectually captivating conception of the restored gospel: God desires all his children to be saved and exalted and has worked out a plan by which they can be. There are no limits on God's redeeming love–no predestination for the elect and damned, no irrevocable assignment to heaven or hell upon death–no limits, that is, except our own individual choices and influence on each other. God struggles with all his power to provide equal opportunity for all who come to the earth. He treats them all with the same unconditional love: "he maketh his sun to rise on the evil and the good, and sendeth rain on the just and the unjust" (Matthew 5:45);

. . . he doeth nothing save it be plain *unto the children of men; and he inviteth them all to come unto him and partake of his goodness; and he denieth none that come unto him, black and white . . . , male and female; and* all *are alike unto God. (II Nephi 26:33; my emphasis)*

He has even provided a way (again, a unique feature of Mormon theology) by which those who are deprived, by human choices and failures, of an opportunity to know and accept the gospel in this life can have such an opportunity after death; in fact a prevailing image we have from Christ is of God standing at the door knocking, continually inviting us to respond.

These unrevealed doctrines–that the priesthood is withheld from blacks because of their descent from Cain or pre-existent choices–come from a very natural, perhaps laudable, desire to explain, give reasons for, a revealed policy. And Bush has shown convincingly what we should have all known, that they are in fact just that: rationalizations, explanations after the fact rather than revealed doctrines from which the policy was derived. The terrible danger, and result, has been the classic problem of the tail wagging the dog. Doctrines, beliefs about the nature of God and man and their relationship, have been derived from policies rather than the reverse. Two books circulating among Mormons and even non-Mormons which exemplify this devastatingly are those by John Stewart, *Mormonism and the Negro* (Deseret Book), and John Lund, *The Church and the Negro* (privately printed). In each of these the concept of a partial God, a respecter of persons, sending his favorite children into more and more favored conditions where they buy their salvation easily by taking advantage of their already superior advantages, is derived from the Church practice of not giving blacks the priesthood. This leaves great concepts of the restored gospel in a shambles. A typical example of the unabashed racism that results, a terrible insult to dark-skinned people such as East Indians, Polynesians, and South Americans, who with Africans make up the majority of God's children on the earth–and will likely before long make up the majority of members of the Church, is the following (Lund, p. 102): "When people rebel against God's commandments, either during their pre-earth life or while in mortality, they are given a dark skin so that those who are of the chosen seed will not intermarry with them." [One of the scandals in present Mormonism is that these books still continue to sell, despite the 1978 revelation which refutes their assumptions. Note added, 1983.]

The matter of distinction on the basis of skin color in the Book of Mormon, and thus the matter of racism toward American Indians, is an entirely separate matter from the Church's policy with respect to blacks of African descent, although non-Mormons have confused the two and Mormons (i.e., Lund and Stewart) have sometimes mistakenly connected the two as mutually supportive evidences for a racist God. That subject deserves a separate essay, but let me merely say at this point that when the Amlicites marked themselves with "a mark of red upon their foreheads," we are told that

thus the Word of God is fulfilled . . . which he said to Nephi: Behold, the Lamanites have I cursed, and I will set a mark on them that they and their seed may be separated from thee and thy seed . . . except they repent of their wickedness and turn to me. (Alma 3:14)

This passage raises the very strong possiblity that the *original* Lamanite "curse" being quoted, from II Nephi 5, as well as this one on the Amlicites, was *propagated by the separated Lamanites themselves*—through marking their own skin, choosing a degenerate life style, and perhaps intermarrying with darker New World peoples around them—and not by a genetically inherited curse from God. At least the commentator in Alma 3 states unequivocally that *every* man that is cursed brings upon himself his own condemnation, and Book of Mormon history is consistent with that claim, because there are no religious restrictions on individual Lamanites such as there are on blacks: Extraordinary efforts are made to establish contact with the Lamanites, and as soon as one chooses to accept the gospel he can participate in it fully and is no longer in any sense cursed. This is a point we fail to make sufficiently clear to modern "Lamanites," such as Polynesians and American Indians, who sometimes suffer seriously under the impression conveyed by false doctrines like that put forth by Lund and Stewart that their skin color is evidence of a cursed and therefore inferior and incapable lineage. Before the end of the Book of Mormon the terms Nephite and Lamanite have no direct reference to ancestry or skin color but are used merely to distinguish between those who accept God and Christ and those who do not, which raises a serious question about the appropriateness of the term "Lamanite" for modern American Indians and Polynesians.

Bush's historical review seems to me to provide the materials for completely demolishing any lingering doubts about whether there is some doctrine, some metaphysical state of the souls of certain human beings manifested in their "blood" or skin color, behind the Church's practice. If such were the case, if there were indeed a specific number of spirits designed to come into the earth with certain crucial restrictions on them, one could reasonably expect that the Lord in his almighty power would provide a way that those restrictions would be applied to those particular souls and no others. With such a good reason God could certainly set up a foolproof means of discrimination; one might, for instance, expect him to mark such restricted spirits infallibly and indelibly, even make them a separate species so that cross-fertilization could not mix things up. At the very least he could inspire his servants, particularly patriarchs, with instant detection. History gives us no assurance of that kind of concern on God's part. Not only (as Bush points out) have many more whites than blacks been denied access to the priesthood because of simple failure on man's part to carry out God's plan of taking the gospel to all, but a certain number of blacks have not had the restrictions applied. At least one, Elijah Abel, was knowingly given the priesthood and enjoyed most of its blessings and powers throughout his life. Certain others known to be blacks may have held the priesthood as well, and there continue to be cases of those who are given the priesthood (and given patriarchal blessings that fail to detect anything unusual) but then, because they unfortunately are faithful enough to the Gospel to do their genealogy, discover a black African ancestor and are asked to *discontinue using* their priesthood (it is not "taken" from them). In addition, in South America (and under a new policy inaugurated under President McKay in South Africa) it is extremely likely that many men of black African descent hold and use the priesthood, because it is not necessary that they demonstrate acceptable ancestry before being given the priesthood where there is no obvious "mark of Cain" upon them. In fact, despite Brigham Young's unequivocal linkage of the two, physical features now have nothing to do with priesthood denial–negroid-appearing Fijians receiving it and white Americans with some black African ancestry not.

Many other minor changes in policy and historical discrepancies documented by Bush show conclusively that God is not acting or requiring his Church to act in a consistent way, which would be necessary if there were a specific number of spirits metaphysically set apart from the rest of us. Especially problematic is Joseph Smith's own teaching on this matter, since there is no available contemporary evidence that he denied blacks the priesthood, and Bush has unearthed, it seems to me, very significant references indicating that, at least in the late 1830s and early 1840s, the First Presidency had no intention to discriminate against blacks in preaching the gospel or bringing them to participate fully in the temple.

But the unrevealed doctrines about blacks are not only *wrong,* they are terribly *dangerous.* Such doctrines are much more racist and demeaning–to blacks in general and to members of the Church, both black and white–than the actual practice of denying the priesthood. They not only warp central life-giving principles of our theology but provide a false theological subsidy for the racism already natural to us as human beings and that, given our history, Americans are especially susceptible to; they also promote lack of courage in meeting a crucial need of our time–to which the Gospel itself calls us–to overcome racial fear and prejudice on this shrinking spaceship earth.

The recent official statements of the Church concerning blacks and the priesthood offer no such subsidy, nor any such doctrinal rationales. These statements simply require Church members to accept, as part of their faith in a divinely directed Church, the revealed *policy* that those of black African descent are not now to receive the priesthood. I accept that, essentially at face value. I do not ordain blacks to the priesthood nor self-righteously (or in any other way) fulminate against the Church or its leaders, nor lobby for a revelation to change things. I trust our leaders are doing their job, seeking and awaiting a revelation, and I believe with all my heart that if such a revelation is received they will in no way hesitate to enforce it, no matter how or where unpopular.

But my Mormonness *wants* a rationale, and though I reject the unrevealed doctrines that I have mentioned as any basis for such a rationale, there is to be found, in our history and that of America and in the theological resources of the restored gospel, a possible reason for the policy that can perhaps help us bear our cross, particularly since my rationale has the advantage of putting blame and the need to change on all of us, not, as is the case with other doctrinal rationales, on the *victims*–the blacks–alone.

I believe that historical conditions in our country, essentially unique in the world, and the resultant attitudes of Church members, brought about a situation in which it was in the best interests of all involved for the Lord to institute a lower law for us to live (denying for a time the priesthood but only to those blacks *of African descent*–those who had been subjected to slavery and its aftermath in our country) until we are ready to live the higher law (accepting blacks fully into the priesthood with all of the natural consequences, including black leadership over whites in the Church and the extremely close relationships and trust that the lay leadership structure of the Church requires). Given its particular nature (lay leadership, strict geographical organization), the restored Church could not, during the period of slavery and its bitter heritage when American blacks and whites would not relate as equals, ease the transition as other churches did by segregating congregations or by keeping blacks out of leadership and priesthood functions through high educational requirements, etc. Thus it seems to me possible to understand that, at least until quite recently, giving blacks the priesthood would have been greatly disruptive to the Church because of reaction both outside and within the Church and thus not a blessing to blacks themselves.

The idea of living a lower law should be a familiar concept to us. The children of Israel had the fullness of the priesthood and the higher ethical law taken from them and were restricted to the Levitical Priesthood and the Mosaic law of performances. Even now in the latter days with the "fullness" of the Gospel available to us we are presently living another lower law, tithing, because of our inability to live fully the higher Law of Consecration of *all* our property and resources to God. The Lord can and does at times reveal policies which it is his will that we practice for our best present good but which he is not very happy about, in the sense that he wishes we were ready to live a higher law and *stands ready to give it to us when we get ready.* I believe that is the case with the Church's policy on blacks and the priesthood. The policy is revealed–at least in the negative sense that the Lord has not changed it, though he clearly has had the opportunity. I don't believe, as some have suggested, that the word can't get through to the Prophet nor that the Church and its leaders have been frozen in a defensive position, resisting this one last surrender to outside secular values. (This interpretation has been suggested by Thomas F. O'Dea in his essay "Sources of Strain in Mormon History Reconsidered" as found in *Mormonism and American Culture*, edited by Marvin S. Hill and James B. Allen.) No, I think rather that we are collectively living out the consequences of historical evil and failure–that of ourselves and of others before us.

There may be nothing at all to my theory. It sounds, when judged by a certain kind of idealism, like a cop-out, a shameful giving in to human weakness, an argument from expediency. But God is certainly not to be understood as *in*expedient. He refers to revealing "what is expedient for you to understand." He gives "milk before meat," bringing us along according to our growing capacities, "line upon line, precept upon precept." If, as it seems, his loving care is extended to all of us and he is willing to work with us where we are in order to be able to get us where he wants us, even instituting lower laws to help us get through some rough periods, then my idea makes some sense. We must all share the blame for a tragic situation, as Americans with our bitter historical burden of slavery and continuing racism, including black Americans who may be in fact in a way "not ready" because they have been forced by that same burden into situations and attitudes in which the priesthood would not be a help. (A thoughtful friend, an historian, suggested to me, plausibly I think, that we have come to such a pass that for our white-dominated church to offer blacks the priesthood would be patronizing, that perhaps they must receive their own prophet and a direct dispensation.)

And some of us in the Church may not yet be capable of participating in the consequences of blacks receiving the priesthood in such a way that it would be a blessing. I don't think the Lord is happy with any such, any more than he is with the increasing number of wealthy Mormons who self-righteously pay their tithing and other "obligations" and then squander the rest of their "increase" on luxuries, forgetting the poor who could use their help to help themselves, in South America or right across town, forgetting therefore the Lord's call for us to voluntarily work towards equality in earthly things, to live the higher Law of Consecration. But the Lord will not give a higher law until it is a blessing, until the Church members or whites or blacks or America or all are finally "ready," until it will be in the best interests of the Lord's plan of salvation for all people.

And therein, perhaps, is the great advantage of such an explanation as mine. I can rationally hope for change without in any sense implying a challenge to the authority of the Prophet, whom I sustain with all my heart, or undermining my faith in the Church as divinely directed and its doctrines as essentially true, which faith is more precious to me than life. The unrevealed doctrines which have been used to rationalize the revealed policy have had as perhaps their most agonizing deficiency that they carry the implication that any change before the end of the world would be unjust. (Why should blacks up to a certain point suffer restrictions and not those after that point, if they all "deserve" such restrictions?)

President Joseph Fielding Smith pointed this out forcibly to me on one occasion; and at the risk of being dismissed as another purveyor of questionable anecdotes about statements of modern prophets I ought to report that experience, not to prove anything, but to keep open some important possibilities. In the summer of 1963, agitation about the Church's policy was at a kind of peak, both nationally and within Church circles. I had expressed myself in Church situations as not being able to square the curse of Cain or the pre-existence "doctrines" with the scriptures, with central principles of the restored gospel, or with my own best thinking and feeling. I was told bluntly that I could not be a Mormon in good standing without accepting those doctrines. I cared deeply about my standing in the Church and relationships with my brothers and sisters and wasn't about to lead a crusade and so was ready to seek an authoritative answer.

It came to my attention that Joseph Fielding Smith (then President of the Quorum of the Twelve Apostles) had published an article in the *Church News* about this matter and in the process had essentially contradicted one of his assumptions in his earlier discussion of the matter in *The Way to Perfection*, then calling blacks an "inferior" race and now specifically saying they were not. Two of my friends who were concerned about the same matter and, as I did, looked at President Smith as the nearly official scriptorian of the Church, made an appointment for us to see him. President Smith was not very anxious to see us since he was being baited from many sources at that time, but after some assurances of our intentions he gave us some time and was particularly gracious when one of my friends, moved I think by the prayer we offered together before going, began the interview by confessing in tears that his original motives for coming had been somewhat contentious.

I told President Smith about my experiences with the issue of blacks and the priesthood and asked him whether I must believe in the pre-existence doctrine to have good standing in the Church. His answer was, "Yes, because that is the teaching of the scriptures." I asked President Smith if he would show me the teaching in the scriptures (with some trepidation, because I was convinced that if anyone in the world could show me he would). He read over with me the modern scriptural sources and then, after some reflection, said something to me that fully revealed the formidable integrity which characterized his whole life: "No, you do not have to believe that Negroes are denied the priesthood because of the pre-existence. I have always assumed that, because it was what I was taught, and it made sense, but *you* don't have to believe it to be in good standing, because it is not definitely stated in the scriptures. And I have received no revelation on the matter." Then it was, as we continued our discussion, that he said, with what seems to be irrefutable logic, that if, as he believed, the reason for the denial was the pre-existence then there could be no expectation that blacks would receive the priesthood in his life, because that would not be fair to those who had been denied it up to that point. [The logic of this also clearly means, of course, that if blacks were ever given the priesthood in this life, that fact alone would prove the "pre-existent choice" notions false. But, in fact, even since the 1978 revelation, some Mormons continue to believe and teach those disproved and dangerous ideas about race, etc., being conditioned upon previous righteousness. Note added, 1983]

Where then are we today? The cross we've hewn for ourselves is painful, embarrassing, humiliating, and ought to–perhaps does–engender humility. On no other issue does our history present us with such a sorry spectacle. It can't be anything but painful to read Joseph Smith, whose vision and mind were so expansive and radically humanitarian on so many other issues (and were also on the race issue towards the end of his life), when he sounds the same racist strains as the rest of American society. It is painful to read Brigham Young (who was right about many things of much more importance than any of his critics were, or nearly everyone else) supporting slavery of blacks and Indians, predicting that the Civil War would not end slavery, repeating the racist myths of his time and even improving on them–in fact, as Bush documents, undercutting any basis to take his teachings as revealed *doctrine* on the subject by including, each time he spoke, things the Church clearly does not now believe. It is shameful to read about even a very few faithful black members of the Church being asked not to come out to meetings or directed to sit in special places to avoid conflicts with white members.

There is nothing about the whole matter in which we can take any comfort, certainly not in the sociological studies of Armand Mauss (see

Pacific Sociological Review, Fall 1966) and others about which some members have been quite enthused because they show that Mormons are *no more prejudiced* than other Americans. In all conscience, given our ideals we should be ashamed that we are not significantly *less* prejudiced. Perhaps the greatest shame is that we in the Church–including our leaders–have been cut off from the major thrust of social conscience in our times, from a social revolution against racism in which we could have exercised beneficial leadership, perhaps even helping to avoid the polarizing bitterness that has wounded our nation. I think Thomas F. O'Dea is right when he says a response to the challenge of that particular social revolution is a telling diagnostic test of the viability of any person's or institution's relation to the challenges of modern life. So far we have not met that challenge well–and by "we," I mean the lay membership of the Church.

What can we do? We can get ready to live the higher law, first by working to root out racism in ourselves through getting to know blacks and something of black aspirations and culture. And we can help get Americans ready, black and white, by working honestly and vigorously to overcome the burden of our racist past. We can become anxiously engaged in the good cause that our Church leaders have already called us to–to see, as they said in their 1969 statement on "the position of the Church with regard to the Negro both in society and in the Church," that "each citizen . . . have equal opportunities and protection under the law with reference to civil rights." We can then go beyond that, as they announce *they* are doing in that same statement, to "join with those throughout the world who pray that all the blessings of the gospel of Jesus Christ may in due time of the Lord become available to men of faith everywhere." If I understand that correctly, it is a call to prepare–by prayer and the action that the gospel makes clear must accompany sincere prayer–for the higher law under which we would be able, as God desires, to extend his blessings to everyone, without discrimination. We can try to do what it seems the First Presidency is doing and has by example called us to do, that is to pray, in private and in our meetings, that the time may soon come when blacks may receive the priesthood and then to act with energy to be prepared for, and thus make possible, that time. This may not at first make our cross easier. In fact, in my experience, our efforts as Mormons to join with others in civil rights actions and to build bridges and respond positively to black aspirations will bring special kinds of misunderstanding and pain and will sometimes make the cross harder to bear. But those efforts may just help the day come when the Lord can extend the fullness of the gospel blessings to all of his children–which will be a great blessing as well to all of us in his Church.

Given at the Symposium on War and Peace at BYU, March 1982, and the Sunstone Theological Symposium, August 1982; published in *Sunstone*, November-December 1982.

CHAPTER 13

CAN NATIONS LOVE THEIR ENEMIES? AN L.D.S. THEOLOGY OF PEACE

The call of Christ is clear: "Love your enemies." But it is so difficult to do that, even in our own families and communities, that many have supposed that such a command could not possibly apply to nations—and few national leaders, Christian or not, have seriously tried to persuade their people to obey it. But Mormon leaders have insisted that the command fits every situation, that it is the only way to peace in any context. In their 1981 Christmas message the LDS First Presidency wrote:

To all who seek a resolution to conflict, be it a misunderstanding between individuals or an international difficulty among nations, we commend the counsel of the Prince of Peace, "Love your enemies, bless them that curse you, do good to them that hate you, and pray for them which despitefully use you, and persecute you; That ye may be the children of your Father which is in heaven" (Matthew 5:44-45). This principle of loving one another as Jesus Christ loves us will bring peace to the individual, to the home and beyond, even to the nations and to the world.[1]

That statement is part of a long LDS scriptural and prophetic tradition of response to the perennial human problem of war. Does that tradition provide a theology of peace, clear and consistent in theory and tested in practice, that could be useful to us in this violent time? I think so. Much of the Book of Mormon deals with violence, and at first glance the various accounts may seem contradictory. There are the "people of Ammon," who provide the most impressive example of rigorous group pacifism I can find in history or literature: They make a covenant to die rather than shed blood, bury their weapons in the ground, and then allow themselves to be massacred rather than break their pledge. However, only twenty-five years later these same pacifists send 2,000 of their sons to war, with a church leader turned military man at their head. The great prophet Mormon, the editor of the book which bears his name, was a military leader from a very young age. Mormon even named his son, who also became a soldier, after Moroni, a general who had lived 400 years before. And Mormon includes, as the last twenty-one chapters of Alma (over ten percent of the Book of Mormon), an extensively detailed and appreciative account of General Moroni's conduct of divinely approved warfare.

It is possible to make a list of LDS scriptures in which God allows war–and match it with another where conflict is forbidden. This may be confusing, but as Hugh Nibley has written:

The contradiction is only apparent, for if one examines the passages on both sides throughout the scriptures, they fall clearly into two categories: general principles and special instances. The verses forbidding conflict are of a general universal nature, while those which countenance it all refer to exceptional cases.[2]

Still, the example of the people of Ammon seems like a special case, precisely because it is so unparalleled, and it is clear elsewhere in LDS theology that what they do is not an automatic result or unqualified expectation for everyone after conversion. But an ideal principle is established, what I would term "effective pacifism": We must do, in love, whatever we can that will *genuinely create peace*, even sacrifice our lives. Mormon clearly views those conscientiously capable of the pacifist decision with great admiration, even as models. He writes, in his characteristic manner of teaching a lesson to his readers, "Thus we see that when these Lamanites were brought to know the truth they were firm, and would suffer even unto death rather than commit sin" (Alma 24:19). And he reports the judgment of Ammon, the Nephite missionary who had converted these people, that they had reached an ethical level superior to his own Nephites:

For behold, they had rather sacrifice their lives than even to take the life of an enemy; and they have buried their weapons of war deep in the earth, because of their love towards their brethren.

And now behold I say unto you, has there been so great love in all the land? Behold I say unto you, Nay, there has not, even among the Nephites. (Alma 25:32, 33)

Without ignoring the high costs (over 1,000 slain), the account also provides unique evidence that the pacifist ethic, which to most of us seems merely idealistic, actually *works*. When the attackers see that these former warlike associates "would not flee from the sword, neither would they turn aside . . . but that they would lie down and perish, and praised God even in the very act of perishing under the sword," they are moved to forbear and indeed many are themselves converted, "for they were stung for the murders which they had committed" (Alma 24:25).

The Nephites, who do not have "so great love," take these pacifists under their protection and are later directed by God to take up arms against the Lamanites. The theological position developed is that known in Christian tradition as the doctrine of a "just war," which maintains that shedding the blood of an enemy can be justified by the rightness of one's cause and the moral restraint of one's methods. Early in the series of battles, Mormon reviews the specific conditions which justified the Nephites in going to war:

They were not fighting for monarchy nor power but they were fighting for their homes and their liberties, their wives and their children, and their all, yea, for their rites of worship and their church. . . . The Lord said unto them, and also unto their fathers, that: Inasmuch as ye are not guilty of the first offense, neither the second, ye shall not suffer yourselves to be slain by the hands of your enemies. (Alma 43:45-46).

The emphasis is on purely defensive war, carried to the point of consistent refusal to annihilate defeated Lamanite armies or even to insist on unconditional surrender. Again and again as soon as Moroni obtains some advantage in a battle he refuses to press it but sends the message "We do not desire to slay you" (Alma 44:1) or "We will forbear shedding your blood" (Alma 52:34). He asks for surrender–but only the surrender involved in the Lamanites returning to their own lands and promising not to attack again.

The major constraint is against bloodthirstiness. From a divine perspective, certain of resurrection and immortality for all and thus most concerned for the state of the soul, it seems that shedding blood can be justified under certain conditions–but delighting in it never. Mormon's great admiration for Moroni is based in good part on the latter's ability to resist, amid all the passions of war that Mormon knew well, the bloodlust that seems to naturally afflict those who train for war and attack other human beings.

Mormon knew how quickly a whole people could be afflicted with the appetite for violence. He saw his own nation decline from being a "civil and delightsome people" until they became "without principle, and past feeling; . . .they have lost their love, one towards another; and they thirst after blood and revenge continually" (Moroni 9:12, 20, 5). At one point Mormon leads his people to a great victory following many defeats. But when they then want to take the offensive and "avenge themselves of the blood of their brethren" who had been slain by their enemies, Mormon refuses to participate and stands instead, under the Lord's direction, as "an idle witness" to his people's deserved destruction (Mormon 3:14–16).

This sounds like an entirely situational ethic. Do the examples cancel each other out? Is the one example of pacifism an aberration? I think not. The especially unified and religiously motivated people of Ammon were moved by their former experiences with violence to covenant upon conversion that under no circumstances, however just, would they shed blood again, and they were capable of enduring the price of allowing themselves to be slaughtered. But a generation later the whole Nephite nation was in danger of extermination—and with them the sacred records and spark of righteousness on the American continent that the Lord needed in order to save not only the Nephites but eventually their enemies the Lamanites and even modern people who would read their record. In this situation, and with a people not as unified and capable of disciplined pacifism as the people of Ammon, the Lord directed waging a just war, with severe constraints on methods and spirit.

But whatever specific response to the varied circumstances and the contrasting values—or the inspired direction of a prophet—may require in a particular situation, the underlying principles do not change: Ultimate concern must be for the character and salvation of those involved rather than apparent right or wrong or justice; revenge is never right, however "justified"; vengeance and bloodthirstiness, very natural dangers even in a just war, must be vigorously resisted, even at great risk, by fighting purely defensively and not insisting on unconditional surrender. As Nibley summarizes the principle, "In the end the most desperate military situation imaginable is still to be met with the spirit of peace and love."

The prophet Joseph Smith, translator of the Book of Mormon, which was explicitly intended to provide essential lessons for modern man, understood this general principle well. In 1833, as recorded in Doctrine and Covenants 98, the Lord taught Joseph a distinction between what is justified and what is *best*. Even in circumstances which would support waging a just war against our enemies, if we have sufficient courage and love to stay with the general principles of promoting peace, there are special rewards, including the promise that the Lord will intervene on our behalf:

And again, if your enemy shall smite you the third time, and you bear it patiently, your reward shall be doubled unto you four-fold. . . .And then, if he shall come upon you or your children. . .I have delivered thine enemy into thine hands. And then *if thou wilt spare him, thou shalt be rewarded for thy righteousness; and also thy children and thy children's children. . . . (D & C 98:16-17; my emphasis)*

Such a vision has been held to consistently by LDS prophets for the subsequent 150 years. This is Brigham Young in 1859, speaking in a passionate satire of nationalistic propaganda, satire that could be applied directly to both sides in the recent Falklands debacle and also in the Lebanon disaster:

Our traditions have been such that we are not apt to look upon war between two nations as murder; but suppose that one family should rise up against another and begin to slay them, would they not be taken up and tried for murder. And why not nations that rise up and slay each other in a scientific way be equally guilty of murder? "But observe the martial array—how splendid! See the furious war horses with the glittering trappings. Then the honour and the glory and pride of the reigning king must be sustained, and the strength and power and wealth of the nation displayed in some way; and what better way than to make war upon neighbouring nations under some slight pretext?" Does it justify the slaying of men, women, and children that otherwise would have remained at home in peace, because a great army is doing the work? No! The guilty will be damned for it.[3]

In the twentieth century the LDS version of a just war has been articulated in direct response to the two World Wars. In April 1917, right after the U.S. officially declared war on Germany, President Joseph F. Smith spoke in general conference against the tendency of Americans to allow patriotism to lead them to madness in time of war, exhorting the Saints to retain their full sense of brotherhood with the Germans living in this country and admonishing those called to fight in the war to "do it with an eye single to the accomplishment of the good that is aimed to be accomplished, and not with a bloodthirsty desire to kill and to destroy."[4]

Twenty-five years later, at the general conference following Pearl Harbor, David O. McKay, of the First Presidency, outlined the conditions under which defensive war is justified, emphasizing carefully the limitations:

Such a condition, however, is not a real or fancied insult given by one nation to another. When this occurs proper reparation may be made by mutual understanding, apology, or by arbitration . . . nor is war justified in an attempt to enforce a new order of government*, or even to impel others to a particular form of worship,* however better the government *or eternally true the principles of the enforced religion may be.*[5]

J. Reuben Clark read a statement of the First Presidency at that same conference which explored at great length the dilemma of those on various sides of a conflict who are called by their governments to fight and possibly shed blood. I sense the anguish the leaders felt as they tried to assuage the anguish of Mormon soldiers serving opposing governments, even fighting each other. Yet the Mormon leaders seem determined to make no compromise with the general principles we have been examining in the scriptures; they make clear that moral responsibility cannot be avoided:

The Church is and must be against war. . . . It cannot regard war as a righteous means of settling international disputes. . . .

But the Church membership are citizens or subjects of sovereignties over which the Church has no control. The Lord Himself has told us to befriend "that law which is the constitutional law of the land" (D & C 98:6).

. . . . When, therefore, constitutional law, obedient to these principles, calls the manhood of the Church into the armed service of any country to which they owe allegiance, their highest civic duty requires that they meet that call. . . . It would be a cruel God that would punish His children as moral sinners for acts done by them as the innocent instrumentalities of a sovereign whom He had told them to obey and whose will they were powerless to resist.[6]

Those "powerless to resist" are innocent, but the First Presidency recognizes that to whatever degree any participant is *able* to be responsible—either as a leader who brings on the conflict or a soldier who can resist an unjust government or who indulges in hatred even in a just cause—he is accountable as a sinner:

There is an eternal law that rules war and those who engage in it. It was given when, Peter having struck off the ear of Malchus, the servant of the High Priest, Jesus reproved him, saying: "Put up again thy sword into his place: for all they that take the sword shall perish with the sword" (Matthew 26:52). The Savior thus laid down a general principle upon which He placed no limitations as to time, place, cause, or people involved. . . . This is a universal law, for force always begets force . . . it is the law of the unrighteous and wicked, but it operates against the righteous who may be involved. . . . That in their work of destruction [innocent participants in war] will be striking at their brethren will not be held against them. That sin, as Moroni of old said, is to the condemnation of those who sit in their places of power in a state of thoughtless stupor, those rulers in the world who in a frenzy of hate and lust for unrighteous power and dominion over their fellow men, have put into motion eternal forces they do not comprehend and cannot control.[7]

Mormon leaders did not hesitate to criticize leaders of the United States as well as those of other countries for ignoring such general principles and perpetrating the brutalities of the Second World War. This is J. Reuben Clark of the First Presidency speaking in general conference just after the war:

As the crowning savagery of the war, we Americans wiped out hundreds of thousands of civilian population with the atom bomb in Japan, few if any of the ordinary civilians being any more responsible for the war than were we. . . . Military men are now saying that the atom bomb was a mistake. It was more than that; it was a world tragedy. . . . And the worst of this atomic bomb tragedy is not that not only did the people of the United States not rise up in protest against this savagery, not only did it not shock us to read of this wholesale destruction of men, women, and children, and cripples, but that it actually drew from the nation at large a general approval of this fiendish butchery.[8]

In much the same spirit, the First Presidency in December 1945 issued a letter to each member of the Utah delegation to the U.S. Congress, outlining seventeen reasons for opposing the "compulsory universal military training" being proposed by the Truman administration. Such a law, they wrote, would "teach our sons not only the way to kill but also, in too many cases, the desire to kill, thereby increasing lawlessness and disorder." The ways of war, they argued, are "wholly un-American." The creation of a military caste would be a threat to the "equality and unity which always characterize the citizenry of a republic." An immense standing army and the "creation of a great war machine" would be a temptation to ambitious dictators intent on the destruction of freedom: "The possession of great military power always breeds thirst for domination, for empire, and for a rule by might not right." The First Presidency warned, in terms exactly prophetic of what *has* happened in the ensuing forty years, that the building of "a huge armed establishment" would contradict any protestations of peace and in fact encourage other nations to follow a similar militaristic course,

so placing upon the peoples of the earth crushing burdens of taxation that with their present tax load will hardly be bearable, and that will gravely threaten our social, economic, and governmental systems. . . . We shall make of the whole earth one great military camp whose separate armies, headed by war-minded officers, will never rest till they are at one another's throats in what will be the most terrible contest the world has ever seen. . . . What this country needs and what the world needs, is a will for peace, not war.[9]

It is clear, then, that LDS leaders have not been content to rest on the doctrine of a just war and the patriotic submission to authority that the World Wars seemed to require. There is clearly in their minds a higher law, which stands in judgment even on the most justifiable efforts of men to defend themselves with weapons. In 1948 Joseph Fielding Smith reviewed for Church members the "law of forgiveness and retribution" in D&C 98 (as referred to above) and also the radical example of perfect pacifism of the people of Ammon in the Book of Mormon. Elder Smith insisted on direct applicability of those standards to present day nations. "This may to the ordinary human being be a hard law to follow," he wrote, "but nevertheless it is the word of the Lord":

Because [the people of Ammon] refused to take up arms to defend themselves, but would rather lay down their lives than shed blood in their own defense, they brought many of their enemies to repentance and to the kingdom of God. This is the doctrine of Jesus as taught in his Sermon on the Mount. If all peoples would accept this doctrine there could be no war.[10]

Of course, all people do not accept that doctrine, but LDS scriptures and prophets have insisted that the individual retains responsibility to live the doctrine, even unilaterally. The Declaration of Belief Regarding Governments and Laws (D & C 134), adopted by the Church in

1835, states that "governments were instituted of God for the benefit of man" and that God "holds men accountable for their acts in relation to them." Men are obliged to "sustain and uphold" their governments only "while protected in their inherent and inalienable rights," first among those being "free exercise of conscience."

The commitment of LDS leaders to such principles of individual responsibility was underscored during the Vietnam War. Some young Latter-day Saints, convinced that their government was asking them to participate in an unjust war, applied for exemption as conscientious objectors. These young men generally faced draft boards that assumed the Mormon emphasis on national loyalty precluded Mormons from conscientious objection. When these LDS men wrote to President McKay about their standing, they received this reply:

As the brethren understand, the existing law provides that men who have conscientious objection may be excused from combat service. There would seem to be no objection, therefore, to a man availing himself on a personal basis of the exemptions provided by law.[11]

Though this certainly did not assume pacifism as *the* Mormon position, the First Presidency clearly placed individual agency to live by the general principle over specific national loyalty. And the letter successfully supported applications of Mormon conscientious objectors.

But the most specific and powerful call to Americans and Mormons to live by conscience and higher law was made in a remarkable prophetic address by President Spencer W. Kimball in 1976. The address was timed to coincide with the American Bicentennial celebrations, when patriotic fervor and national self-satisfaction were at a high. President Kimball accused Americans, specifically pointing to his own Mormon people, of worshiping the false gods of material possessions and pleasures and of relying on the arm of flesh, the carnal security of military armaments, rather than trusting the God of Israel and living his law:

We are, on the whole, an idolatrous people—a condition most repugnant to the Lord. We are a warlike people, easily distracted from our assignment of preparing for the coming of the Lord. When enemies rise up, we commit vast resources to the fabrication of gods of stone and steel—ships, planes, missiles, fortifications—and depend on them for protection and deliverance. When threatened, we become anti-enemy instead of pro-kingdom of God; we train a man in the art of war and call him a patriot, thus in the manner of Satan's counterfeit of true patriotism, perverting the Savior's teaching [that we love our enemies].

We forget that if we are righteous the Lord will either not suffer our enemies to come upon us—and this is the special promise to the inhabitants of the land of the Americas (see 2 Nephi 1-7)—or he will fight our battles for us.[12]

President Kimball then articulated precisely the central pragmatic concept of the LDS theology of peace—that enemies cannot be defeated, but they can be changed into other than enemies by true principles of love, and God will provide the power to do that if we will trust him and pay the price of trying things his way:

What are we to fear when the Lord is with us? Can we not take the Lord at his word and exercise a particle of faith in him? Our assignment is affirmative; to forsake the things of the world as ends in themselves; to leave off idolatry and press forward in faith; to carry the gospel to our enemies, that they might no longer be our enemies.[13]

President Kimball has, of course, continued to preach this doctrine, notably in the message last Christmas which insists that nations as well as individuals can learn to love their enemies and also in the earlier statement opposing basing of the MX missile system in the western United States:

Our fathers came to this western area to establish a base from which to carry the gospel of peace to the peoples of the earth. It is ironic and a denial of the very essence of that gospel, that in this same general area there should be constructed a mammoth weapons system potentially capable of destroying much of civilization.[14]

Let me now briefly apply this theology in judgment on some recent wars and suggest how it might guide us in the future decisions of our country and our individual consciences. In general, the extraordinary prevalence and horror of wars since 1914 seem to be a result of the combination of modern technology with mediocre or actually sinful leaders, those David O. McKay identified in 1942 as "rulers in the world who in a frenzy of hate and lust for unrighteous power and dominion over their fellow men, have put into motion eternal forces they do not comprehend and cannot control." Certainly in the First World War, "the war no one wanted," mutual hate and miscalculation by inept leaders initiated the conflict, and lack of rational ability to adjust prolonged the horror: The Austrian, German, and Russian leaders, seeing themselves as honorable and superior and their opponents as inferior and diabolical, escalated their hostile behavior, ignored the reactions of those around them, and led their nations to destruction. French and English leaders reviled the "Huns," persisted in committing such follies as cavalry charges against machine guns, and destroyed a whole generation of their young manhood. Even after victory the peace settlement imposed at Versailles was a "victor's peace." Its vengeful humiliations rankled in the German spirit and added fuel to the postwar economic disasters that helped bring Hitler to power (and which we–merrily dancing the Charleston–did nothing to prevent as we finally had the good sense to do after the Second World War).

The main lesson of the "Great War" of the forties is that even a just war can be conducted immorally or ineffectively when judged by larger ends or higher principles than merely winning the war. The United States won the peace to some extent with the Marshall Plan, one of the few acts between belligerent nations in this century that (despite its inception in pragmatic anti-Communism) seems entirely consistent with Christ's teachings. This effort brought an economic recovery to our former enemies that continues to have lasting benefits as they have now become our friends and helpful competitors–certainly one example of President Kimball's injunction and promise "to carry the gospel to our enemies, that they might no longer be our enemies." But we also brought great and prolonged suffering and created the specter of nuclear destruction that continues to haunt us, because we let the end justify the means and gradually accepted bombing of civilian populations as a weapon. Lewis Mumford has documented[15] how we slowly surrendered to our own military leaders and turned from abhorrence of the German practice of such bombing at the beginning of the war to retaliation in kind and finally to acceptance without a qualm of the obliteration of Dresden and Berlin and Hiroshima–a moral blindness President J. Reuben Clark so graphically denounced. And I am convinced that by our vengeful insistence on "unconditional surrender" we prolonged the war, created a situation that seemed to justify the atomic bomb, and helped ensure Russian dominance in Eastern Europe.

That same blindness to the costs and impermanence of a humiliatingly imposed victor's peace or a devastating total defeat led to serious mistakes in Korea. I find John G. Stoessinger's analysis in *Why Nations Go to War* convincing.[16] The decision to repel aggression was justifiable and conducted with initial restraint. But when victory seemed assured, General MacArthur and then President Truman were tempted to *offensive* action–first the crossing of the 38th parallel into North Korea and then a drive toward the Yalu River border with China. Proceeding without respect for either the United Nations or Communist China, MacArthur provoked Chinese intervention that probably prolonged the war another eighteen months and turned it into one of the bloodiest wars of this century: 34,000 Americans dead, perhaps 1.5 million Korean and another 1.5 million Chinese casualties. And the war that might have, with continued restraint, stopped an aggression without lasting bitterness and enhanced the United Nations, ended indecisively. Two Koreas emerged–both fully armed, hostile dictatorships–and the United Nations was seriously weakened as a neutral arbitrator by being drawn onto the side of a victim of aggression who in turn became the aggressor.

A similar temptation seems to be afflicting Israel: It has long been the victim of irrational hatred, terrorism, and aggression but now seems to lack the humility and courage to resist inflicting on others what has been inflicted on itself. All its heroic resistance and rolling back of its enemies has not bought Israel the security it craves. In fact the one clear lesson seems to be that the victor's peace imposed on Egypt in 1967, when Egypt lost the Sinai, continued to fester until a near defeat of Israel and then a more equitable ceasefire finally helped lead to negotiations and a peace treaty. And that required a unilateral act of courageous love to break the impasse, when Anwar Sadat risked everything to reach out to his enemies.

But the lesson seems lost, and Israel, in the name of avenging a few hundred of its people killed by Palestinian rockets and terrorism, has killed thousands of Lebanese as well as Palestinians and probably incurred the lasting enmity of entire new groups and a whole new generation. Even it if it had completely destroyed the Palestinians in Beirut, hundreds of thousands of enemies would continue elsewhere until there is someone with the largeness of mind and heart to sacrifice Israeli-occupied land and temporarily risk Israeli security enough to provide a permanent solution to Palestinian homelessness and consequent resentment–to turn enemies into something else and thus bring the only real security and peace.

But we Americans cannot be proud of our own record, especially in Vietnam. That war is perhaps still too close to us to analyze sensibly, but let me risk a few judgments in the light of the theology I have described. On the basis of the evidence available,[17] I believe that in Vietnam we not only failed to act in Christian love so as to turn enemies into friends but we turned potential friends into bitter enemies. Ho Chi Minh led his people as our ally against the Japanese and looked to us as an example and champion in his legitimate quest for independence from French colonialism—but in vain. And after he defeated the French, if we had sustained his efforts under the Geneva accords of 1954 to hold national elections that our own leaders admitted would have brought him legitimately to power, Vietnam could still have emerged as a united, certainly Communist, country, but probably as friendly to us and progressive as China is now. But our anti-Communist panic led us twice to betray Ho Chi Minh in favor of colonial or minority governments—not because they were more legitimate but merely the ones that we *preferred*. We became increasingly involved in the ensuing civil war and finally, directly contrary to the principles for a just war outlined by David O. McKay, waged an offensive war, far from our borders, "in an attempt to enforce a new order of government," against the majority will, on the Vietnamese.

I feel certain that Communism is on balance a disaster for most of those brought under its sway, especially because of the massive curtailment of individual freedom (continuing defections from Vietnam indicate that even former Viet Cong are learning this), and it may well be that for many individuals it is better to be dead than to be Red. But the very principle of agency so endangered by Communism as to make that cliche sometimes true requires that we recognize that *we have no right to make such a decision for other people,* as it seems we tried to do in Vietnam.

What, finally, of our failure in the long cold war with Russia, with its corollary nuclear escalation, that now costs hundreds of billions of dollars a year and seems to lead toward an abyss. The history of efforts to control atomic weapons and then to disarm is one of irrational mistrust between the superpowers—continued unwillingness of each to exhibit the faith in the other that it demands the other to have in it. Even the farsighted Baruch plan, designed for international control in 1946 when the U.S. still had an atomic monopoly, insensitively placed Russia in an inferior position by denying it the right to continue its own research and by requiring its economic submission to an international body it did not trust. There followed a long struggle between the U.S. and Russia over which would come first, disarmament or mechanisms for inspection and control. Stoessinger describes the dilemma:

Though both powers accepted the principle of simultaneous disarmament and control, they were unable to translate it into practice. Each side continued to postpone making the greater sacrifice, *and instead encouraged the opponent to take the first step.*[18]

The story is almost amusing, like one of little boys with fragile egos quarreling–except that this failure of imagination and courage not only now costs many times what it would take to solve world hunger and bring adequate medical care and education to all in the world who need it, but it has produced a world of potential nuclear accidents, of proliferation to nations (even terrorist groups) capable of nuclear blackmail, and of weapon building that gathers momentum in a way that points to catastrophe.

Beyond a radical critique of most of the conduct during conflict of most contemporary governments, including our own, LDS theology offers a guide to better conduct. I believe its fundamental message is that "effective pacifism"–even unilateral disarmament *if* accompanied by massive efforts to extend intelligent, creative, tough-minded but loving help to other nations, particularly our chief "enemy" the Soviet Union–is the ideal solution, the only one that could make our enemies no longer enemies and that would make us fully worthy of God's assistance and protection. But since we are not, with our allies or even as a single nation, capable of such unified love of our enemies and faith in God rather than the arm of flesh, a compromise solution, based on the restraints of a purely defensive just war must be worked out. That solution must be guided, however, by the principles inherent in the ideal solution, which stands in judgment on anything less.

A first step would be to work toward loving our enemies by knowing them as humans like ourselves, by resisting the usual mindless stereotyping of Russians as universally crude, deceitful monsters intent on our enslavement and ourselves as noble, generous saviors fit to release them from their enslavement. This means resisting the demagoguery of press and politicians. It means studying Russian and Chinese and Eastern European cultures and languages, visiting behind the Iron Curtain–but getting to know individual people in depth rather than superficially. If only five percent of our monstrous military budgets were spent on exchange of peoples between our nations for such study we could send a million persons each year (and as a result could well be motivated to find ways to reduce those budgets much more than five percent). It is likely that we can only gradually be weaned away from placing our faith in weapons and in an escalating balance of terror based only in paranoid actions and reactions. But we must try.

Loving our enemies means, I believe, that we would resist at every point the idea increasingly promoted by our present government that we should attempt to collapse the Russian (or Polish) economy as a means to bringing about revolution and a government more to our liking. In the first place, it is highly unlikely we could succeed, given the resilience of the peoples involved and the military power of their governments, and it is even more unlikely on the evidence of history that the chaos resulting from such a collapse would bring to power a less repressive government. We would be much better advised to look to our own economy, which may be in as great danger as the Russian–and to our basic principles, which call us to help not hurt our enemies, so they will no longer be our enemies.

Perhaps, given the realities of the cold war, we must work mainly through private people-to-people agencies to love our enemies. Some of us, mainly in Utah, conducted a campaign this past year called Food For Poland, cooperating closely with the Polish American Congress and Catholic Relief Services. Our success seems small compared to the need. But we did help send perhaps $1 million in food and medicine ($100,000 worth given by the LDS Church and much of the rest by Mormons), and in visits to the Polish community in Chicago and to Poland itself we felt the power of love changing people's hearts and saw that our efforts brought hope and courage to people far out of proportion to the physical help.

President Reagan cut off $800 million in aid to Poland for 1982. Perhaps twice that much (but still less than one percent of our military budget), invested in 1981 in an imaginative, well-designed Marshall Plan for the economic recovery of Poland–and implemented through Solidarity and the Catholic Church–might well have obviated the need for martial law, bound us in friendship to that country, and provided the crucial resources for their remarkable "renewal" to continue. We may soon have another chance to do something like that, as the suffering this winter worsens and the Polish government seeks help, but I wonder if our leaders are planning for such positive measures. If we could be willing to help build a genuinely neutral, still socialist but experimental and developing Poland, it might well be as acceptable to Russia as Finland is, and it would be a great example to other countries who might see how to develop greater freedoms without antagonizing Russia by seeming to threaten her national security–and thus could help to diversify the world from its dangerous bipolar division.

To touch the heart of an enemy and heal divisions is difficult–among the most difficult and important of human duties. It requires risk, imaginative effort to overcome suspicion, hard-headed negotiation and calling to repentance at the right moment–followed by an increase of mercy and generosity. But each of us has had enough experience at the personal level to sense that it can be done and something of how it could be done between nations. For instance, it is impossible to judge precisely the relative U.S.-Soviet strength: Which is better, our advantage in flexibility of delivery systems or their advantage in "throw weight"? In any event each has sufficient power to destroy the other totally, many times over. And if the Soviets really have the nuclear superiority and the ambition to rule the world that some of our political leaders are claiming (as an excuse to escalate our own arms buildup), Russia would already have used that power to destroy or at least blackmail us. We should resist therefore the current obsession of our government to become exactly "equal" with Russia before we can seek a bilateral nuclear freeze or arms reduction. Both sides will always be able to use that argument–until doomsday. One side must have the courage to accept rough parity (such as I believe we now have), stop threatening and "catching up," then trust in the basic principles for reducing enmity we have reviewed and act so as to entice the other side to do the same. Since we claim to be a Christian or at least morally superior nation, why shouldn't we be first? At the very least, we must resist any ambitions to "roll back" Communism through regaining nuclear superiority and threatening to launch a "winnable" nuclear war if the Soviets do not retreat. There is growing evidence that some in our government are pushing arms build-up because they have precisely those ambitions–a clear violation of President McKay's warning against offensive war.

If we are individually to assist in finding solutions, we must replace thoughtless fear of Communism with faith in Christ's commandments. In President Kimball's phrase, we must leave being "anti-enemy" and become "pro-kingdom of God." President McKay helped us look beyond systems to people and to principles of peace:

No matter how excellent [Nazism, Fascism, Communism, or Capitalism] may seem in the minds of their advocates, none will ameliorate the ills of mankind unless its operation in government be impregnated with the basic principles promulgated by the Savior of Men. On the contrary, even a defective economic system will produce good results if the men who direct it will be guided by the spirit of Christ. Actuated by that spirit, leaders will think more of men than of the success of a system. Kindness, mercy, and justice will be substituted for hatred, suspicion, and greed. There is no road to universal peace, which does not lead to the heart of humanity.[19]

All our experience shows that in the course of arguments about equality, former injuries and injustices, and who deserves what, none of us will see peace between nations. LDS teachings witness that it is only in treating our enemies with the respect and justice we want for ourselves–and then in mercy rather than retribution, in "perfect love" that "casteth out fear"–that the eternal influences that lead to peace can be released.

Notes

1. *Church News*, 19 December 1981, p.2.
2. Hugh Nibley, "If There Must Needs Be Offense," *Ensign* 1 (July 1971):54.
3. *Journal of Discourses*, 16 vols. (London: Latter-day Saints' Book Depot, 1854-86), 7:137.
4. Joseph F. Smith, *Eighty-Seventh Annual Conference of the Church of Jesus Christ* (Salt Lake City, Utah: Deseret News, 1917), p.4.
5. David O. McKay, *One Hundred and Twelfth Annual Conference of the Church of Jesus Christ* (Salt Lake City: Deseret Book, 1942), p. 72; my emphasis.
6. McKay, pp. 94-95.
7. McKay, p. 95.
8. J. Reuben Clark, *One Hundred and Seventeenth Semi-Annual Conference of the Church of Jesus Christ* (Salt Lake City: Deseret Book, 1946), p. 88.
9. *Improvement Era* 47 (February 1946):76-77.
10. Joseph Fielding Smith, *Church History and Modern Revelation*. Second Series (Salt Lake City: Council of the Twelve of the Church of Jesus Christ of Latter-day Saints, 1953), p. 193.
11. Letter signed by Joseph Anderson for the First Presidency, January 1968, reprinted in *Dialogue: A Journal of Mormon Thought* 3 (Spring 1968):8.
12. Spencer W. Kimball, "First Presidency Message: The False Gods We Worship." *Ensign* 6 (June 1976):6.
13. Kimball, p. 6
14. "First Presidency Statement" of 5 May 1981, *Ensign* 11 (June 1981):76; my emphasis.
15. Lewis Mumford, "The Morals of Extermination," *The Atlantic Monthly* 204 (October 1959):38-44.
16. John G. Stoessinger, *Why Nations Go To War* (New York: St. Martin's Press, 3rd ed., 1982), pp. 55-80.

17. Analysis and bibliography is available in Ray C. Hillam, Eugene England, and John Sorenson, "Vietnam: A Roundtable," *Dialogue: A Journal of Mormon Thought* 2 (Winter 1967):69-100 (reading suggestions on p. 80).
18. Stoessinger, pp. 219-220; my emphasis.
19. David O. McKay, *One Hundred and Fifteenth Semi-Annual Conference of the Church of Jesus Christ* (Salt Lake City: Deseret Book, 1944), pp. 80–81.

Read for the Women's Conference, BYU, February 1983, and the East Coast meetings of the Association for Mormon Letters, May 1983; a shorter version published in *Exponent II* (Spring 1983).

CHAPTER 14

WE NEED TO LIBERATE MORMON MEN!

In the past twenty years an increasing number of voices, male and female, from novelists to theologians, from heretics to housewives, have claimed that the rights and freedoms of women have been severely restricted under various patriarchal systems, particularly religious ones—and that women have thus been suppressed, prevented from their possible development and expression as creative, free human beings. Mormonism, with its strongly authoritarian male priesthood and family centered theology, has been attacked as an extreme example of this suppression by religious patriarchy. Marilyn Warensky, in her book *Patriarchs and Politics*, claims that "In the Mormon experience can be found the ideal case in support of feminism against any patriarchal society" because it "demonstrates how patriarchal power ultimately and inevitably becomes confining to women." After reviewing Dostoevsky's account of the Grand Inquisitor, who claims it is inevitable that humans give up painful freedom for the safe bonds of religion, Warensky claims that Mormon women "have not only accepted the security of religion, with its mystery and miracle, but have also embraced patriarchal authority as a necessary part of that religion." Another noted critic of patriarchies, Sonia Johnson, of course has made the same claim. Others, Mormon women who are not at all heretics, have made similar complaints, though in milder tones. Even Linda Sillitoe and Mary Bradford, both of whom seem to me much more liberated than suppressed by the patriarchy—and certainly more liberated than most men I know—were worried a few years ago that Mormon women were writing mainly through a "mask of maleness." Bradford urged Mormon women, "Reveal yourselves, sisters. Risk it! Risk it!"[1]

I am naturally skeptical about *any* sweeping claims, but more to the point, I have found nothing to support these claims in my own experience with Mormon women, especially Charlotte England. However, many bright and good people feel *something* is wrong, so I began to look for evidence one way or the other in my own field of scholarship, Mormon literature.

The evidence, I am convinced, shows that Mormon women are more free, more daring, inventive, original in thought and unique in voice than Mormon men. In quantity and quality of literary production, certainly one of the great measures of freedom and creativity, they are more liberated than men under the "patriarchy." In the first generation of writers after the Restoration, roughly 1830-1880, Mormon women wrote more than fifty percent of our best journals, diaries, letters, autobiographies, poems, and hymns. But that was not just an unusual, anomalous nineteenth-century phenomenon. In the twentieth century, after a fallow period from 1880 to 1930, a second generation of first-rate writers developed, from 1930-1960. Our best two Mormon novels, which come from that period, are by women. Our two most innovative histories were also written then–and by women. In the third generation of Mormon writers, since 1970, which contains such quality it looks to many of us like "The Dawning of a Brighter Day,"[2] *all* of our collections of personal essays,[3] about fifty percent of our finest individual essays and poems,[4] and many of our best short stories are by women.[5] Scanning down a select bibliography of Mormon literature I compiled lately, I find it clear that in every period and most genres more than half of our best, most challenging original work is by women.[6] The most challenging, insightful, and successful independent journal in nineteenth-century Mormonism was the *Women's Exponent.* And in 1982, when I began to make this investigation, the three modern independent journals of Mormon thought and literature, *Dialogue, Exponent II,* and *Sunstone*, were all edited by women. Contrary to the claim that the Mormon patriarchy suppresses its women more than its men–and does so more than other cultures, I can find no other culture, or nation, contemporary or historical, in which such a preponderance of creative thought and writing is by its women.

How can we explain this evidence? Is it a case of opposition and struggle against oppression producing, by natural selection, a hardier stock, more feistiness and rebellion and thus freedom and creativity in the women? Or is it that the patriarchy–because it is inherently corrupt in its reliance on power–corrupts, enfeebles, and makes cowardly and inarticulate its men. Or that the pressures of career and priesthood responsibility simply keep them too busy, or too deprived of the necessary solitude? Or is it that Mormonism inherently contains liberating forces, challenges, paradoxes, spiritual trials and exaltations that women have, for whatever cultural reasons, learned to respond to better than men? I am persuaded that not only is the gospel true but that our Church and our culture have the greatest *potential* for stimulating creativity, so I opt for the third alternative and rather than presuming to say much about women will explore how men can more effectively grasp their opportunities. But first we'll consider the first two possibilities and look at what Mormon literature itself can tell us.

At the end of Solzhenitsyn's novel, *The First Circle*, a marvelous revelation occurs. Innokenty, a Soviet security official who in a sudden moment of compassion had tried to warn by phone someone about to be arrested, has been identified and is himself arrested and taken to Lubyanka prison. As his freedoms are removed and a process of dehumanization begins, a remarkable thing happens. Innokenty begins to see things, feel things, think things he had never before–in his life of privilege and ease and oppression of others: "He had had money, good clothes, esteem, women, wine, travel, but at this moment he would have hurled all those pleasures into the nether world for justice and truth . . . and nothing more." He learns to perceive, to genuinely experience and value simple freedoms and skills. After one guard has ripped all the buttons off his tunic but another has given him a needle and old buttons, he learns for the first time to sew on buttons:

Unable to draw on thousands of years of experience, he then invented sewing for himself. . . . [T]his deliberate, concentrated work not only killed time but also quieted Innokenty completely. His emotions fell into place, and he no longer felt either afraid or despondent. He could perceive that even this legendary pit of horror, the Lubyanka Prison, was not totally fearsome, that there were people of flesh and blood here too. Oh, how he would like to meet them.

After a long, harrowing time, bread and tea are brought him. He has no desire for food but for the first time in his life genuinely tastes his tea: "With a shudder of happiness Innokenty drank the second cup, without sugar but sensing sharply the aroma of the tea. His thoughts brightened to a clarity he had never known."

This moving image of human response to opposition suddenly makes clear one subtle message of the whole novel: That the "zeks," the political prisoners who staff the technical institutes of Moscow, slave labor suppressed under Stalin's patriarchy, forced to work long hours without reward or power or the usual freedoms, these men and women are much more intellectually alive, inventive, interesting, moral, free in important ways, even happy, than their oppressors. This is, of course, one of Solzhenitsyn's great testimonies about the "gulag," that for all its evil, it contained in remarkable spiritual freedom the true soul of Russia, stimulated the best creativity, produced some of the highest Sainthood in the modern world.

This is not a new idea. The literature of Western Civilization is full of powerful images of *men* reaching heights of spiritual power or literary creativity when made powerless in prison or exile or by some other suppression: Socrates, Christ, Boethius, Thomas More, John Bunyan, Henry David Thoreau, Joseph Smith, Gandhi, Solzhenitsyn, Martin Luther King. In *Civil Disobedience* Thoreau described the principle in ringing and influential words:

Under a government which imprisons any unjustly, the true place for a just man is also in prison. . . . It is there that the fugitive slave and the Mexican prisoner on parole, and the Indian come to plead the wrongs of his race, should find them; on that separate but more free and honorable ground, where the State places those who are not with her but against her—the only house in a slave-state in which a free man can abide with honor.

But Thoreau taught the more general principle as well—the *danger* of being conscripted into the power structures, seduced into the quest for wealth and stature, of any oppressive system, the *value* of being instead among the oppressed, the outcast, even the imprisoned, for the perspective it gives. He quotes Confucius: "Statesmen and legislators, standing so completely within the institution, never distinctly and nakedly behold it." Thus, Martin Luther King saw and wrote better about America from Birmingham Jail. Gandhi, as we can see again in the current film, when in prison was the freest man in South Africa; later, when he was near death with fasting against oppression, he was the most alive person in India.

In *The Scarlet Letter* Nathaniel Hawthorne gives a powerful example of the possibility that oppressive limitations can also be strangely liberating in a *woman.* Of his heroine, Hester Prynne, he writes:

She assumed a freedom of speculation, then common enough on the other side of the Atlantic, but which our forefathers, had they known it, would have held to be a deadlier crime than that stigmatized by the scarlet letter. In her lonesome cottage by the seashore, thoughts visited her, such as dared to enter no other dwelling in New England. . . . Had [her child] never come to her from the spiritual world, she might have come down to us in history as the foundress of a religious sect. She might, in one of her phases, have been a prophetess.

Is it a similar patriarchal oppression, like that of the Puritans, and loneliness, like Hester's, that have produced the free and creative, maturely speculative and spiritual, even prophetic, voices of Mormon women? Partly, but much more is involved.

Consider Eliza R. Snow, married to the first two Prophets of Mormonism and sister to another, a Mormon woman to whom the term "prophetess" was literally given—as well as "poetess," "priestess," and "presidentess," even "the president of the female portion of the human race." She was certainly not suppressed—or isolated. She greatly influenced the development of almost all the Church's auxiliaries: Relief Society, Primary, young women's and young men's groups; she published nine books, volumes of poems, many hymns—most notably "Oh My Father," which remains one of the most popular and influential Mormon hymns. It is the single most powerful source for what may be our single most powerful new doctrine in Mormon thought, that of a Heavenly Mother. That doctrine nails down firmly the otherwise somewhat vague implications of Joseph Smith's eternalism: the doctrine that we have existed eternally as separate, unique individuals— and always will— but that our individuality can only be fully realized, its potential completely developed, in an eternal, fully sexual union of opposites, that in fact God is not a single lonely male or female but an eternal creative partnership. That gives us our highest vision of the future and of the present, and, as Maureen Beecher has reminded us, Wilford Woodruff pointed out how fitting it was that the Lord revealed this profound doctrine through one of his daughters.[7]

Eliza was certainly the appropriate choice. Let's listen to her voice in what I think perhaps the crucial period in her discovery of self, of her seeking and receiving the spiritual gifts commensurate with that calling. Her "Trail Diary" from Nauvoo to the Great Salt Lake is known but not well enough known and is now out of print. She found her essential self in the black death and black mud of Winter Quarters, and in keeping her journal, honestly and revealingly as she did, she provided one of the central values of good literature, a catalytic aid in our own search for self. The desperate trek across Iowa and the great plains winter endured in caves and lean-to cabins was perhaps the most harrowing trial of the early Church. For those who did not die, or leave, it was a dark night of the soul and a being pushed back to basics, to frontiers of selfhood, from which they emerged discovered selves reborn. I feel certain this happened to Brigham Young. We have more direct evidence that it did to Eliza. What is most moving and to me makes her record fine Mormon literature is not so much how much of self she exposes but what she reveals of the *process* of her discovery of self. We meet her at first as the spirited, intelligent, and perceptive but also petulant, self-indulgent, and self-righteous young woman who had been Joseph Smith's secret wife and is now uncertain of her status–nominally under Brigham Young's care, but shunted off to travel with a troubled family she guiltily detests, and constantly seeking reassurance through blessings and counsel from authorites such as Brigham Young and Heber C. Kimball.

But after the chastening of that winter a fine, patient strength, directness, and sense of humor slowly emerge, climaxing, in the spring, with one of the most remarkable outpourings of spiritual power and intelligence in religious history, among Eliza and others of the women of Winter Quarters; they taught each other the doctrine of the kingdom and spoke and sang in tongues and laid their hands on their sick and afflicted sisters and blessed them to health.

Saturday, May 1. This afternoon had a most glorious time at br[other] Leonard's. Sis. Sessions presided–present: Moth[ers] Chase, Cutler, Cahoon, Sis[ters] Whitney, Kim[ball], Katherine, Lyon, Buel, Knight, etc.–spoken by the spirit of prophecy that the Pioneers were well, happy & were in council–that tomorrow they will have a greater time of rejoicing than they have ever had.

Patty Sessions' diary of that day reports:

Sylvia and I went to meeting to Sister Leonard's. None but females there. We had a good meeting. I presided. It was got up by E. R. Snow. They spoke in tongues; I interpreted. Some prophesied. It was a feast.

Here is another report from Eliza, on the trail west:

Friday, June 18. Had a treat of a spirit in the wagon. Sis. Moore & sis. Sess[ions] p[rese]nt. In the aft. attended meeting at sis. Beaches'–most of br. Pratt's fam[ily] pr[esen]t–had a refreshing time. Sis. Sess[ions] & I went to br. Hunter's, found sis. H[unter]–went into the wagon–I spoke to br.

H[unter] in the gift of tongues, sis. S[essions] interpreted, after which br. H[unter], sis. S[essions] & I laid hands on sis. H[unter]'s head and rebuk'd her illness & blessed her. I then sang a song to them & sis. S[essions] sang the interpretation. Susanna present & arose & bless'd sis. H[unter].

In September, Eliza's wagon train met Brigham Young's group that was returning from the Salt Lake Valley settlement to Winter Quarters, where he would remain until spring, while she went on to Salt Lake; she writes:

Before the Pioneers left, Brigham came to the carriage and blest us. I ask'd who was to be my counsellor for the year to come. He said Eliza R. Snow. I said, "She is not capable." He said, "I have appointed her president."

I see this passage as ironic and deeply revealing. Both she and Brigham Young well knew that she had developed into a woman of marvelous spiritual daring and stature and had a resulting self-confidence and sense of self that could allow her to playfully pretend to her former dependence but with complete assurance, in both of them, that she was, whether he appointed her or not, now indeed "president" of her own soul.

Now listen to a very different voice, Mary Goble Pay, a pioneer woman essentially unknown to any but her family and small Utah community–no prophetess or president of anything prominent. Hers is a voice of spiritual nobility, revealed in the purity and understatement of a prose that is shaped toward genius not by any training or models, but by character and by honest response to great historical and personal events. It is a voice probably not approached, certainly not surpassed, by any Mormon man of the time. Her luminuous account of the sufferings of her family in the handcart disaster, devoid of any self-pity or excess of sentimentality, is quite flat. It sees clearly the detailed, hard surface of life and also its depth. It is *moving* in the finest sense. As we read of her endurance, at the age of thirteen, through the death of two sisters and her mother and then the loss of her own feet, then see her victory over that handicap and her long life of faith and service, we are motivated not only by passive wonder at a great human being but to an active sense of our own possibilities as human beings and children of God:

My mother had never got well, she lingered until the 11 of December, the day we arrived in Salt Lake City 1856. She died between the Little and Big Mountain. She was buried in the Salt Lake City Cemetery. She was 43 years old. She and her baby lost their lives gathering to Zion in such a late season of the year. My sister was buried at the last crossing of the Sweet Water.

We arrived in Salt Lake City nine o'clock at night the 11th of December 1856. Three out of four that were living were frozen. My mother was dead in the wagon.

Bishop Hardy had us taken to a home in his ward and the brethren and the sisters brought us plenty of food. We had to be careful and not eat too much as it might kill us we were so hungry.

Early next morning Bro. Brigham Young and a doctor came. The doctor's name was Williams. When Bro. Young came in he shook hands with us all. When he saw our condition our feet frozen and our mother dead tears rolled down his cheeks.

The doctor amputated my toes using a saw and a butcher knife. Brigham Young promised me I would not have to have any more of my feet cut off. The sisters were dressing mother for the last time. Oh how did we stand it? That afternoon she was buried.

When we had been in Salt Lake a week, one afternoon a knock came at the door. It was Uncle John Wood. When he met Father he said, "I know it all Bill." Both of them cried. I was glad to see my father cry. Uncle said for him to pack up and we would start right away. That night we got to Centerville. There Aunt Fanny was waiting for us at Brother Garns. We stayed there that night. The next morning we went to Farmington and stayed there until the following April. My father married again.

Instead of my feet getting better they got worse until the following July I went to Dr. Wiseman's to live with them to pay for him to doctor my feet. But it was no use he said he could do no more for me unless I could consent to have them cut off at the ankle. I told him what Brigham Young had promised me. He said all right sit there and rot and I will do nothing more until you come to your senses.

One day I sat there crying. My feet were hurting me so—when a little old woman knocked at the door. She said she had felt someone needed her there for a number of days. When she saw me crying she came and asked what was the matter. I showed her my feet and told her the promise Bro. Young had given me. She said, "Yes, and with the help of the Lord we will save them yet." She made a poultice and put on my feet and every day after the doctor had gone she would come and change the poultice. At the end of three months my feet were well.

One day Doctor Wiseman said, "Well, Mary, I must say you have grit. I suppose your feet have rotted to the knees by this time." I said, "Oh, no, my feet are well." He said, "I know better, it could never be." So I took off my stockings and showed him my feet. He said that it was a miracle and wanted me to tell him what I had been doing. I told him to never mind that they were now healed.

I have never had to have any more taken from them. The promise of Brigham Young has been fulfilled and the pieces of toe bone have worked out.

I had sat in my chair so long that the cords of my legs had become stiff and I could not straighten them. When I went home to my father and he saw how my legs were we both cried. He rubbed the cords of my legs with oil and tried every way to straighten them, but it was of no use. One day he said, "Mary I have thought of a plan to help you. I will nail a shelf on the wall and while I am away to work you try to reach it." I tried all day and for several days. At last I could reach it and how pleased we were. Then he put the shelf a little higher and in about three months my legs were straight and then I had to learn to walk again.[8]

What about the twentieth century? I mentioned our two best novels, which are Virginia Sorensen's *The Evening and the Morning* and Maurine Whipple's *The Giant Joshua.* Sorensen and Whipple were part of our second major literary generation, what Edward Geary has called "Mormondom's Lost Generation."[9] They were guilty of a certain patronizing tone, even of their own quaint forms of provincialism, in their reaction against Mormon provincialisms. They were, as Virginia Sorensen characterized herself, "in the middle–incapable of severe orthodoxies." But, better than any of our male writers, Sorensen and her protagonist in *The Evening and the Morning*, Kate Alexander, understood sin very well, its complex beginnings in small, tragic misunderstandings and impulses, its power to require one to persist when the pains and costs become much greater than the pleasures and rewards.

Whipple's *The Giant Joshua* is the richest, fullest, most moving, the *truest* fiction about the Mormon pioneer experience–one of the best about any pioneers. It gives, better than any of our male-written histories or biographies or novels, the human cost of pioneering and the faith that was willing to meet the cost and the human results won in the struggle. It is a most direct and perceptive access to understanding Mormon experience; it is our finest fictional access to our roots as Mormons and as Rocky Mountain, high-desert people, our most profound imaginative knowledge of the spiritual ancestors of us all, the Dixie pioneers.

Also in that second generation of writers were two women who made courageous and far-reaching breakthroughs in Mormon history: First was Fawn Brodie's *No Man Knows My History* (1946). It has many faults, the main one being that Brodie's considerable rhetorical skill is used, under the guise of objective scholarship, to bring Joseph Smith powerfully alive—but only as the engagingly clever charlatan Brodie had to see in him after she had rejected his Church. But the scholarship, particularly in non-Mormon sources, really is there, for the first time, and much Mormon historical scholarship since has been spent in responding to or imitating that breakthrough. The other is Juanita Brooks' *Mountain Meadows Massacre* (1950), the first book by a Mormon historian to deal directly and fully with an incontrovertibly tragic mistake, a sin, by our own people.

What about our contemporaries, the third generation of Mormon writers—again, a majority of them women. These writers, compared to most of those of the previous generation, are characterized by various kinds and degrees of sincere commitment to the unique and demanding religious claims of Mormonism as well as its people, history, and culture—and they can be devastatingly critical of the world, of Babylon. But they are also clear-sighted in their analyses of Mormon mistakes and tragedies, both historical and present, in some cases *more* incisive because less naive and more emphatically involved themselves in Mormon conflicts and mistakes. Lavina Fielding Anderson, past president of the Association for Mormon Letters, in her Presidential Address (January 1983), described how this new voice is developing in fiction, as we move beyond the sentimental literature of the late nineteenth century that persists in our official magazines and popular novels and also beyond the somewhat alienated fiction of the 1930s and 1940s such as in Sorensen and Whipple:

> *The pretty romances, the cute tales of cute adolescents, and the melodramatic historical fiction that constitutes the majority of published works in the field of Mormon literature today consists mostly of cliches borrowed from the larger world of literature. The cheap and easy fiction seems preoccupied with its audience, deals in simple conflicts, simply resolved, flops brokenbacked between preaching and entertaining, and usually considers the craft of fiction as relatively unimportant. I see the new Mormon fiction as attempting something more ambitious. It is literature of intelligent affirmation, not of alienation, fiction that takes as its province the hitherto unexplored field of spiritual realism.*

A fine new term that—spiritual realism—and Anderson goes on to describe it:

In spiritual realism, the conflicts that a character may encounter in his or her social settings are primarily important as they provide information about the interior spiritual life of that person. The experiences move the person toward a greater understanding of the ambiguous nature of human good and human depravity. They affirm or challenge the reality of God. They illuminate by recording those perplexing moments when prayers are not answered and the equally perplexing moments when they are. They shoulder the burden of a community with a vision of holiness and unity that stands in contrast to its inevitable pettiness and cruelties of daily living. They attempt to make sense out of a large picture of human interaction that includes the values of faith, commitment, deepest doubts and anger focused on a seemingly uncaring God and swelling rejoicing and gratitude focused on a seemingly loving and watchful God.

This is a crucial point. It describes what Mormon women have, for whatever reasons, done more often and better than men: that is, look at the depths and heights of human experience, not just the middle ground. Anderson herself gives us one of the finest examples of "spiritual realism" in her June 1982 Exponent Day Dinner Speech; published in *Exponent II*, it is entitled "On Being Happy: An Exercise in Spiritual Autobiography"[10] and exemplifies the special voice we men need to listen to and imitate–clear, elegant but witty, contained, noble but unselfconscious, afraid neither of pain nor proper piety, clearly witness both to the hard surface of life and to its deeper mysteries, attuned to both the body and the spirit:

In 1973, I accepted a position on the Ensign *staff and moved to Salt Lake City. Making that decision was difficult for me, not only because I felt that I had finally hit my stride in my chosen field, but because I didn't know if I wanted to work for the Church. I'd already seen some of the difficulties an official publication has when I'd worked for the* Daily Universe *at Brigham Young University. As I was praying about what the right thing would be to do, the answer I got was a curiously oblique one but exactly the right one. (Many of my prayers are answered by a distinctively sarcastic personage whom I've come to regard as a kind of guardian angel.) It assured me that my friendship with Karen would not suffer. I hadn't realized it myself, but that question–which I had not been asking–was the only one I needed the answer to. So I went.*

After summarizing her unusual courtship with Paul Anderson, marked by her resistance due to being "thoroughly and happily single," she describes her struggle to find the right questions to ask in her prayers about marrying Paul and then continues:

I received extremely clear information about all of those topics. I received insight into my attitudes about privacy, money, priesthood, professionalism, and ability to communicate that was somewhat shocking though not, I'll have to admit, very surprising. But possibly the most important question that I asked was, "What kind of person is Paul?" In answer to that question, I had the closest thing to a vision I have ever experienced. A personage with a definable personality told me, almost in so many words, "Let me show you how I feel about Paul," and then I experienced that person's feelings for Paul: the deepest, most profound sensations of love and a respectful savoring of personality. There was not a question in my mind that I was in the presence of someone who knew Paul differently and better than I did or possibly could know him, someone who loved him totally. I acquired an awesome amount of respect for Paul quite suddenly.

There were other issues to be worked through, but one sunny day, as I knelt again in prayer, I asked again, "Should I marry Paul?" expecting to learn of a new question I should ask. Instead, I was distinctly told, "You have enough information to make that decision now." I was stunned. I was supposed to make the decision? Yes. There was a long internal pause, a kind of mental breathholding, then I said, still on my knees, "Yes, I will marry Paul." The reaction could not have been more vivid, an explosion of pleasure and excitement like being in the center of a fireworks display. It surprised me, pleased me, gratified me, and humbled me simultaneously. I knew that all of these emotions were not my own, and the delight shared with other presences who cared about the decision was reassuring in ways I don't even know how to begin to describe. One of the consequences has been that I have never had to question the initial rightness of the decision nor had to wonder if I made a mistake. (That's been important. I may be crazy about Paul, but I'm not crazy about being married.)

There are, of course, other such voices: There is Carole Hansen, who, in "The Death of a Son," was the first Mormon to tell us *in faith* of priesthood blessings that seemed to fail.[11] There is Claudia Bushman, writing of death with a majestic honesty and assurance not heard among Mormon men since John Taylor wrote (see D&C 135) about Joseph Smith's:

When I entered the room I came face to face with reality, for there was my mother, cold and dead. Her naked body had been laid out under a sheet on a high platform. Her face and hair had been nicely done, and she looked as if she were asleep. Although I knew why we had come, the shock of seeing her there, her presence so familiar and so different, distressed me greatly. [*My sisters and I] wept a few tears, trying to accept and understand the great and alarming mystery before us, and then we set to work.*

Action may not always solve problems, but it temporarily removed the need to try. The question of how to confront death was put aside when the practical need became how to put complex garments on an inert and somewhat stiff figure. Aunt Jane taught us some of the necessary techniques as we went along. We worked together turning the body on one side and the other, in easing here and slipping under there. They had brought in an iron and a little board for us to touch up some of the clothes. We bustled about as if this were some regular housekeeping task, as it has been for women over the ages.

We put on the garments and the slip and the new dress. She wanted to wear her own temple robes so we put those on, including the brilliant green apron I had once embroidered for her, easily the brightest in any temple session. I also made some little white velvet and felt shoes for her for temple wear, but she had considered them too fragile to use. She had written that she would like to wear them for the occasion. In working these little shoes over her stiff, cold feet, I overcame any aversion I first felt about touching the dead.

After Mother was all dressed, we stayed around for quite a time discussing arrangements. By then we were more comfortable with her body, and one or another of us held her hand as we talked. She felt just the same, just cold.

We stepped out when the men came to transfer her body to the coffin, a white one as requested with some gold accents. We felt good about the way she looked. We added a favorite piece of music to the coffin, "Ah, love, but a day, and the world has changed. . . ," and a ring we had found in a drawer dating from my parents' early courtship. I felt that our morning's work had been well done.[12]

How I yearn to know how other Mormon men feel in the face of such unusual experience. We know much more about Mormon women's feelings.

There is Dian Saderup, a young woman who wrote the extraordinary story "A Blessing of Duty" that appeared in *Sunstone* a few years ago[13]; it is a finely tuned, uncompromising but compassionate, creation of the feelings of a young mother, worn and torn to near exhaustion and despair by all the demands made on her, yet unsentimentally enduring in faith. (We don't yet have male voices creating for us how her husband, a weary, enduring elders' quorum president, might feel.) Here is Saderup's voice, in a personal essay that bravely and tenderly reports, again for the first time in Mormon literature, from inside a bishop's court. She goes to support a friend who has sinned seriously and persistently; she has herself been somewhat inactive, alienated, but has now begun to feel the spirit return to help her help her desperate friend:

I sat next to Carol in a big shiny dark wood chair—the kind I remember seeing on TV's Divorce Court *as a child. The Bishop was there, and so were his two counselors and the ward clerk. The clerk asked my name, then asked me to spell it so he'd get it right on the official record. He was a small, dark-complexioned man with a harelip. He didn't say anything else the whole time, but sat like a silent mole burrowed into the corner, his head bowed over the endless notes he scratched on his paper. The first counselor sat across the large conference table from me. He looked about thirty-two, had deep acne scars on his face, and wore a plaid, imitation-Pendleton jacket over his broad thin shoulders and spider arms. His smile was wide and spread slowly across his face when the Bishop introduced him to me: unlike both Carol and me, he hadn't had braces on his teeth as a teenager. His eyes were the gems of his body—glittering, translucent stones set in an ill-cut length of pitted hardwood. They were the color of Bear Lake. They were intelligent and kind eyes. I don't remember the second counselor very well. He sat directly to my right, three seats down, out of my immediate line of vision. He smiled whenever I glanced his way, and as I talked, marched the fingers of his left hand, which was stretched in front of him, silently upon the table from index to pinkie, forward and back, like a four note scale repeated again and again on the piano. The Bishop asked me to tell a little about myself, then with a question mark in his voice said, "Carol tells us you are an active, committed member of the Church." The past year was my business, and God's. I said, "Yes, I am."*

Then I started talking, explaining what I knew of Carol and her problems over the years. Much like the night I prayed with Carol when she was so upset long ago at BYU, the words flowed and I can't remember now what exactly I said: things, I think, about her father, her deep— if not apparent— feelings for the Lord and the Gospel, and her terrible frustration at her failures to live faithfully. At some point she reached over and took hold of my hand. Then a strange thing happened, strange for me at least: I started crying, so hard that I couldn't talk for several minutes. I rarely cry in private (especially not of late) and almost never in public, but the steel in me that had been so mysteriously softening over the past hour suddenly melted completely, like ice in fire. I remember a symposium on world religions I attended several years ago at BYU. A holy man from India spoke on the Buddhist (or was it Hindu?) belief system. Using a fable, he explained that the ultimate transcendence of the world and its cares for his people lay in experiencing what he could only describe as an "unutterable gush of compassion," whether for an individual or the whole of humanity. Sitting in the Divorce Court *chair in this Mormon Bishop's office, I experienced a pure and purifying "gush of compassion" for Carol, a giant surge of the gift of comfort. Carol began to cry and her mascara ran in black streams down her cheeks. The Bishop lowered his head. The first counselor rubbed his scarred face with three flat fingers, his Bear-lake eyes all the more bright from unspilled tears. The second counselor's fingers marched silently. The clerk's pencil stopped. When I could finally talk again I said, "I guess that's all I have to say."*

The Bishop asked Carol a few more questions, and then she and I stood up to leave the office while he and his counselors deliberated.

He rose and came to her, taking her hand. He spoke quietly, and said, as nearly as I can remember, "The Lord is full of grace, Carol. Let yourself accept that and take joy in his gifts. In my life I've had moments of peace and inspiration and encouragement from our Heavenly Father. Sometimes they even come when I know I'm not really worthy and I think he's furthest away. Just remembering those moments helps me get through the dark times in the way I should. He loves us. You're a precious girl." It was the first time I'd ever heard a Bishop say the word grace.[14]

It was another of God's daughters, Linda Sillitoe, who was the first modern Mormon to reach back to our foremother, Eliza, and daringly speculate about that most fundamental metaphysical idea–the eternal, *married* companionship of the Gods, as she does in her poem "Song of Creation."[15] And it was another daughter, Eileen Kump, who in her story "Sayso or Sense"[16] took on one of the most explosive subjects in Mormonism, one that derives from that eternal companionship of the sexes–that is, authority in the priesthood as it affects men and women; and Kump there handles that difficult subject more helpfully and yet more delicately than any *man* has, except Joseph Smith, in the 121st section of the Doctrine and Covenants. But then he also was writing from prison, as well as bravely and clearly– from Liberty Jail, in 1839, as part of a letter to the Saints:

The rights of the priesthood are inseparably connected with the powers of heaven, and . . . the powers of heaven cannot be controlled nor handled only with the principles of righteousness.

. . . when we undertake to . . . exercise control or dominion or compulsion upon the souls of the children of men, in any degree of unrighteousness, behold the heavens withdraw themselves.

We have learned by sad experience that it is the nature and disposition of almost all men, as soon as they get a little authority, as they suppose, they will immediately begin to exercise unrighteous dominion.

No power or influence can or ought to be maintained by virtue of the priesthood, only by persuasion, by long-suffering, by gentleness and meekness, and by love unfeigned.

. . . let virtue garnish thy thoughts unceasingly; then shall thy confidence wax strong in the presence of God; and the doctrine of the priesthood shall distil upon thy soul as the dews from heaven.

The Holy Ghost shall be thy constant companion, and thy scepter an unchanging scepter of righteousness and truth; and thy dominion shall be an everlasting dominion, and without compulsory means it shall flow unto thee forever and ever.

That passage is the clearest warning anywhere about the destructiveness of seeing priesthood as power rather than duty to serve–a warning both to men who think they have such power and to women who want to get it. And it shows how clearly the role of oppressor is more destructive to the oppressor than to the oppressed, whether in a patriarchy or a matriarchy.

But many Mormon *men* as well as women have understood the 121st section and resisted the seductions of authority. Where are their free and creative voices? Of course, some are being heard, but perhaps too many Mormon men are emulating the wrong voices. The Mormon patriarchy tends to produce, as models for men, the firm, invulnerable voice of success: the voice in the middle, about setting goals, establishing yourself, and being simply good, not about the dark night of the soul or its exaltation. That is the voice we hear most–or think we hear–from bishops, stake presidents, and general authorities, even academic leaders. May I suggest that we all, men and women, listen more closely to certain other voices as well: Read the women I have mentioned and other new voices that are developing in the third generation of Mormon writers–our contemporaries, an excellent sampling of which is gathered in Mary Bradford's recent collection, *Mormon Women Speak* [17].

But there are men with that voice of spiritual realism too, some, if we need it, men of authority. Spencer W. Kimball gives us, sometimes very subtly, the evocative, risky, vulnerable prophetic voice, as well as the safe priestly one. Read the parts of his journal quoted in the biography by Edward and Andrew Kimball or the separately printed excerpt,

One Long and Sleepless Night,[18] overwhelming in their revelation of his own sense of inadequacy but determination, of both his pain and his profound spiritual encounters. Read his fierce denunciation, in 1954, of Mormons who hold aloof from the Indians,[19] or the 1976 rebuke of our materialism and jingoism in "The False Gods We Worship,"[20] or his attack on Mormon blood sports in the 1978 address, "Don't Kill the Little Birds."[21] A new volume, *The Teachings of Spencer W. Kimball,* is a good place to start.[22] And we might read LeGrand Richards (or better, get tapes if we can), to hear his gentle, fierce voice, his stark testimonies, his emotions uncensored by the teleprompter.

We men have failed to listen carefully to the voice of prophetic warning, even from other men, and have not let that voice affect our own. For instance, in a First Presidency Statement in 1969 Hugh B. Brown encouraged us to pray for the time when all men could hold the priesthood. Most of us did not listen and respond; President Kimball offered such prayers and received a revelation. After that revelation Elder Bruce R. McConkie pointed out that President Kimball had gotten the revelation because he asked in faith and wanted an answer: "It was a matter of faith and righteousness and seeking on the one hand, and it was a matter of the divine timetable on the other hand."[23] Elder McConkie also stated that because of the revelation there was new meaning in a familiar scripture (II Nephi 26:33): "[Christ] inviteth them all to come unto him and partake of his goodness; and he denieth none that come unto him, black and white, bond and free, male and female . . . and all are alike unto God, both Jew and Gentile." According to Elder McConkie, "Many of us never imagined or supposed that these passages had the extensive and broad meaning that they do have," and it seems to me he calls us to greater vigilance against such misunderstanding in the future. But I don't see many of us men creatively exploring how it is that we may *still* misunderstand how *male* and *female* are alike to God just as we used to misunderstand how black and white were. For instance, I still hear men repeat the deceptively belittling speculation that women cannot be Sons of Perdition–seeming to imply that women are too righteous, but really implying that women without the priesthood can't know enough. And few men, compared to the increasing number of women, are thinking about and questioning the most sexist idea in Mormonism: that polygamy is the ideal, celestial state of marriage–which is, in fact, a most questionable idea.

We need to listen to the voice of Elder B. H. Roberts, who, after quoting Josiah Royce's description of two kinds of religious disciples, the mere partisans, who expound and defend "faithful to one formula," and those who "bring to the new teaching, from the first, their own personal contribution," writes this:

I believe "Mormonism" affords opportunity for disciples of the second sort: nay, that its crying need is for such disciples. It calls for thoughtful disciples who will not be content with merely repeating some of the truths, but will develop its truths; and enlarge it by that development. Not half–not one-hundredth part–not a thousandth part of that which Joseph Smith revealed to the Church has yet been unfolded, either to the Church or to the world. The work of the expounder has scarcely begun. The Prophet planted by teaching the germ-truths of the great dispensation of the fulness of times. The watering and the weeding is going on, and God is giving the increase, and will give it more abundantly in the future as more intelligent discipleship shall obtain. The disciples of "Mormonism," growing discontented with the necessarily primitive methods which have hitherto prevailed in sustaining the doctrine, will yet take profounder and broader views of the great doctrines committed to the Church; and, departing from mere repetition, will cast them in new formulas; cooperating in the works of the Spirit, until they help to give to the truths received a more forceful expression *and carry it beyond the earlier and cruder stages of its development.*[24]

Let me add to that a confirming modern testimony from a woman, Lavina Fielding Anderson in that Presidential Address quoted earlier:

I had an experience this summer [at a gathering of Mormon women in Nauvoo] that has made me think about that particular vow of consecration [that Mormons make in the temple] in a new way. Catherine Stokes, a black convert in a Chicago ward, related the experience of going to the temple for the first time. "I took my blackness with me," she said, "and that was part of what I consecrated." She told of the woman who assisted her in the initiatory ordinances, barely able to articulate through her tears, and apologizing at the end because she had not wanted her personal emotions to interfere with Cathy's experience. "But I've never had the privilege of doing this for a black woman before," she explained, "and I'm so grateful." Cathy reassured her, "That's all right. That's one of the things I can do for you *that no one else in the temple today could do." As she summed up the experience, she added, "My blackness is one of the things that the Lord can use if he wants to"–and apparently it has been a most successful collaboration.*

I realized I had always assumed that the Lord wanted only my strengths, my abilities, and my competencies. It had not occurred to me that qualities I considered to be unique idiosyncracies or even weaknesses might be equally useful to him but that I, in wrongful humility, was withholding them from consecration.

And if those witnesses seem too remote or unspecific or unauthoritative, if we need a modern prophet to make us as brave as women in exploring both the tragedies and the exaltations of our faith, listen again to the voice of Spencer W. Kimball:

For years I have been waiting for someone to do justice in recording in song and story and painting and sculpture the story of the Restoration, the reestablishment of the kingdom of God on earth, the struggles and frustrations*; the* apostasies and inner revolutions and counter-revolutions *of those first decades; of the exodus; of the* counter-reactions*; of the transitions; of the persecution days; of* the miracleman, *Joseph Smith, of whom we sing "Oh, what* rapture *filled his bosom, For he saw the living God."*[25]

NOTES

1. Mary L. Bradford, from an address, "The Secret Sharers: Utah Women Writers," delivered at the Utah Retrenchment Society meetings, April 1976, and quoted in Linda Sillitoe, "New voices, New Songs: Contemporary Poems by Mormon Women," *Dialogue* 13 (Winter 1980): 48.

2. See my essay, "The Dawning of a Brighter Day: Mormon Literature after 150 Years," *BYU Studies* 22 (Spring 1982): 131-60; also printed in *After 150 Years*, Thomas G. Alexander and Jessie L. Embry, eds. (Midvale, Utah: Signature Books, 1983), pp. 95-146.

3. *Mormon Sisters*, Claudia Bushman, ed. (Cambridge, Mass.: Emmeline Press, 1976; rpt. Salt Lake City: Olympus Publishing Co., 1982); *Sister Saints*, Vicky Burgess-Olson, ed. (Provo, Utah: BYU Press, 1978); and *Mormon Women Speak*, Mary Lythgoe Bradford, ed. (Salt Lake City: Olympus Publishing Co., 1983).

4. See especially essays published in various Mormon publications by Lavina Fielding Anderson, Mary Lythgoe Bradford, Claudia Lauper Bushman, Judy Dushku, Dian Saderup, and Laurel Ulrich; and see poetry by Elouise Bell, Marilyn Brown, Carol Lynn Pearson, Vernice Pere, Linda Sillitoe, and Emma Lou Thayne.

5. See stories published in Mormon publications by Eileen Kump (and her collection, *Bread and Milk and Other Stories*, published by BYU Press, 1979), Phyllis Barber, Karen Rosenbaum, Dian Saderup, and Linda Sillitoe.

6. See the select bibliography appended to my essay on Mormon literature, cited above in note 2.

7. Wilford Woodruff, "Discourse," *Latter-day Saints' Millennial Star* 56 (9 April 1894): 229; cited in Maureen Ursenbach Beecher, "The Eliza Enigma," *Dialogue* 11 (Spring 1978): 37.

8. Published in *A Believing People: The Literature of the Latter-day Saints*, Richard H. Cracroft and Neal E. Lambert, eds. (Provo, Utah: BYU Press, 1974; rpt. Salt Lake City: Bookcraft, 1979), pp. 143-150; the quotation is from p. 145.

9. Edward Geary, "Mormondom's Lost Generation: The Novelists of the 1940s," *BYU Studies* 18 (Fall 1977): 89-98; see also his "The Poetics of Provincialism: Mormon Regional Fiction," *Dialogue* 11 (Summer 1978): 15-24. Sorensen's *The Evening and the Morning*, published by Harcourt, Brace, and Co. in 1949, is now out of print; Whipple's *The Giant Joshua*, first published by Houghton Mifflin in 1941, was reprinted in Salt Lake City by Western Epics in 1976.

10. Published in *Exponent II* 9 (Fall 1982): 1-3.
11. Carole Hansen, "The Death of a Son," *Dialogue* 2 (Autumn 1967): 91-96.
12. Claudia Lauper Bushman, "Light and Dark Thoughts on Death," *Dialogue* 14 (Winter 1981): 169-77.
13. Dian Saderup, "A Blessing of Duty," *Sunstone* 4 (May-June 1979): 17-20.
14. Dian Saderup, "The Grace of the Court," *Inscape* 2 (Fall-Winter 1983): 44-58.
15. Linda Sillitoe, "Song of Creation," *Dialogue* 12 (Winter 1979): 95.
16. Eileen Kump, "Sayso or Sense," in *Bread and Milk and Other Stories* (Provo, Utah: BYU Press, 1979).
17. See my review of this collection in *Sunstone Review* 3 (April-May 1983): 29-31.
18. Spencer W. Kimball, *One Long and Sleepless Night* (Salt Lake City: Bookcraft, 1975).
19. Spencer W. Kimball, "The Evil of Intolerance," *Improvement Era* 57 (June 1954): 423-26.
20. Spencer W. Kimball, "The False Gods We Worship," *Ensign* 6 (June 1976): 3-6.
21. Spencer W. Kimball, "Strengthening the Family," *Ensign* 8 (May 1978): 45–48.
22. *The Teachings of Spencer W. Kimball*, Edward L. Kimball, ed. (Salt Lake City: Bookcraft, 1982).
23. Bruce R. McConkie, "All Are Alike Unto God," speech given 18 August 1978, collected in *Charge to Religious Educators* (Salt Lake City: The Church of Jesus Christ of Latter-day Saints, 2nd ed., 1982), p. 152.
24. B. H. Roberts, "The Book of Mormon's Place," *Improvement Era* 9 (1906): 712-13; my emphasis.
25. Spencer W. Kimball, "The Gospel Vision of the Arts," *Ensign* 7 (July 1977): 5; my emphasis.

The opening statement for a defense of Mormons as Christians, sponsored by *Sunstone,* May 1983; a version of this to be published in *BYU Today,* Summer 1984.

CHAPTER 15

WHAT IT MEANS TO BE A MORMON CHRISTIAN

Three years ago I conducted a group of Mormon students through the ruins of the Palace of Caiaphas, not far from Gethsemane, where Christ was taken after his suffering in the Garden. He was there arraigned, abused, probably beaten, illegally tried before being taken before Pilate the next morning. As my group moved on through the dungeons, I stopped to look back into a room built like a huge bottle, with only a top entrance where Christ may well have been lowered by his bound hands to spend part of the night after being tortured. I heard a group behind us–Methodists I learned later–stop and softly begin to sing a hymn, one I didn't know but was deeply moved by, about Christ being wounded for us. I felt solidarity with those pious believers in Christ as Savior, shared their trust in the efficacy of his suffering and death as the ultimate and necessary source of our salvation, and wept a bit with them. Later that day, our group had its own time of hymn singing and reading from the New Testament, at the Garden Tomb, which is preserved in refreshing simplicity by British Protestants. We sang some hymns most Christians would recognize, like "I Know That My Redeemer Lives" and "There is a Green Hill Far Away," and also some that bear our own particular Mormon Christian witness, like this one by Eliza R. Snow:

How great the wisdom and the love
That filled the courts on high
And sent the Savior from above
To suffer, bleed, and die!

His precious blood he freely spilt;
His life he freely gave,
A sinless sacrifice for guilt,
A dying world to save.

Then each of us meditated by ourselves, walking through the garden and into the tomb. As I stood inside the tomb vestibule, through the window I heard a mother, American Evangelical Protestant I would guess from her idiom, telling her young son about the resurrection and, with tears in her voice, bearing her witness to him that Christ had indeed risen from the grave and therefore all people, including his dead grandparents, would be raised too.

We visited other places in Israel that are sacred to many because of Christ, such as Bethlehem, and some of my students were disappointed–as others, especially Protestants, have told me they were–because the sites were built over with churches or encrusted with the paraphernalia of Catholic worship: lamps, crosses, etc. But I found myself able to be moved deeply by such places–because of the evidence there of hundreds of years of humble pilgrimage by Christians to those spots sacred in tradition. I felt part of a great community of faith, one of the millions over the centuries moved by our hope in Christ to make a pilgrimage there–to places made sacred not only by Jesus but by all those of us who go there to worship him as our Divine Savior. We returned to our study center in England where I continued with new vigor and understanding to teach my Mormon students two things: that they were part of an ancient religious tradition which they should know and appreciate, from the Old Testament prophets and forerunners to the New Testament apostles and evangelists and the early Church fathers, then the great scholastics and cathedral builders of the Medieval age of faith, to the great reformers and martyrs and translators, Luther and Calvin, Tyndale and Wycliffe, Thomas More and Charles Wesley, and, in America, Roger Williams and Jonathan Edwards. But that they also had their own special witness to bear, their own tradition, with its own special emphases and precious revelations, which at its best taught them both to identify with that great Christian tradition and to challenge it and other religious traditions, in love, with their own unique Christian witness.

I find the basis for this difficult, seemingly contradictory, stance in the New Testament. Paul taught it this way: "Prove all things; hold fast that which is good" (I Thess. 5:22). And in rereading the New Testament I have found that stance verified constantly by Christ. He does not use the term Christian, of course, and he proposed no creed. But while Jesus defines his followers as uniquely open and loving, universal in their sympathy and acceptance of others, just as he is the universal Savior, he also defines them as standing clearly for something *specific* and committed to bear witness of that to others. It is something rather simple: First he calls for *faith* in himself, Christ, as uniquely the Savior of mankind; second he asks commitment to and expression of *hope* in him through initial baptism and then regular symbolic renewal through the sacrament of the last supper, partaking of his body and blood in remembrance and to preserve the Holy Spirit with them; and finally, besides faith and hope, he commands what Paul designated "the greatest of all," *charity*: "A new commandment I give unto you, That ye love one another; as I have loved you, that ye also love one another. By *this* shall all men know that ye are my disciples, if ye have love one to another" (John 13: 35; my emphasis).

But what kind of love? "God so loved the world, that he gave his only begotten son, that whosoever believeth in him should not perish, but have everlasting life" (John 3:16). It is *unconditional* love, not constrained by differences in belief–or even by others' wrong doing. Paul exclaimed, "While we were yet sinners, Christ died for us"(Romans 5:8). And Christ called upon his disciples to "Love your enemies, bless them that curse you, do good to them that hate you, and pray for them which despitefully use you, and persecute you. That ye may be the children of your Father which is in heaven" (Matthew 5:44-45). Christ gave a simple test by which to know those following this direction–in other words, by which we may *best* recognize true Christians: "Ye shall know them by their fruits. . . . A good tree cannot bring forth evil fruit, neither can a corrupt tree bring forth good fruit" (Matthew 7:16, 18). And he was tolerant in the application of that test, restricting it to deeds, not ideas or professions or creeds:

John answered him saying, Master, we saw one casting out devils in thy name, and he followeth not us: and we forbad him, because he followeth not us. But Jesus said, Forbid him not: for there is no man which shall do a miracle in my name, that can lightly speak evil of me. For he that is not against us is on our part. (Mark 9: 38-40)

Christ would leave it to *no one* to define Christ–or Christians–for others: "If any man say unto you, Lo here is Christ, or there; believe it not. For there shall arise false Christs, and false prophets, and shall shew signs and wonders; insomuch that, if it were possible they shall deceive the very elect" (Matthew 24: 23-24). Instead in the very next chapter of Matthew, he gives one simple test by which we will all be judged by God and must judge ourselves, as to whether we are among Christ's sheep, whether we are "Christians":

For I was an hungered, and ye gave me meat: I was thirsty, and ye gave me drink, I was a stranger, and ye took me in: Naked and ye clothed me: I was sick and ye visited me: I was in prison and ye came unto me. . . . Inasmuch as ye have done it unto one of the least of these my brethren, ye have done it unto me. (Matthew 25:35-40)

And a few pages later we have Christ's simple, final commission to his disciples: "Go ye therefore, and teach all nations, baptizing them in the name of the Father and of the Son, and of the Holy Ghost" (Matthew 28:19).

Mormons meet these simple criteria, established by Jesus Christ himself, not perfectly but well, as well as any other groups calling themselves Christian. We therefore have as much right, no more, no less, to call ourselves Christian. I ask that Mormons–and all other Christians–be respected in that right, and be loved and accepted in that spirit, especially by any who would themselves claim to be Christian. As I understand the New Testament a basic test of whether one *is* Christian is his love and tolerance of others, however different their theology. Thus the commonly asked question whether Mormons are Christian can be in itself an unChristian question, even a direct offense to Christ–unless perhaps if it is asked purely in the spirit of a quest for the mutual understanding and love that he taught. Let me try to promote that spirit here.

But first let us face honestly the fact that the question of whether Mormons are Christian currently rises most often out of a growing intolerance of and persecution of Mormons, a specific, planned, public attack, making use of public media, sponsored by some Christian churches and Christian presses and broadcasting stations as well as individuals. It is an attack that has many of the same characteristics and spirit as the shameful extremes of anti-Masonic and anti-Catholic movements of the nineteenth century and of anti-Communism and especially anti-Semitism in our recent past: It is clearly motivated by fear and jealousy. It indulges in stereotypes and name-calling. It does not engage in careful, honest exploration of issues with a view to finding truth together and living in love together. Instead, by combining obscure, unofficial statements by various Mormons it creates a parody of our theology which most Mormons themselves would reject and then attacks that parody as a "cult." It creates fear and irrational prejudice (exactly as has been done against Jews) by calling up images of wicked, secret rites, of mass deception, of sexual looseness, of unbridled political and economic power and conspiracies. We forget easily: A book like Peter Bart's *Thy Kingdom Come*, which uses precisely the techniques of Nazi propaganda, would not be endured in this country if it were about Jews. Because it is about Mormons it is praised. Most Christians are not inclined, I trust, to use these techniques and excesses, and so I hope we can do something constructive in dialogue with each other. My purpose here is to affirm what it means to be a Christian, to suggest how we could all be better Christians, and to try to show how differences between Christians can provide an opportunity to learn from, rather than attack, each other.

Dictionaries, other generally accepted sources, and common sense all suggest there are three ways the term Christian is properly used: first, to designate those who claim to follow Christ, whatever the variants of their theology; second, to indicate those who confess a particular set of beliefs that is generally defined as Christian; and third, to identify those who live in a certain way generally called Christian. On the first category there can be no argument. Mormons have as much right to *call themselves* Christian as anyone. Who then has the right to judge them on the second and third categories: creed and ethical standards?

Mormons find it ironic to be labeled non-Christian at a time when they have been among the few Christian groups standing firm against various liberal Protestant and Catholic attempts to demythologize the New Testament accounts of Christ, to make Christ more a mystical, symbolic idea than a literal, redeeming, divine person. Mormons are aghast at the general loss of belief in a literal bodily resurrection guaranteed by Christ, at the declining belief in Christ's literal return to the earth to reign over a real millennium, at the retreat among Christians, sometimes led by their ministers, from definite ethical standards about care of the body, about chastity, about abortion and euthanasia, about the evils of war and luxury. We are appalled by an increasing relativism and purely situational ethic generally in Christianity.

But Mormons do differ theologically from other Christians in some important ways—and certainly Mormons, both individually and as a group, fail to live fully the high ethic of Christ-like love. And that is what we should discuss, for understanding and improvement. My initial and minimal point is that the doctrinal differences are not departures from the scriptures but merely from other Christian interpretations, whose proponents have no more right to claim orthodoxy than Mormons, and that the ethical failures are certainly no greater than those of other Christians. We are sinners all.

Mormons affirm, with the New Testament and all Christians, that we are saved by Christ. The question is *how?* Appeal to the Bible has not kept Christian groups from wide diversity on that question. Medieval Catholicism, for political and economic as well as theological reasons, moved to the position that Christ's salvation was administered only through the Church and specifically through a form of works that required participation in Church-administered sacraments, including penance and forgiveness of sins. This allowed the monstrous but logical perversion by Tetzel, the sale of "indulgences" or payment, even in advance, for sins. Obviously the idea of salvation by works is dangerous, pernicious, offensive to the New Testament message–and Luther and later Calvin were properly offended. They brought the Reformation to life in the energy of rediscovered personal choice and commitment to Christ and the sense of his grace as central to salvation. Mormons believe these Reformers were inspired directly by God, and Mormon scriptures and official doctrines all affirm unequivocally that salvation, all of it and in every sense (including "exaltation"), is by and through the grace of Christ (see especially Doctrine and Covenants 20:30–31, where both of the technical theological terms, "justification" and "sanctification," are used to affirm full dependence on Christ's grace).

But Luther and Calvin, over-reacting to the extremes of Tetzel's narrow view of salvation, went to their own narrow, and unscriptural, extremes. The official Lutheran movie of the life of Martin Luther shows him at the crucial moment, in his monk's cell, reading the crucial passage from Romans,"that a man is justified by faith." And the movie unashamedly shows Luther writing in the margin: *sola*, alone. But the New Testament *does not say* we are saved by faith *alone*; it makes the importance of works and ordinances clear in many places and many ways (and not just in the Book of James, which Luther tried to demean by calling it the "straw" epistle because it clearly contradicted his extreme position). The New Testament shows that grace is essential but not absolute, or sufficient. *Solafideism* (salvation by faith alone) is as unscriptural as Tetzel's reliance on hypocritical works, on *buying* salvation. And so is Calvin's set of logical extremes: predestination to salvation or damnation, the irresistibility of God's grace upon those he chooses to save, the perseverence in grace of those so chosen, despite all appearances in their evil actions to the contrary. We must *respond* to grace, grow in grace, show forth *fruit* meet for salvation. The Mormon position is that we are saved by grace, that salvation is a free gift, made available only through the life and teaching, the suffering and death of Christ. But Mormon theology recognizes the crucial role of agency; it posits the genuinely free will of God's children and thus their ability and need to accept the gift of grace and grow in it through that continuing acceptance and response–that is, through sincerely performing the ordinances and producing sincere and obedient good works. We define faith, as ordinary usage certainly suggests, as *behavior* based on *commitment*, that is, as *including* good works.

But Mormonism is not a mere *amalgam* of salvation by grace and works, both of which notions are subject to severe abuses. Works, as Tetzel showed Luther, can be performed hypocritically or out of cultural habit, not out of faith in Christ. It would be foolish to rely on them as a basis for salvation. But the notion of grace alone can be just as easily perverted. It can, as Paul warned, be license to sin or, as Protestants themselves constantly warn, can take the form of "cheap grace"; as they sometimes ironically express the danger, "The world is admirably arranged. God likes to forgive sinners. I like to sin." Emphasis on grace can also suggest a God who created beings and a world out of nothing, for no discernible purpose, puts them through incredible suffering and exposes them to all forms of evil, and then chooses to lift *some* out of the mire through his inscrutable grace. Life thus may seem to be an incomprehensible game played by a sadistic God, and the huge loss of faith in modern times seems to me directly related to such a view, one an emphasis on "salvation by grace alone" inevitably promotes.

Mormon Christians believe that salvation is neither an incomprehensible game of irresistible grace nor something that can be hypocritically bought with the appearance of good works. We believe in the New Testament call to *become* new creatures in Christ. Salvation is not an exterior thing, merely given or bought, but a genuine becoming, a complete, absolute, gradual (or sometimes sudden) permanent change to a new being; it is made possible only through Christ but is also only possible through our own unforced choice to respond to him and grow in his grace through the sacraments and service. Salvation is ultimately a matter of what we *are* when we face Christ at the judgment bar. It is not merely what *he* has made us, for then he would be entirely responsible for what we were or *were not*, and it is not merely what *we* have made ourselves, because we could have made *nothing* of ourselves without Christ's grace. Christ's gospel is the *power* of God unto salvation; his teachings and his unconditional love, expressed ultimately in Gethsemane and on the cross, uniquely give us power to repent, to become and remain "new creatures." The Book of Mormon makes that central Christian affirmation this way:

That great and last sacrifice will be the Son of God, yea, infinite and eternal. And thus [*Christ*] *shall bring salvation to all those who shall believe on his name; this being the intent of this last sacrifice, to bring about the bowels of mercy, which overpowereth justice, and* bringeth about means *unto men that they* may *have faith unto repentance. (Alma 34:15; my emphasis)*

It can be said that such a comprehensive view of salvation—as involving grace *and* works *and* ordinances in a realistic integration that leads to genuine repentance and newness—is *more* logical and scriptural than the limited concepts espoused by other Christian groups. It can be said that Mormon doctrine, which explicitly provides for that same process of salvation for *all* mankind, living and dead, before and after Christ, is most fully in the universalist spirit of Christ himself—"Salvator Mundi," savior of all the world. And such claims *have* been made, to the convincing of many converts to Mormonism, including intelligent, well-trained ministers, priests, and lay theologians. But Mormons do not thus claim to be the *only* Christians or exclude any groups which make claim to be so. We recognize that the experience of Atonement with Christ through his grace and through our response is not so much a matter of theology as experience. People with widely varying concepts of how it happens can experience that Atonement and enter the strait gate. The whole point of our message to the world is to *add*, to provide, on the basis of modern revelation, additional, clarifying concepts, new witnesses that will increase and expand others' faith in Christ.

As a young missionary in Samoa I once taught a fine woman who was listening to me only out of cultural politeness until I told her that Christ's salvation would apply to her pagan ancestors whom she knew had been idolatrous, even cannibalistic. It could apply, not through some incomprehensible "Kings-X," such as that God sent them to earth at the wrong—or right—time and so excused them from having to have faith in Christ and live his commandments. It applied because those ancestors were alive in the spirit world, were there hearing the gospel preached, and were committing themselves to Christ, aided by the love of people on this earth expressed as they performed baptism and other ordinances with and for them. Her eyes filled with tears. Already a Christian, she became a Mormon Christian, not in *rejection* of Christ or her faith in him but with *additional* understanding and rejoicing in his universal saving grace.

As a student I sat in a class in Christian ethics at Stanford University and heard the great Presbyterian theologian, Robert McAfee Brown, with tears in his eyes, say he was considered a heretic in his church because he could not accept the traditional Protestant concept of final judgment at death; he could not conceive of a God who was limited in his saving love and power, who had to stop it merely because we died. He imagined that in *some* way Christ continued to teach and love those of us who had no or little chance to know him on earth and that, therefore, there must be a continuing way to repent and be saved. I could tell him something specific about that way because of revelation to modern prophets that has come not in contradiction to the New Testament but in clarification of the scriptures on Christ's preaching to the dead and on vicarious baptism for the dead. Surely Mormonism is not *less* Christian because it is *more* comprehensive and universalist in its understanding of Christ's saving role.

How about Mormon ethics? The question is often whether *Mormons*, as well as Mormon ideas, are Christian. Mormon *ideals* are certainly as high as others! Our personal morality—respect and care for the body, honesty, chastity, in both the expressed ideals and in statistically measured practice—is impressive to outside observers and bears visible fruit in the health and appearance, the longevity and stability of our people, families, and communities. But what about the ultimate ethic of Christlike love—constant unselfish service to the hungry, homeless, and imprisoned and genuine love of, even service to, our enemies. Here Mormons, like all Christians, fall short. But it is not because of a lack of proper belief and leadership. The Book of Mormon teaches the ethic as clearly and unequivocally as the New Testament, in some ways more clearly. For instance, it includes the only account in scripture—or in history, that I can find–of a group living out the love ethic to its ultimate consequences in personal sacrifice and redemptive power. They allow themselves to be massacred rather than take up arms, and their example moves their attackers to repentance–just as Christ taught love like his *would* do: It is the love, the only love, that changes people, makes enemies no longer enemies. It absorbs and does away with evil rather than striking back in retribution and passing the evil on; it is a love that stands in judgment over all our talk as Christians and as a so-called "Christian" nation about protecting our rights and our so-called national "security."

I stand condemned by that ethic, but my Mormon faith and Mormon teachings call me to change–and I am slowly changing. Ten years ago, as a president of an LDS branch in Minnesota I was approached one Sunday at church by a man who, it became apparent to me as we talked, badly needed food. I was in another town far from home; I didn't have any money with me; and, as I tried to help or find a way to help, I couldn't seem to find one that wouldn't have made his plight public in a way unacceptable to him, a way that didn't shame him. Finally, as I pressed various ways of getting money or food to him he literally rushed away and left me helpless. That night, lying sleepless, and freed from my public self-consciousness and uncertainties about how to give, I was able to think of at least five good ways I could have helped and that he might have accepted, but it was too late.

Just last month, as bishop of a new BYU student ward, I had another such opportunity and was able to respond immediately with my own and Church resources. I have learned in ten years to better understand and respond in grace to Christ's New Testament command to "Give to him that asketh thee, and from him that would borrow of thee turn not thou away" (Matthew 5:42), but I have learned also by responding better to Christ's teaching to the Book of Mormon prophet, the great King Benjamin:

Ye will administer of your substance unto him that standeth in need; and ye will not suffer that the beggar putteth up his petition to you in vain. . . . Perhaps thou shalt say: The man has brought upon himself his misery; therefore I will stay my hand, for his punishments are just–But I say unto you, whosever doeth this the same hath great cause to repent and except he repent hath no interest in the Kingdom of God. (Mosiah 4:16-18)

The Book of Mormon makes the connection between our generous, graceful, Christ-like giving and our own salvation absolutely explicit: *And now, for the sake of . . . retaining a remission of your sins from day to day, that ye may walk guiltless before God–I would that ye should impart of your substance to the poor, every man according to that which he hath, such as feeding the hungry, clothing the naked, visiting the sick and administering to their relief, both spiritually and temporally, according to their wants. (Mosiah 4:26)*

It is when we entirely separate our concept of worthiness, of a person's Christian commitment, from such *visible* righteousness, that we get in deep trouble. Yes, overt works can be hypocritical, but that hypocrisy too, over time, will become visible, especially at the level of the highest ethic, sacrificial love. Not many are willing to die, or give up all their substance–not willing to come forth and lay it at the apostles' feet, as the New Testament Christians did–merely to *appear* to be righteous. They only persist in doing so, only *endure* in good works to the end, because of their faith given in grace by Christ.

The Puritans in America made some serious mistakes in this matter of judging visible righteousness. They believed that good works were not efficacious to salvation and therefore rejected the great Catholic tradition of ethical discipline and careful, responsible moral judgment. This led to a combination of moral insensitivity and arrogance that has become a Puritan stereotype and a dangerous element in the American character. But, in contradiction, because of their emphasis on will, on a person's *decision* to follow Christ in response to his election, and because of their growing anxiety to know, and also to *show*, by the visible means of good works, who was indeed among the elect, Puritans also became the most energetic activists in history–except perhaps for Communists, who, like the Puritans, believe everything is determined and individual effort *meaningless*!

Such ironies and contradictions abound in human experience. But for the Puritans the irony became tragic. The Half-Way Covenant was instituted in the second generation of Puritan America to give some kind of status to children of the original covenanted Christians, children who had not chosen for themselves and made explicit commitments based on the experience of grace like their fathers. But by the third generation the implicit contradiction surfaced tragically and ultimately destroyed Puritanism, both ethically and intellectually.

The Puritans attempted to hold onto an absurd, morally bankrupt theological contradiction, what could be called "The Puritan Fallacy": that salvation was willed and controlled by God, but that people–such as witches and adulterers–could be held responsible and punished, unto death, for their actions, as if they had willfully abandoned God's supposedly irresistible grace. But then again, people could be judged to be witches, not because they *did* evil things but because people accused them of being such and claimed, or appeared, to be affected by their supposed demonic power. The key was the acceptance of "spectral evidence": admitting to the courtroom evidence based on the assumption of the devil's power over even apparently good people and his ability to possess them and use some form of them, their "specters," to evil ends despite all rational, empirical evidence in their actual lives to the contrary–for instance, condemning as a witch the most righteous, pious matron of the community on the claim of jealous, addle-headed servant girls that her ghostly form had possessed them. Hawthorne's story "Young Goodman Brown" is about this fallacy–and about the consequent destruction of souls, not the souls of supposed witches and devils but of those like young Goodman Brown who leave "Faith" and enter the devil's territory by taking spectral evidence seriously. Of course, modern psychology has helped us see that what they were doing was "projection"–seeing evil, actually conjuring it up, where they unconsciously most feared and suspected it in themselves.

What is the modern equivalent of spectral evidence? It is a good German acquiescing in, even secretly approving, the transportation to a death camp of his Jewish neighbors, believing the Nazi *assertion* that Jews are part of an international conspiracy that is destroying the German economy rather than believing the visible evidence of long years of good neighborliness. In our country's famous case of Robert Oppenheimer, it is the acceptance by certain anti-Communists–jealous or fearful people who disagreed with his morals and political ideas–of innuendo and genuine uncertainty about his *past*; it is their letting that be more important than his long, persistent history of faithful service and trustworthiness and his obvious *present* character–and being willing to destroy him on that evidence. It is *anyone* accepting the mere claim that Mormons are not Christian on the spurious evidence of an isolated quotation from some Mormon's unofficial book or even private conversation or an anecdote about some Mormon's uncharitable action–letting that be more important than a careful look at the central body of constantly preached Mormon doctrine concerning Christ and constantly practiced Mormon worship of Christ and the consistent Christian service of most Mormons. And–as I shall discuss briefly–it is a Mormon judging other Mormons by their political beliefs, their theology, by mere opinions rather than their total lives, especially their visible works.

My father's great-grandmother hid under hickory bushes with her mother and watched mobs of professed Christians burn her home in Nauvoo, Illinois, and then walked 1,200 miles to worship Christ freely and well. My father's grandmother, alone on a homestead in Idaho while her husband preached Christ crucified in a foreign land, so sick she could not get up for help, called her tiny children, including my grandmother, around her and asked them to pray to Christ for her because Christ loved little children and would hear them–and she was healed. My father left home at seventeen to work in a railroad shop far away, got up at 5:00 each morning to read the scriptures, and received a vision in a dream of Jesus Christ, calling him to lifelong service and consecration–a call he and my mother have fulfilled. As a boy I knelt with him in our wheatfields as he reaffirmed that consecration, and I felt directly the confirming presence of the Savior. There are Mormon men and women I know who are fully consecrated, like the early Christians. Avoiding all recognition, not imagining they are in any way buying salvation, they use their God-given talents to serve others; some earn in the process large amounts of money, which they in turn, beyond very frugal means for the simplest standard of living, come forth and lay at the apostles' feet for the service of Christ.

Now, when someone says to me that these people are not Christian, he offends me deeply and does something very dangerous to our human community. He is using his own esoteric, idiosyncratic definition of "Christian," essentially as a person who does not agree with *him*–a definition so trivial as to be meaningless–or else he is delivering a divisive insult which is destructive to the harmony of our society and the building of Christ's kingdom, an insult that is itself perhaps the most dependable evidence that someone is not Christian.

Martin Luther, the great, inspired Reformer whose 500th birthday we celebrate on November 10 of this year, once wrote:

The Kingdom of God is like a besieged city surrounded on all sides by death. Each man has his place on the wall to defend and no one can stand where another stands, but nothing prevents us from calling encouragement to one another.

It would be tragic if we Christians, standing each in our different places, were to desert our place on the wall against death—against our true enemies, the world, the flesh, and the devil—and, accepting spectral evidence from the father of lies, were to turn on each other. We have no business but to call encouragement to each other.

Let me suggest an appropriate way for Christian groups to do this. Just as Paul suggested we have different gifts as individuals that together, recognized and appreciated by each other, can edify the whole body of Christ, so the differing emphases of Christian groups, recognized and appreciated, can edify the whole body of Christians. When I was a student at MIT and attended the Cambridge Branch of the Mormon Church, there was a Quaker meeting house just across the green, and with that more relaxed schedule we used to have, with time between meetings, I would go to the Quaker worship service for an hour of absolute quiet, broken only by a very occasional speaker. It was a marvelous change from the rather hectic, child-filled Mormon sacrament meetings, and I was sometimes envious. But after a time I realized that I missed, in the Quaker meetings, the meaningful content of sacrament prayer and doctrinal sermon and personal testimony, and I wished for some kind of combination.

About that time a decision was made by the Mormon Church not to have music during the passing of the bread and water to the congregation, and I found that the island of quiet and contemplation I had yearned for was there for me if I sought and concentrated on it. But attending the Quaker meeting, with its extreme form, had identified for me my need and helped me find it. I'll always be grateful.

And I'm grateful that I lived for five years among Lutherans in Minnesota and learned the joy of a concentrated sense of grace, of gratitude for God's gift of life and salvation. I had a Lutheran friend in Minnesota who would occasionally choose a day in the future, at random, circle it on his calendar with bright rings and rays and declare it a personal "celebration day"—celebration of his joy in the grace of Christ. I loved that and learned from him how to better break out into celebration as well as to be a responsible Latter-day saint, working out my salvation in fear and trembling. But I think *both* are needed.

Mormons do tend to overemphasize their works sometimes, usually in overreaction to a challenge from someone who overemphasizes grace. Someone quotes Ephesians 2:8 ("For by grace are ye saved through faith") and we turn quickly to James 2:17: ("Even so faith, if it hath not works, is dead, being alone"). Such mere opposition is no solution. We need to look carefully at the other testament of Christ, the Book of Mormon, and at the whole New Testament, to see if a complete picture, including the proper place of both faith and works, is apparent. James teaches that faith can be dead, without works, and Mormon gives, in a passage that every Baptist should love, the best attack on infant baptism imaginable, arguing that works, including ordinances like baptism, without sincere, knowing commitment, is what he calls "dead works." Mormons can be, have been, guilty of dead works; Protestants I know can be, have been, guilty of dead faith. Let us learn from each other to avoid both, rather than merely fighting over emphases that are both wrong by themselves.

My great concern is that these processes of learning from each other, rather than improving, in our modern, ecumenical, supposedly enlightened 1980s, seem to be breaking down. What do we have instead: Respectable Christian presses publishing books like Gordon Fraser's *Is Mormonism Christian?* (Moody Press, 1982), which does not enter into serious doctrinal discussion but takes the low road of implying that Mormonism is ethically corrupt and a dangerous conspiracy—all through the use of isolated quotations, misrepresentations, half-truths, and outright slander. Christian groups, in cooperation with "Ex-Mormons for Jesus," have produced a movie, *The Godmakers*, which desecrates the most sacred religious rites and covenants of the Mormon people and engages in direct falsehood in its implications about Mormon teachings and practices and the effects of Mormonism on a particular, real family. These groups, as well as others who have illegally printed stolen and personal documents (including some of my own), clearly believe their intolerant ends justify their immoral means. But, you may say, those are aberrations which Christians in general abhor as well. And it is true that a Presbyterian minister in Mesa had the Christian morality and courage to denounce *The Godmakers*. But the fact is that Christian churches in Provo, Utah, and Boise, Idaho, and Los Angeles, and Washington, D.C., etc., have used their facilities, which are dedicated to the work of Christ, to show that scurrilous movie and to sponsor those dishonest people. I cannot believe that Christ is pleased.

Christians cannot give platforms to such people and disassociate themselves from their illegal methods and unChristian purposes. I appeal to Christians to withdraw support from all who do these things. As the minister in Mesa said, if you allow such methods, which are exactly those of anti-Semitism, to be used in our society against Mormons, those methods can be used against other Christian and religious groups as well. I appeal to you to turn your recognition of differences from Mormon Christians into a basis for our learning from each other and appreciating more fully the fullness of God's grace as he works with all people to fulfill his purpose of salvation through Christ. For those who cannot, I offer this witness: You will wear out your lives fostering bitterness and destructiveness that will turn and sweep you up in it, and you will reap disappointment by and by. What you are doing is more unChristian than anything you accuse Mormons of, even if it were true. If Mormons are wrong in their beliefs, then invasion of privacy, slander, and desecration are not what they need but rational discourse, love, and testimony. If you cannot give that, Christ at the judgment bar will say to you, "Depart from me. . . . Inasmuch as ye did it not to one of the least of these, ye did it not to me" (Matthew 25:41, 45).

Finally, let me say something to my fellow Mormons. I am very proud that our Church does not engage in the practices of some others: We do not misuse our energies or our Church facilities and various media to attack other churches or condemn their members; the Church does not even engage in conflict with those who unfairly and immorally attack us as non-Christian cultists. But we do something that does us much damage and is in fact unChristian: We use spectral evidence on each other. We sometimes judge each other as unacceptable, not on the evidence of a demonstrated lack of love and good works, but on someone's claim that we are unorthodox or inactive, because we have unpopular theological or political beliefs. Within Mormonism there is a great range of thought and action, all of it still within the generous limits of what Christ defined for his disciples and within any reasonable definition of a Mormon Christian—that is, one who proclaims openly his faith in Christ as Savior of all mankind, living and dead, who manifests that faith by baptism into a new life, continually renewed through the ordinances, and who shows forth good fruits of his faith by attempting to love unconditionally, as Christ did.

But some of us too often fail on that last point, which would require that we not presume to judge others' faith and hope. Three examples: First, when I helped found *Dialogue*, I was disappointed to find that some Mormons, directly contrary to Christ's witness that anyone not against us is for us, assumed that any publication not officially Mormon was *anti*-Mormon. Some who actually knew me, contrary to the direct evidence of my continual service and good works in the Church, believed the spectral evidence of rumors that I was an apostate and sinner, even practicing polygamy. Second, far too many religious or political liberals I know at BYU assume that conservatives like George Pace and Orrin Hatch and their supporters are insensitive, warmongering, racist, and sexist troglodytes–in a word not really Christian; they believe this purely on the spectral evidence of the assumed consequences of such people's religious or political *beliefs* and contrary to all the evidence daily that such "iron rodders" are as generous, kind, and reasonable–as Christian–as themselves. Third, especially right now, when the Church is increasingly attacked from outside, in some of the ways I have described, I find it appalling that many Mormons are drawing in, hunkering down defensively, turning with suspicion on each other and cutting themselves off from each other as well as many good non-Mormon Christian and Jewish and agnostic friends.

We need to consciously open ourselves to all the friends we have, join with all Mormon Christians and then all Christians and all others of good will. The Kingdom of God is like a besieged city surrounded by death. We will each have our unique place on the wall to defend. We will be different in belief and expression, in mode of worship and ideas. And no one can stand where another stands. But we can be anxiously engaged in calling encouragement to one another. If we cannot do that we will surely be fulfilling the frightening prophecy Christ made to his former-day disciples about what could happen among his latter-day disciples just before his second coming:

Ye shall be hated of all nations for my name's sake. And then shall many be offended, and shall betray one another, and shall hate one another. . . . And because iniquity shall abound, the love of many shall wax cold. But he that shall endure unto the end, the same shall be saved. (Matthew 24: 9-13)

In a time of increasing persecution, a terrible "iniquity" that Mormon Christians can commit is certainly to "betray one another" and hate each other, or even let their love wax cold. True disciples of Christ, true Christians, will ignore persecution and resist the paranoia it naturally brings, will bend their energies to loving and serving others, whatever their differences, and thus will endure and be saved.

Read at the Association for Mormon Letters in Boston,
June 1982,
and published in *Dialogue*, Winter 1983.

CHAPTER 16

ENDURING

Edgar to Gloucester in *King Lear*:
. . . Men must endure
Their going hence, even as their coming hither.

June 1982

I grew up in a safe valley. The years five through twelve, when we are most sensuously attached to the landscape—and when, I think, the foundations of identity are firmly laid—I lived in gardens and wheatfields. They had been claimed a generation before from desert knolls and sagebrush flats but were now constantly fruitful, watered by canals or sufficient rain for dryland grains and surrounded by low mountains that were protective, inviting, never fearful. We hiked into the mountains for deer and trout to supplement our meat, eaten sparingly from the pigs butchered each fall, or sometimes we rode out to look for horses that had strayed and, once a year, on the Sabbath nearest the 24th of July, with all the Sunday School, we went in cars to have classes out of doors and eat a picnic together and explore those safe canyons of Cherry Creek or Nine Mile that brought us our water.

Even when I found a perfect flint arrowhead and a large flawed spearhead on one of those picnics, I did not imagine the blood. Instead I thought about coming there to live, in a rock cave I had found high in the canyon—perhaps with Dee Christiansen, my companion in Saturday-long Tarzan adventures, perhaps with Margene Ware, my first serious love (Moral and practical details absolutely did not intrude into such fantasies).

I wanted safe and secret places even within that safe valley. And I found or made them. The canal was one. It moved slowly along the east side of the valley, no more than two feet deep except at "The Diversion," where a falls as the canal divided created a spice of danger. Submerged in the rich muddy water with a straw for air or lying on the farm road bridge while it seemed to move backward over the surface flowing just a few feet below, my mind would flow to a safe world inside me.

And there was the vacant lot across from Grandma Hartvigsen's that grew pepper weeds three feet high, dense and fragrant, perfect for making trails and hidden nests. There was the cottonwood, with a large cup where the first branches separated, that stood right at the corner of Grandpa's barn and could be reached from the roof. And the little grove of fruit trees, part of the old homestead out on what we still called the Coffin place, preserved from my father's relentless consolidating of those old 160-acre holdings–each with log cabin and well and outbuildings and trees–into large, uninterrupted fields to fit the economies of the shift from horses to tractors. This grove was not leveled partly because it was watered, along with a lovely line of cottonwoods, by overflow from the town reservoir, built on our northern boundary to hold the stream from Nine Mile. Dad kept Peter Coffin's old house and barn to store machinery in, and we always parked the truck there and ate our lunch in those trees, on that fresh, grassy bank, adding watercress from the little overflow stream and sometimes plums or apples from the neglected grove.

The subtlest bliss from such safe and cozy places came each spring. It was a bliss mostly of the mind because I could only be in such a place occasionally and briefly–but my heart yearned, on early May mornings, when the brisk Southern Idaho wind still moved the tops of sagebrush along our fencelines and I could look down as we passed in the truck and see, among the clumps of sage, small patches of last year's dead grasses, with just a scatter of new blades coming through and a few small flowers. I knew those places were warm and fragrant, humming with tentative insect life. When I would sometimes, on a Saturday, walk out to the "ranch" (as we called it, though any livestock that might justify that name were gone), carrying an extra dessert for Dad's lunch or a hoe to work at the potato patch we planted, during the war, by a spring in the lower 320, I could sometimes stop and hide for a time under the sagebrush out of the wind. I could crush the small gray-green, velvet leaves from the strangely dead-looking branches until the air was sharp with sage or hold my fingers close until the smell went back into my throat. There would be one or two mild yellow buttercups, with five waxed petals, concavely shaped as if still ready to close quickly around the orange center. And by late May a few wild honeysuckles, the blossoms washed pink and detachable, made to be plucked off delicately and delicately set between the lips so the tube under the blossom could be sucked for the smallest, most delicate taste, deep on the tongue.

But most of all I was drawn to secret places I made, like the huge lilac clump at Dee's grandmother's, where we had cut out the inner branches for our hiding place and could strip to our shorts, creep out and run wild across the lawn and garden, through the barns, and even sneak into her cellar for a can of tuna fish and retreat through branches to lie still as she walked by, calling Dee. Or the place I fashioned at the back of our woodpile where I could be completely hidden and watch crazy old Brother Nelson do his chores, mumbling passages of scripture to himself, and where I hid the revolver a friend, who had stolen it from home, gave me to keep. I would nestle in among the logs and boards, hold the gun in both hands and think about using it to kill deer when I took my mate off to Cherry Creek. One day it was gone.

Our valley began just outside the rim of the Great Basin, at the point we called Red Rock, where the waters of ancient Lake Bonneville had once worn through the Nugget sandstone formation and drained out into what became the Portneuf and Snake Rivers, leaving a mile-wide scar and finally a slough moving slowly through cattailed bottom lands that gave us our name, Marsh Valley. The slough provided poor fishing–mostly chubs and suckers–but attracted great flights of geese in the fall that swept up to our stubble fields to feed at night and moved to the north in huge, constantly reforming wedges. I may have sensed from them that our valley was part of something larger, but surely I knew so when my parents suddenly went off forty miles to Pocatello late one night in Grandpa's new hump-backed Mercury, leaving me in Grandma's care, and came back after a week with my baby sister. Or when I sat in Grandpa's lap, playing with his gold watch chain and listening to the strange, emphatic voices emerging from the static of his Philco. Prophets, I was told, at general conference in Salt Lake City. But even the Second World War seemed far away, unconnected, intruding only for moments when I rushed outside at a sudden roar one overcast morning to see a strange, double bodied, P-38 fighter plane just passing over our house on its way hedgehopping down the valley toward Pocatello under the low clouds. Or when the oldest Bickmore boy was shot through the chest by a sniper on Okinawa and came home to tell about it in sacrament meeting.

> Hamlet to his friend:
> *There are more things in heaven and earth, Horatio,*
> *Than are dreamt of in your philosophy.*
> *But come–*

My father knew of larger things than our valley, and he included me easily. He had left home at seventeen, learned to paint the fine interiors of Union Pacific passenger cars, and lived alone, rising early to read the Book of Mormon and *The Discourses of Brigham Young.* When he spoke of Nephi and Alma and Moroni or of Joseph and Brigham and Heber I felt his love for me. When he said Christ had appeared to him in a dream and told him the Book of Mormon was true, I knew it had happened. And as I rode with him to do his share on the Church's welfare farm, or to the store or the wheat elevator or the machinery shop or from neighbor to neighbor, to borrow and return, to ask for help and give, to buy and sell, I saw him doing the truth and felt safe.

One June dawn we drove toward the reservoir farm for a day of weeding the fallow ground. He would drive the tractor. I was old enough to ride the twenty-four-foot rod weeders, jumping off to tromp away stubble as it accumulated around the goosenecks and rods. That morning, as he often did, he stopped the truck and took me to see how the wheat was heading out in that lower 320. We kept our feet between the rows as we walked out on a ridge, I just learning how to imitate his motion of plucking a stalk to examine critically its forming kernels. He asked me to kneel with him, and he spoke, I thought to Christ, about the wheat. He pledged again, as I had heard him at home, to give all the crop, all beyond our bare needs, to build the kingdom, and he claimed protection from drought and hail and wind. I felt, beside and in me, something, a person, it seemed, something more real than the wheat or the ridge or the sun, something warm like the sun but warm inside my head and chest and bones, someone like us but strange, thrilling, fearful but safe.

How is it then that sometime in those years I first felt my own deepest, most hopeless, fear, the fear of being itself? It is a fear I have never been able to write about until now nor imagined anyone else knew about or could understand, a fear so fundamental and overwhelming that I feel I must literally shake myself from it when it comes or go mad. And yet I felt it as a child in that safe valley. I've forgotten, perhaps blocked away, the time it first came. Probably it was during one of those long summer evenings when Bert Wilson and I would sleep out on our large, open front lawn and watch the stars come. The stars in that unpolluted sky were warm and close and dense and, as I began to learn from my father, who taught early morning seminary, about the worlds without number God had created and that we had always existed and always would, destined to explore and create forever in that infinite universe, it was exciting, deeply moving at times, to look into those friendly fires that formed patterns in the night and stretched away beyond my comprehension.

But one evening there began to come moments when I could feel moving into my mind, like a physical presence, the conviction that all was quite absurd. It made no sense at all that anything should exist. Something like nausea, but deeper and frightening, would grow in my stomach and chest but also at the core of my spirit, progressing like vertigo until in desperation I must jump up or talk suddenly of trivial things to break the spell and regain balance. And since that time I am always aware that that feeling, that extreme awareness of the better claim of nothingness, lies just beyond the barriers of my busy mind and will intrude when I let it.

Much later, of course, I learned about existential anxiety and the Christian sense of total dependence, of contingency, and I heard about the question Paul Tillich's daughter asked him, "Why is there something and not nothing?" But I believe these are quite different things from what I feel. My own deep fear seems unique, precisely because of those unique Mormon beliefs that have given me my greatest joy and security. It is one thing to wonder, as traditional Christians do, why an absolute, perfectly self-sufficient God would bother to create me and this strange, painful universe out of nothing, to feel the proximate mysteries of this "vale of tears" but also an utter dependence on an ultimate being who can indeed reduce me and the universe to nothingness and thus painlessness again—or to feel Albert Camus' desperate bitterness about a universe that has produced beings like us, with our constant yearning for meaning and permanence, but which seems to answer with absurdity and annihilation. But my own experience with God and this universe has produced not only dependence but identity. I have felt confirmed in my own separate, necessary, and unquenchable being. I had no beginning, not even in God. And the restored gospel provides the best answers–the most adventuresome and joyful–to the basic questions about how I came to be here and about my present and future possibilities. But there finally is no answer to the question of why and how I exist in my essential being. I just always have, and that is where my mind balks in horror, perhaps at its own limitations. I just cannot imagine how it could come to be that there is existence *or* essence–how there could be something instead of nothing. And the answer of Joseph Smith, that it did not *come* to be but simply always *was*, is marvelous–until I let the horror intrude.

Joseph Smith to the family of King Follett:
All the minds and spirits that God ever sent
into the world are susceptible of enlargement.

I know a young couple whose two-year old boy, because of cerebral palsy, is a spastic quadriplegic, apparently blind and deaf. His twin brother is perfectly healthy. As a new high councilman, I gave a sacrament meeting sermon at my assigned ward on the grace of Christ, his unconditional love for sinners. Susan, the mother, came up, grateful for what I'd said and wanting to talk more about how she could cope with her struggles and feelings, her guilt about her son. What neglect had caused the fever in the hospital that produced the palsy? Or, if a genetic "accident" was to blame, why had God allowed–or caused–it? Why had priesthood blessings that promised recovery not yet been fulfilled? How could she go on holding Allyn almost twenty-four hours a day to keep him from bracing back and choking. How could she be forgiven for her anger at him, striking him, sometimes wanting him dead. I felt she needed most to rest and offered to hold Allyn while she had an undisturbed Sunday School hour with her husband. Then we talked later in the afternoon.

I wasn't much comfort. I could testify about Christ's understanding and unconditional acceptance of her and about the real benefits to her son of gaining a body, however imperfect now, and of feeling her love while he lived, however dimly. But I could not tell Susan I found Allyn's trouble a blessing in disguise or evidence he was an especially righteous spirit who had volunteered for such trouble or that he would be compensated in some extra way in the next life—that is, beyond the marvelous opportunity to grow and be tested in a normal body during the millennium. She listened, wept, disagreed, accepted some things. I offered our family to care for her twins occasionally so she and her husband could get away to rest and to renew their own relationship, which had, she said, suffered.

Recently in her sacrament service, I heard Susan sing "I Walked Today Where Jesus Walked," and more recently I heard her give a spiritual living lesson in Relief Society on apostasy, talking forthrightly about her own struggles with personal apostasy when priesthood blessings seemed to fail and when she felt unacceptable to God and unable to continue to endure. She warned her sisters to constant vigilance. I feel warned of two things: that holding little Allyn while Susan has an hour with her husband is at least as important as my words and that she sings and teaches and bears her testimony more maturely and movingly now and also continues to suffer terribly while she endures.

In an interdisciplinary colloquium for freshmen I teach with four colleagues, I've been learning about genetic problems that produce malformations in children. As the sex cells divide, the complicated process of meiosis, by which the chromosomes are reduced from forty-eight to twenty-four, sometimes produces broken and reattached parts—translocations—or duplications in some eggs and sperm cells and, of course, missing or partial chromosomes in their divided opposites. Many of these accidents (statistics all nicely predictable) are lethal, resulting after fertilization in miscarriages or stillbirths, but some produce living children. Down's syndrome children are the result of such translocations, but there are also many others, rare but real, hidden away from our usual experience. The frequencies are surprising—one in every 700 births is Down's syndrome (now being called trisomy 21 to clearly identify the problem and the chromosomes—a duplication or a segment attachment to chromosome number 21, making it "three-bodied"). Jean de Grouchy's *Clinical Atlas of Human Chromosomes*, which is amply illustrated with photographs of the victims of chromosomal aberrations, is a kind of chamber of horrors of deformed, doomed children: grotesquely cleft palates in Patau's syndrome (one in 5,000 births), flexion deformities in Edwards' syndrome (one in 8,000). In some texts a refrain comes at the end of each description: "the mean survival time is about 2½ months, 90 percent of all cases dying within a year" of birth, or "mean survival 3 months, 80 percent dying in the first year." Is it a relief to know that most such terribly deformed children do not live long? But some do, with retardation, shortened, skewed limbs, impossibly positioned fingers and toes, clubfeet.

The sex chromosomes, X and Y, most commonly cause abnormalities through duplications, though a missing X in females produces Turner's syndrome: tiny body, sterility, low mathematics IQ, webbing on the neck. An extra X in men produces Klinefelter's syndrome: some female body characteristics, sterility, low verbal IQ. Extra X's can occur up to a total of six, producing lower and lower IQ, but perhaps most trying to a believer in moral agency is the single extra Y in men, which produces a tall, powerful body and impulsive behavior that easily becomes anti-social. Victims of this chance occurrence in cell division (one in 1,000 births) have forty times the chance of others to end up in a penitentiary.

One syndrome, designated 5p monosomy (a missing part of chromosome 5), produces some facial and bone deformations and very severe retardation but not high fatality. Its deformation in the larynx produces a distinctive cry, like that of a kitten, which gives the syndrome its more common name, "cri du chat"–cry of the cat. What do parents endure when they first hear that cry from their newborn–and then as the years go and the cry diminishes and a characteristically wide-eyed, almost jawless face develops in a child who will live long, without language, with an IQ under twenty? If the figure one in 50,000 births is right there must be over 4,000 sets of such parents in this country, perhaps 80,000 in the world.

A few months ago we read, with surprising calm it seems to me, of the parents in Bloomington, Indiana, who were able to get medical and legal support for a decision not to perform the difficult but feasible surgery needed to save their Down's syndrome child–designated "Infant Doe." Their lawyer called it "treatment to do nothing." Columnist George Will called it homicide. Since the case apparently would not have been filed–probably not allowed–if the child had not had Down's syndrome, the logic of the decision suggests that parents have the right to kill through neglect–and why not more directly?–a child that they decide is a huge trouble. And surely, then, it would seem society must have the right to relieve itself of those who come to us through "wrongful birth," the tortured phrase that has developed in recent litigation aimed at doctors whose advice or decisions leads to safe delivery of severely deformed or retarded babies who could have been aborted.

So far the courts have been willing only to assess the doctors the costs for care of such "wrongful births"–not to establish punitive damages.

I know of a couple whose first baby was born with a gaping cleft lip, the eyes squeezed almost into a cyclops, no muscle tone, and profound retardation. It lived ten days, requiring very expensive care at enormous cost to the parents. A chromosomal check available in recent years revealed the mother to be a carrier of trisomy 13, Patau's syndrome, and the doctors presented the options: no more children except by adoption, amniocentesis in future pregnancies to check the chromosomes of the fetus and abortion in case of abnormality, or having children with a certain percentage of carriers and abnormal births. On the basis of their opposition to birth control and abortion (and thus to amniocentesis that would assume abortion as an option), and with faith in an optimistic priesthood blessing and strengthened by the fasting of their ward and stake, the couple went ahead with another child. It was born with trisomy 13, lived thirty-three days, and put the parents in debt over $100,000.

> Jesus Christ to Joseph Smith:
> *Fear not even unto death; for in*
> *this world your joy is not full,*
> *but in me your joy is full.*

A year ago, while we were in England, Charlotte learned that her mother, Josephine Johnson Hawkins, had cancer of the pancreas. There was an exploratory operation. The decision was not for the dangerous surgery or traumatic chemotherapy that had little chance of helping but for a peaceful final few months. When Charlotte came home in July she found her mother wasted but still hoping. She had had a blessing, she said, that she would recover. Charlotte decided to do what could be done, found a doctor willing to do limited chemotherapy, brought her mother to her own bed (I moved to a cot in my study), and together with her sisters set about making Josephine well. They cooked tempting food to keep up her appetite against the nausea of painkillers, bathed her, and helped her to the bathroom (finally carrying her) to avoid the discomfort of bedpans. Charlotte was determined and the doctor encouraging until one day in late August when he saw that the chemotherapy was just not working and stopped it. Josephine told me she thought she could have the faith to make the promise work, but there was so much pain and she was so tired. Charlotte kept trying, fiercely believing in the promise, hoping. Our daughters lay on the bed with Josephine, held her in their arms and talked about canning apricots with her years ago. She died on October 2. The last month she slowly turned a deep golden color from the jaundice.

I have long thought that Josephine Hawkins took too much onto herself, keeping her own hurts inside, interceding for others in potential conflicts, absorbing others' weaknesses, letting any damage be done to *her* feelings, letting mercy rob justice. The internal stress she invited may well have brought on her cancer and killed her, and I felt for a long time she was foolish. But I decided in that last month that she was right. And she was also right about jokes. She never could get the punchlines straight and always marred a funny story in the telling so that the humor came against herself rather than whoever was the butt of the joke. I used to be condescendingly amused, merely tolerant, but I've decided she felt intuitively that nearly every joke is at someone's expense. She took the expense. I think she was right to do so, whatever the cost.

Since last fall Charlotte hasn't slept well. She wonders about that promise to her mother and about fighting to hold on so long, prolonging the pain, straining her bonds with her sisters. And she takes the children's troubles more onto herself and doesn't tell jokes very well.

> Christ describing the last days to his
> apostles just before leaving them:
> *Then shall many be offended, and shall betray*
> *one another, and shall hate one another.*
> *And because iniquity shall abound,*
> *the love of many shall wax cold.*
> *But he that shall endure unto the end,*
> *the same shall be saved.*

On 13 May 1981, an attempt was made on the Pope's life at his public audience in St. Peter's Square. I was in the throng, next to his car, just reaching out to touch his hand. My mind formed clearly two partly visual, mostly verbal images: first, John Paul II, a man of God, is shot, hurting terribly, will die; and second, Poland's Solidarity, which this man inspirited, and Lech Walesa, to whom this man conveyed symbolic spiritual power, are finished. When I learned that night on the train away from Rome that the Pope had survived I knew it was a miracle—for him and for Poland. I learned of another miracle in the summer when the Polish military leaders, by refusing to use force against fellow Poles, apparently prevented the Communist Party from destroying Solidarity. In the fall I began to wake in the night and think about the coming winter. With Poland's economic problems still unsolved because of the continuing power struggle, I knew that hunger could defeat Solidarity. Food riots could justify internal suppression or external intervention. Another miracle was needed. Those images of the Pope and Walesa returned. I couldn't sleep.

Finally I began to explore. I found that most people felt deep concern and admiration for Solidarity and wanted to help but didn't know how. Agencies like Catholic Relief Services and Polish National Alliance were sending food but not enough and were not doing large-scale publicity that might attract help from non-Catholics and non-Poles. Through Michael Novak, a Catholic lay theologian who had met in Rome with Solidarity leaders, I was able to get in contact, by phone to Warsaw, with Bronislaw Geremek, chief advisor to Solidarity. He said the children were starting to die of dysentery. He asked that we send dried milk, detergents, and technicians to help them build privately controlled small businesses and that we do it soon, by plane. We organized Food For Poland, a non-profit public foundation for tax-free contributions, and had a planeload of food and arrangements almost ready for a donated flight when martial law was declared December 13.

All flights were grounded. Geremek was one of the first arrested (I saw his name on a list in *Time* on Christmas day), and from a letter smuggled out later we learned he went on a hunger strike in January and then was punished with an unheated room. Our government cut off its aid and vacillated on private aid like ours. We weren't certain food would get through. Finally it became clear through messages from Poland and successful shipments from Western Europe that the military was not interfering; our State department gave approval and on January 6 we sent our first shipment, by truck, then train and Polish ship to Gdansk. Since then we have sponsored a National Day of Fasting, made five more shipments of food, medicine, clothing, detergents, and sent one of our trustees along with one plane load to Warsaw to verify first-hand the proper distribution to those most in need. Our national director went a few weeks ago to Gdansk to observe distribution of our largest shipment, which included 90,000 pounds of milk from the LDS Church.

We have been responsible for adding perhaps $1 million worth of supplies to the Polish Relief effort. That is pitifully little–the equivalent of one extra good meal for the three million Polish children, aged, and families of imprisoned Solidarity members who are in greatest need. Our government cut off $800 million in aid just for this year. And I am convinced that perhaps twice that much, invested one year ago in a massive Marshall Plan to Poland, focused on improving farming efficiency and on building small, privately controlled industries and businesses, would have provided enough economic resurgence and enough return to Poland's traditional productivity to enable Solidarity's nonviolent success and a gradual development of basic freedoms. But now the stalemate drags on. Someone tried to kill the Pope again, one year later, this time with a bayonet. Poland is not in the news, and people don't think much now about helping.

During January and February I woke very early each morning, thinking of the mistakes I was making as an English professor trying to raise funds, the missed opportunities, inept public relations–not enough hard-nosed pushiness, not quick enough tough-minded assessment of how we were being used by others to their own advantage. I thought of the people I met each day, or talked to on the phone, who could give $1 million easily but didn't, or the families who fasted and sent all they could, but only once, or students and faculty who helped a while and then disappeared. And I lay awake thinking of Bronislaw Geremek in his cold cell and of thousands of families with father or mother or both interned or dismissed from jobs–and knowing we were failing them. I thought of a film I saw in December made by a French journalist of an interview with Lech Walesa held just a few days before the December 13 crackdown. Walesa sat holding his daughter, with a portrait of John Paul II in the background. He said, "I must remember that even if my dream of a free Poland is achieved, it could be taken away in a day. Disaster can come anytime, as it has in the past. I must be ready for death. I could die at any time and must be prepared while I continue to work."

Recently we've decided we may have to discontinue Food For Poland before long. We've failed to get major corporation or foundation support or the help of a popular entertainment figure–both of which seem necessary to keep up momentum. And I am ready to admit I do not have the gifts–or the stomach–to make a career of fundraising. I do not lie awake much any more. When I do it's usually to hold

Charlotte, who sometimes has bad dreams. We get up very early and, as the days begin to shorten, play tennis for half an hour in the cool shadow of Y Mount.

And for the first time in over a year I've begun occasionally to let the fear of being slip into my mind. Sometimes I look up from a book or the typewriter and the world is only whirling quanta of energy, reflecting all its seductive impressions of color from a palsied and blank universe. If I let it (sometimes I invite it), the horror deepens, because neither that atomized, inertial, spinning chaos nor my strange ability to sense and order and anguish over it have any real *reason* to exist. I want to take refuge in the mystery that an absolute God made it all out of nothing and will make sense of it or send it back to nothing, but Joseph Smith will not let me. There must be opposition or no existence. Is it more difficult or easier to take my problems to a God who has problems?

Nephi bidding farewell to his people:
If ye shall press forward,
feasting upon the word of Christ, and endure
to the end, behold thus saith the Father:
Ye shall have eternal life.

Postscript: December 1982

In September, at the equinox, I was called to be bishop of a newly formed student ward. I have stewardship of 120 young couples, most already beginning to have children. The first thing the Lord told me, when I began to think and pray about staffing the ward, as clearly as I have ever been told anything, was to call Susan as my Relief Society president: to be in charge of all the women, their religious instruction, their compassionate service, their sisterhood, their training as wives and mothers. It made no sense: Susan was still burdened greatly by her struggles with Allyn, with her husband, with herself. Dale had left school to cope with their enormous financial burdens and was planning to move them to Salt Lake. But the call was clear and they accepted.

Susan immediately visited every family and established the crucial foundation for making a ward community. She has opened herself and her life entirely to her sisters and conducts all her interviews, her meetings, her casual conversations with the same absolute honesty and down-to-earth forthrightness. The women—and their husbands—experience quite directly the struggles, the ups and downs of anguish and hope, the need for help, and the enduring courage through which she lives day by day.

I've tried to be that open and direct as a pastor. I speak for a few minutes in nearly every sacrament meeting, very personally, about the realities of my life with Charlotte, our sorrows, our decisions, our faith, and I teach the family relations class each Sunday for all the newlyweds in the ward. I spend many hours with people in trouble: couples who have hurt each other until they can't speak, lonely husbands, burdened with past sins and present insecurity, women who can't have children and women who are having too many. I talk about the problems Charlotte and I have had, how we have hurt each other and suffered and learned and got help and endured. How the Lord has tried to direct us from place to place across the country–toward unforeseeable service and learning and away from ambition for luxury and prestige. I call people to the regular positions but also to special assignments: a couple to help take care of Allyn in sacrament meeting, another to work with an alcoholic living in our area separated from his family. I see people changing, marriages beginning to work again, people helping without being called, people making moral decisions–to pay income tax on tips from years back, not to sue someone who has wronged them. I see Susan, now three months pregnant, smiling often.

Reality is too demanding for me to feel very safe any more in the appalling luxury of my moments of utter skepticism. God's tears in Moses, chapter seven, at which the prophet Enoch wondered, tell me that God has not resolved the mystery of being. But he endures in love. He does not ask me to forgo my integrity by ignoring the mystery or he would not have let Enoch see him weep. But he does not excuse me to forgo my integrity by ignoring the reality which daily catches me up in joy and sorrow and shows me, slowly, subtly, its moral patterns of iron delicacy.

Food For Poland has continued. We have been accused of glory-seeking, of being liberals indulging in do-goodism instead of the true religion of doctrinal purity, and by some of being traitors: giving aid to the enemy in time of war. But we are sending, in cooperation with the LDS Welfare program, another large shipment of food and clothing to help the Poles through this winter. Charlotte's father, after a year of trying it alone, will be coming to live with us soon. Our third daughter, who was born with a diaphragmatic hernia and who almost died from a resulting intestine block last June while she was on a mission, came home, was operated on, slowly recovered, and is going back into the field in January. Our oldest daughter is in love. I lie awake sometimes now, as the nights begin to shorten, my mind besieged by woe and wonder.

Edgar to his blind father in *King Lear*:

. . . Men must endure
Their going hence, even as their coming hither.
Ripeness is all. Come on.